On Melville

On Melville

The Best from *American Literature*

Edited by Louis J. Budd and Edwin H. Cady

Duke University Press   Durham and London 1988

© 1988 Duke University Press
All rights reserved
Printed in the United States of America
on acid-free paper ∞
Library of Congress Cataloging-in-Publication Data
appear on the last printed page of this book.

Contents

Series Introduction

From Vol. 1, no. 1, in March 1929 to the latest issue, the front cover of *American Literature* has proclaimed that it is published "with the Cooperation of the American Literature Section [earlier Group] of the Modern Language Association." Though not easy to explain simply, the facts behind that statement have deeply influenced the conduct and contents of the journal for five decades and more. The journal has never been the "official" or "authorized" organ of any professional organization. Neither, however, has it been an independent expression of the tastes or ideas of Jay B. Hubbell, Clarence Gohdes, or Arlin Turner, for example. Historically, it was first in its field, designedly so. But its character has been unique, too.

Part of the tradition of the journal says that Hubbell in founding it intended a journal that should "hold the mirror up to the profession"—reflecting steadily its current interests and (ideally) at least sampling the best work being done by historians, critics, and bibliographers of American literature during any given year. Such remains the intent of the editors based at Duke University; such also through the decades has been the intent of the Board of Editors elected by the vote of members of the professional association—"Group" or "Section."

The operative point lies in the provisions of the constitutional "Agreements" between the now "Section" and the journal. One of these provides that the journal shall publish no article not approved by two readers from the elected Board. Another provides that the Chairman of the Board or, if one has been appointed and is acting in the editorial capacity at Duke, the Managing Editor need publish no article not judged worthy of the journal. Historically, again, the members of the successive Boards and the Duke editor have seen eye-to-eye. The Board has tended to approve fewer than one out of every ten submissions. The tradition of the journal dictates that it keep a slim back-log. With however much revision, therefore, the journal publishes practically everything the Board approves.

Founder Hubbell set an example from the start by achieving the

almost total participation of the profession in the first five numbers
of *American Literature*. Cairns, Murdock, Pattee, and Rusk were
involved in Vol. 1, no. 1, along with Boynton, Killis Campbell,
Foerster, George Philip Krapp, Leisy, Mabbott, Parrington, Bliss
Perry, Louise Pound, Quinn, Spiller, Frederick Jackson Turner, and
Stanley Williams on the editorial side. Spiller, Tremaine McDowell,
Gohdes, and George B. Stewart contributed essays. Canby, George
McLean Harper, Gregory Paine, and Howard Mumford Jones appeared as reviewers. Harry Hayden Clark and Allan Gilbert entered
in Vol. 1, no. 2. Frederic I. Carpenter, Napier Wilt, Merle Curti,
and Grant C. Knight in Vol. 1, no. 3; Clarence Faust, Granville
Hicks, and Robert Morss Lovett in Vol. 1, no. 4; Walter Fuller Taylor, Orians, and Paul Shorey in Vol. 2, no. 1.

Who, among the founders of the profession, was missing? On
the other hand, if the reader belongs to the profession and does not
know those present, she or he probably does not know enough.
With very few notable exceptions, the movers and shakers of the
profession have since the beginning joined in cooperating to create
and sustain the journal.

The foregoing facts lend a special distinction to the best articles
in *American Literature*. They represent the many, often tumultuous
winds of doctrine which have blown from the beginnings through
the years of the decade next to last in this century. Those articles
often became the firm footings upon which present structures of understanding rest. Looking backward, one finds that the argonauts
were doughty. Though we know a great deal more than they, they
are a great deal of what we know. Typically, the old best authors
wrote well—better than most of us. Conceptually, even ideologi-
cally, we still wrestle with ideas they created. And every now and
again one finds of course that certain of the latest work has rein-
vented the wheel one time more. Every now and again one finds
a sunburst idea which present scholarship has forgotten. Then it appears that we have receded into mist or darkness by comparison.

Historical change, not always for the better, also shows itself in
methods (and their implied theories) of how to present evidence,
structure an argument, craft a scholarly article. The old masters
were far from agreed—much to the contrary—about these matters.

But they are worth knowing in their own variety as well as in their instructive differences from us.

On the other hand, the majority of *American Literature*'s authors of the best remain among us, working, teaching, writing. One testimony to the quality of their masterliness is the frequency with which the journal gets requests from the makers of textbooks or collections of commentary to reprint from its pages. Now the opportunity presents itself to select without concern for permissions fees what seems the best about a number of authors and topics from the whole sweep of *American Literature*.

The fundamental reason for this series, in other words, lies in the intrinsic, enduring value of articles that have appeared in *American Literature* since 1929. The compilers, with humility, have accepted the challenge of choosing the best from well over a thousand articles and notes. By "best" is meant original yet sound, interesting, and useful for the study and teaching of an author, intellectual movement, motif, or genre.

The articles chosen for each volume of this series are given simply in the order of their first publication, thus speaking for themselves and entirely making their own points rather than serving the compilers' view of literary or philosophical or historical patterns. Happily, a chronological order has the virtues of displaying both the development of insight into a particular author, text, or motif and the shifts of scholarly and critical emphasis since 1929. But comparisons or trend-watching or a genetic approach should not blur the individual excellence of the articles reprinted. Each has opened a fresh line of inquiry, established a major perspective on a familiar problem, or settled a question that had bedeviled the experts. The compilers aim neither to demonstrate nor undermine any orthodoxy, still less to justify a preference for research over explication, for instance. In the original and still current subtitle, *American Literature* honors literary history and criticism equally—along with bibliography. To the compilers this series does demonstrate that any worthwhile author or text or problem can generate a variety of challenging perspectives. Collectively, the articles in its volumes have helped to raise contemporary standards of scholarship and criticism.

This series is planned to serve as a live resource, not as a homage to once vibrant but petrifying achievements in the past. For several sound reasons, its volumes prove to be weighted toward the more recent articles, but none of those reasons includes a presumed superiority of insight or of guiding doctrine among the most recent generations. Some of the older articles could benefit now from a minor revision, but the compilers have decided to reprint all of them exactly as they first appeared. In their time they met fully the standards of first-class research and judgment. Today's scholar and critic, their fortunate heir, should hope that rising generations will esteem his or her work so highly.

Many of the articles published in *American Literature* have actually come (and continue to come) from younger, even new members of the profession. Because many of those authors climb on to prominence in the field, the fact is worth emphasizing. Brief notes on the contributors in the volumes of their series may help readers to discover other biographical or cultural patterns.

Edwin H. Cady
Louis J. Budd

The Anatomy of Melville's Fame

O. W. Riegel

THE extraordinary enthusiasm for Herman Melville in recent years among persons who had not previously heard of him has led to two erroneous conclusions: first, that Melville's contemporaries were blind to the significance of his work, and, second, that until the beginning of the revival of the last decade Melville was completely forgotten.

I

There is sufficient evidence to show that Melville's contemporaries were fairly well aware of his intentions. The sea romances, *Typee* and *Omoo,* are praised today for the same virtues that were observed in the 1840's, and the attacks upon Melville's later and more philosophical works arose not so much from a lack of comprehension in the critics as from a dislike for the philosophy which they understood only too well. For instance, *The Democratic Review* (July, 1849) pointed out that "Mardi is an allegory that mirrors the world," but the critic was "saddened" because Melville "seems to think that the race is in a vicious circle, from which we cannot escape."[1] A similar point of view was expressed by *The Literary World* (August 21, 1852) in a review of *Pierre:* "The most unmoral *moral* of the story . . . seems to be the impracticability of virtue. . . . But ordinary novel readers will never unkennel this loathsome suggestion."[2]

Melville was attacked by his contemporaries, it is true, for the failure of his later work as literature, but modern critics at the height of the Melville boom have passed virtually the same unfavorable judgments. Compare, for example, the critique published in *The Athenæum* in 1852, which called *Pierre* "a prairie in print, wanting the flowers and freshness of the savannahs, but almost equally puzzling to find a way through it,"[3] with Lewis Mumford's comment, "It is the failure of *Pierre* as literature that draws our attention to

---

[1] *The United States Magazine and Democratic Review,* XXV, 44 (July, 1849).
[2] *The Literary World,* XI, 118 (August 21, 1852).
[3] *The Athenæum,* XXV, 1266 (November 20, 1852).

Melville's predicament as a man,"[4] or with H. M. Tomlinson's description of *Pierre* as "a tragic and noteworthy failure."[5] The tone of the modern critics is more sympathetic, but the judgment of *Pierre* as literary art remains much the same.

An apparent exception to the general comprehension of Melville's meaning was the inability or the unwillingness of British critics to see in *Moby Dick* anything more than a poorly constructed whaling story. As early as December, 1851, *Harper's Magazine,* an American journal, said that "beneath the whole story the reader may find a pregnant allegory,"[6] but the British, with an amazing stupidity, never recognized the possibility of a philosophical interpretation. They tested *Moby Dick* by the canons of unity, coherence and emphasis, and found it wanting. *The London Examiner,* for instance, found that in *Moby Dick* "all the regular rules of narrative or story are spurned and set at defiance."[7] *The London Spectator* remarked that "such a groundwork is hardly natural enough for a regular-built novel, though it might form a tale, if properly managed." *The Spectator* censured Melville for "beginning in the autobiographical form and changing *ad libitum* into the narrative."[8]

Indeed, there was always a sharp difference of opinion between British and American criticism of Melville during his creative period, a fact which has not hitherto been stressed by Melville's biographers. Ill feeling, national pride, and a patronizing attitude toward America help to explain the severe condemnation by the English of Melville's "Yankeeisms" and "Go-ahead method." They also help to explain the unexpected English praise of *The Confidence Man,* a book which nearly every one else has whole-heartedly damned. For instance, *The Westminster Review* (July, 1857) said: "Perhaps the moral is, the gullibility of the great Republic when taken on its own tack."[9] Had Americans felt more cultural pride and less inclination to grovel before British oracles, Melville might have become then, as he is now, a great hero of American national consciousness.

[4] Lewis Mumford, *Herman Melville* (New York, 1929), p. 218.
[5] H. M. Tomlinson, Introduction to *Pierre* (New York, Dutton, 1929), p. xv.
[6] *Harper's Magazine,* IV, 137 (December, 1851).
[7] *The Examiner,* November 8, 1851, p. 709.
[8] Reprinted in *The International Magazine,* IV, 602 (December, 1851).
[9] *The Westminster Review,* XII, 311 (July, 1857).

Melville's genius was, indeed, recognized by the critics who undertook to evaluate his work as a whole: Philarète Chasles (*Revue des Deux Mondes,* May 15, 1849),[10] Fitz-James O'Brien (*Putnam's Monthly,* February, 1853),[11] "Sir Nathaniel" (*The New Monthly Magazine,* July, 1853),[12] and others clearly apprehended Melville's power, although they might quarrel with him over stylistic excesses or his offenses against the proprieties and evangelical morality, such as references to smoking the vile weed, drinking spirituous liquors, and cohabiting with Polynesian maidens.

II

The second myth, that after the close of the first productive period Melville was almost completely forgotten, is simply false. It is true that little evidence of the continuation of an enthusiasm for Melville can be found in the literary histories and text-books. Beginning with the Duyckincks' *Cyclopædia of American Literature* and Gostwick's *Hand-book of American Literature,* Melville found a place in a considerable number of academic works; but these notices, in general, reveal a dismal ignorance both of the man and of his work. Academic criticism abounded in plagiarism and paraphrase of previous criticism, and it was apparent that few of the literary historians bothered to read Melville with any degree of critical insight, if at all. More important as indicative of an abiding interest in Melville were the references to him by men of letters and literary amateurs on both sides of the Atlantic. The extent of the interest in Melville among the reading public can never be determined accurately, because the opinions of ordinary readers do not often find their way into print; but a sufficient number of professional writers left comments on Melville to prove the existence of a following, however small it might be. Among the more important men who were admirers of Melville at one time or another during the "dark" periods before 1919 may be mentioned Robert Louis Stevenson, Charles Warren Stoddard, Sir Alfred Lyall, John La

[10] Philarète Chasles, "Voyages Réels et Fantastiques d'Hermann Melville," *Revue des Deux Mondes,* II (new period), 541-570 (May 15, 1849).

[11] Fitz-James O'Brien, "Our Young Authors—Melville," *Putnam's,* I, 156-164 (February, 1853).

[12] "Sir Nathaniel," "Herman Melville," *The New Monthly Magazine,* XCVIII, 300-308 (July, 1853).

Farge, Robert Buchanan, Henry S. Salt, Arthur Stedman, Titus Munson Coan, W. Clark Russell, J. M. Barrie, Frank Jewett Mather, Jr., Archibald MacMechan, William Morris, and Theodore Watts.

III

Contrary to the popular impression, the recent revival of interest in Melville is not the first, nor even the second or third, attempt to rehabilitate the author's reputation. It is possible to demark at least four or five movements which sought to reawaken a general interest in Melville. The first occurred in England in the middle 1880's, with Robert Buchanan and Henry S. Salt as the chief advocates.[13] Another occurred in England and America after Melville's death (1891), when new editions of four of the books were published.[14] Professor William P. Trent mentioned a "revival of interest" in Melville—and deprecated it—in 1903.[15] Another revival, which resulted in the acknowledgment of *Moby Dick* as Melville's masterpiece and one of the greatest sea books in all literature, began in 1914 with Professor Archibald MacMechan's essay on the White Whale.[16] The last revival began with the Melville Centenary in 1919 and still continues.

[13]*Cf.* Robert Buchanan, "Socrates in Camden," *The Academy*, XXVIII, 102-103 (August 15, 1885).

The Letters of Robert Louis Stevenson, South Seas Edition, edited by Sir Sidney Colvin New York, 1925), III, 71.

Henry S. Salt, "Herman Melville," *The Universal Review*, IV, 78 (May, 1889).

Henry S. Salt, "Imperial Cockneydom," *The Scottish Art Review*, II, 186-190 (November, 1889).

Letter from W. Clark Russell to Herman Melville dated July 21, 1886, published in *The New York World*, October 11, 1891, p. 26. In this letter Russell wrote, "Your reputation here [England] is very great."

[14] *Cf.* Richard Henry Stoddard, "Herman Melville," *The Mail and Express*, XX, 5 (October 8, 1891).

Arthur Stedman, "Marquesan Melville," *The New York World*, XXXII, 26 (October 11, 1891).

W. Clark Russell, "A Claim for American Literature," *The North American Review*, CLIV, 138-149 (February, 1892).

Henry S. Salt, "Marquesan Melville," *The Gentleman's Magazine*, CCLXXII, 248-257 (March, 1892).

This is only a partial bibliography of notices of Melville published during the years 1891 and 1892.

[15] *Cf.* William P. Trent, *A History of American Literature, 1607-1865* (1903), New York, 1929, p. 390.

A commentary on the interest in Melville at this time may be found in an article on Herman Melville by Frank Jewett Mather, Jr., published in *The Saturday Review of Literature*, V, 945-946 (April 27, 1929).

[16] *Cf.* Archibald MacMechan, "The Best Sea Story Ever Written." In *The Life of a Little College* (Boston, Houghton Mifflin, 1914), pp. 179-198.

The divergent character of the various revivals is important. In the first two or three Melville was talked of only as a writer of "travel books," the author of the charmingly exotic *Typee* and *Omoo*. H. S. Salt's comment in *The Scottish Art Review* (November, 1899) was typical: *"Typee* takes precedence of all his other writings, in merit no less than in date."[17] When *Moby Dick* emerged in 1914, it was as a glorified sea and whaling story. MacMechan, who set the tone of this revival, was not interested in the philosophy and allegory of *Moby Dick* so much as in its "expansiveness" and "freedom from rules and conventions." The Whitman vogue was in full swing. To MacMechan, Melville was the "Walt Whitman of prose."[18]

The most recent Melville boom began with a repetition of orthodox judgments,[19] and a new note did not enter criticism until the publication of Frank Jewett Mather's articles on Melville in *The Review* in August, 1919.[20] The Centenary reawakened interest in Melville both in England and in America, but again there were important national differences. The English have always been interested in Melville as a writer of travel literature and of books about the sea. Since 1919 English criticism has concerned itself chiefly with style and story. Its main characteristic has been its enthusiasm for *Moby Dick,* an enthusiasm which partly atones for former blindness.[21] But it is an enthusiasm for *Moby Dick* as the whaling epic. English criticism has been, therefore, stylistic and literary, and it is a significant fact that John Freeman's most original contribution to Melville criticism has been his analysis and literary appraisal of the poems.[22] Carl Van Doren could speak in 1921 of the "greater re-

---

[17] *Op. cit.*, p. 186.   [18] *Op. cit., passim.*

[19] *Cf.* the Centenary articles in *The New York Times*, LXVIII, July 27, 1919, Section 3, p. 1; *The New York Evening Sun*, XXXIII, August 1, 1919, p. 16; *The New York Evening Post*, CXVIII, August 2, 1919, p. 6; *The New York Tribune*, LXXIX, August 4, 1919, p. 8. In England, F. C. Owlett, "Herman Melville (1819-1891): A Centenary Tribute," *The London Bookman*, LVI, 164-167 (August, 1919).

[20] Frank Jewett Mather, Jr., "Herman Melville," *The Review*, I, 276-278 (August 9, 1919), and I, 298-301 (August 16, 1919).

[21] *Cf.* Viola Meynell, "Herman Melville," *The Dublin Review*, CLXVI, 96-105 (January, February, March, 1920).

E. L. Grant Watson, "Moby Dick," *The London Mercury*, III, 180-186 (December, 1920).

Augustine Birrell, "The Great White Whale," *The Athenæum*, January 28, 1921, pp. 99-100.

F. L. Lucas, "Herman Melville," *The New Statesman*, XVIII, 730-731 (April 1, 1922).

[22] John Freeman, *Herman Melville* (New York, Macmillan, 1926).

vival interest" in England,[22a] but he was not speaking of the great Melville boom which is still going on in this country. The "new" Melville criticism, the reinterpretation of the character of Melville and of his work in the light of modern psychology and philosophy, is essentially an American phenomenon.

IV

The recent revival of interest in Melville has been attributed by some to "the spirit of the age." This is undoubtedly true, but "spirit of the age" is a term difficult to define, and one that leaves the inquirer groping for more ponderable reasons. Some have emphasized the appeal of Melville's boldness and expansiveness, which were the same qualities that attracted Professor MacMechan in 1914. A more distinctive characteristic of the third decade of the twentieth century may be its devotion to psychological history, to "case histories" of spiritual struggle and conflict, to the spectacle of man against the world, to all evidences of psychological maladjustment: a devotion induced by the recent enthusiasm for psychology as well as by the post-war psychosis of futility, of futility and defiance.

Mather's importance as a critic of Melville arises from the fact that he was one of the first to see clearly Melville's personal struggle with a perspective on the Victorian age. The point of view was elaborated by Professor Weaver in his biography: "Indeed, Melville's complete works, in their final analysis, are a long effort towards the creation of one of the most complex, and massive, and original characters in literature: the character known in life as Herman Melville."[23] This sentence, indeed, sounds the keynote of the new criticism. For what that "Herman Melville" character is which has been discovered by recent critics, and its meaning to modern life, one must go to the works and the biographies. The important point is that the new interest in Melville is not so much belletristic as biographical, and it is the biographical interest that is responsible for the gradual reclamation of the literary "failures." The unpopular works, even *Pierre* and *The Confidence Man* and

[22a] Carl Van Doren, *The American Novel* (New York, Macmillan, 1921), pp. 75-76.
[23] Raymond M. Weaver, *Herman Melville: Mariner and Mystic* (New York, Doran, 1921).

Clarel, have been brilliantly gilded and festooned and illuminated with modern effects, and so rescued from the limbo.

The biographical enthusiasm reached its climax in D. H. Lawrence's *Studies in Classic American Literature* (1922), Carl Van Vechten's essay in *The Double Dealer* (January, 1922), and especially, in Lewis Mumford's *Herman Melville* (1929). Van Vechten clearly revealed the attitude of this group of critics:

> In spite of all the detractors, I think . . . the day may come when there will be those who will prefer the later Melville just as there are those who prefer the later James, those who will care more for the metaphysical, and at the same time more self-revealing works, than for the less subtle and more straightforward tales.[24]

The excitement over Melville as a man may be held responsible for the sometimes excessive praise of his writing, for the elaboration of awful but often improbable "hidden meanings,"[25] and for the amusing contradictory opinions among enthusiastic critics. To Lewis Mumford, for instance, Melville is always a conscious artist;[26] to Van Wyck Brooks he is an unconscious artist.[27] To M. Josephson, Melville is an "escape" writer;[28] to Mumford he is a realist in the deepest sense.[29] Other examples may be found in the criticism of the last ten years, but these will suffice to show the lack of agreement on the more strictly literary aspects of Melville's work.

V

In spite of the enthusiasm of the Melville boom, there has been, and there still is, a strong dissenting opinion. *Pierre,* it seems, is as difficult to read as ever. Here again there seems to be a difference

---

[24] Carl Van Vechten, "The Later Work of Herman Melville," *The Double-Dealer,* III, 12 (January, 1922).

[25] *Cf.* D. H. Lawrence, *Studies in Classic American Literature* (New York, Seltzer, 1923).

Lewis Mumford, *Herman Melville* (New York, Harcourt, 1929).

W. S. Gleim, "A Theory of Moby Dick," *The New England Quarterly,* II, 402-419 (July, 1929).

[26] Lewis Mumford, "The Significance of Herman Melville," *The New Republic,* LVI, 212-214 (October 10, 1928).

[27] Van Wyck Brooks, *Emerson and Others* (New York, 1927), p. 181.

[28] M. Josephson, "Transfiguration of Herman Melville," *The Outlook,* CL, 809 (September 19, 1928).

[29] Lewis Mumford, *Herman Melville* (New York, 1929), pp. 228 and 195.

between English and American criticism, the conservative American critics being suspicious of blurb and exaggeration, and the English being unwilling to evaluate Melville on other grounds than those of intrinsic literary merit. A reviewer in *The Freeman* (October 26, 1921) expressed the cynical American point of view:

Well it was only a question of time: sooner or later the darkness that surrounds this extraordinary man was certain to yield before our indefatigable national appetite for investigation and research. Next year Melville will have been forgotten again. . . . But for the next six months there is to be a Melville boom. Ishmael is to emerge at last: he is to have his little hour. And there will be a few hundred or a few dozen readers, moreover, who, discovering him for the first time in this limelight, will seize upon his gift as a permanent possession.[30]

Frank Jewett Mather, Jr., commenting on Lewis Mumford's biography, said: "Indeed there is some exaggeration in the general envisagement of Herman Melville as a Prometheus too lonely even to attract the vultures."[31] Professor Weaver limits Melville's claim to fame to three exploits: the literary discovery of the South Seas; the creation, with Dana, of a new world of literature of the sailor; and *Moby Dick,* which reveals a great imagination.[32] But Professor Weaver seems to be doubtful, as he revealed in private conversation, of Melville's claim as a literary artist.

It ought to be remembered that the epic hero, the "Herman Melville" of the modern critics, is an American created by Americans. Differences in national psychology may account for the failure of the English to catch the spark of enthusiasm for this figure. Much of the English criticism has been, therefore, literary and conservative. Michael Sadleir said in 1922: "Apart from *Moby Dick,* the neo-Melvillian has little beyond patronizing approval for the books of his hero." Even *Moby Dick* was over-praised:

In some degree the worship of *Moby Dick* and the comparative neglect of the other work are inevitable corollaries to the Melville boom at its present stage. During the first period of any new æsthetic wonder, the peculiar transcends the normal in the imagination of disciples. . . . In

---

[30] "A Reviewer's Notebook," *The Freeman*, IV, 166-167 (October 26, 1921).

[31] Frank Jewett Mather, Jr., "Herman Melville," *The Saturday Review of Literature*, V, 945-946 (April 27, 1929).

[32] Raymond M. Weaver, "Herman Melville," *The Bookman*, LIV, 323 (December, 1921).

years to come, when the glamour of oddity has paled a little, it will be admitted that the book labours under a sad weight of intolerable prolixity.[33]

Probably the most sober appraisal of Melville's work has come from an Englishman, H. P. Marshall. *Moby Dick* is in a class by itself. *Redburn, Typee, Omoo,* and some of the *Piazza Tales* deserve to be read for their style as well as their matter. Badly written but interesting, *Mardi* and *Pierre* are books that publishers would call "human documents." But *Israel Potter* has only moments, *White Jacket* is ordinary, and *The Confidence Man* is "extremely dull and monstrously constructed."[34]

VI

One may suspect that the Melville *culte* is not so large as the mass of recent notices of Melville would seem to indicate. It may be limited, indeed, to those who find in the "Herman Melville" of the recent biographies a kindred spirit, or a life which embodies their own psychological conflicts. The whole subject of Melville's reputation is extremely interesting because it has unusually sharp contrasts and because it permits us to see the complicated process of literary apotheosis going on all around us at the present moment. Perhaps the "spirit of the age" will soon become sufficiently corporeal to enable us to see why there has been such a strong Melville revival in this generation. Although Herman Melville has a throne in our literary Valhalla, it may perhaps be seen, after the rosy clouds have rolled away from the pedestal, that he is balanced precariously on a chair with a single leg, and that made of whale-bone, like the leg of Captain Ahab.

[33] Michael Sadleir, *Excursions in Victorian Bibliography* (London, Chaundy & Cox, 1922), p. 218.
[34] H. P. Marshall, "Herman Melville," *The London Mercury,* XI, 58-59 (November, 1924).

Herman Melville's "I and My Chimney"

Merton M. Sealts

T HE FIVE years between the publication of *Moby-Dick* and his advent to the Holy Land were the most crucial in Melville's long life. . . ."[1] So Raymond Weaver has written of the obscure period in Herman Melville's career between 1851 and 1856 which included the writing of *Pierre* (1852), a number of short stories and sketches for periodicals (1853-1856), and *The Confidence-Man* (1857). At this time Melville was living at Arrowhead, his farmhouse near Pittsfield, Massachusetts, which provided the setting for some of his less familiar prose. Such is the case with "I and My Chimney," a short sketch in a humorous vein probably written near the end of 1855,[2] in which "Melville makes the old chimney at Arrowhead the chief character in a sketch of his domestic life at Pittsfield. . . ."[3] But the story, as will be shown, is more than a mere descriptive sketch: it is Melville's subtle comment on a major spiritual crisis of his life. The clue to certain elements in *Pierre* is also afforded by an understanding of Melville's procedure in writing "I and My Chimney."

A brief account of the plot of the story should be useful in fur-

[1] In the Introduction to his edition of Melville's *Journal up the Straits, October 11, 1856-May 5, 1857* (New York, 1935), p. xii.

To Herman Melville's granddaughter, Mrs. Eleanor Melville Metcalf, and to the Committee on Higher Degrees in the History of American Civilization, Harvard University, I am indebted for permission to quote from manuscript material as indicated below. This material, hitherto unpublished, is now in the Melville Collection of the Harvard University Library. Mr. William Braswell of Purdue University has also allowed me to quote from his unpublished dissertation, *Herman Melville and Christianity*. For these and other favors connected with the preparation of this article, I am grateful.

[2] A study of the number and frequency of Melville's contributions to periodicals, including *Israel Potter* (1855, but first published serially), indicates that none of this work remained long in manuscript. "I and My Chimney" was written enough in advance of March, 1856, to appear in *Putnam's Monthly Magazine* for that date, yet it was not reprinted with other pieces from *Putnam's* in Melville's *Piazza Tales* (1856). A letter of March 24, 1856, from Melville to his publishers, Dix & Edwards, accompanied his return of corrected proofs of *The Piazza Tales* (*Family Correspondence of Herman Melville, 1830-1904, in the Gansevoort-Lansing Collection*, ed. V. H. Paltsits, New York Public Library, 1929, p. 12). Allowing the necessary time for transactions with the publishers and printing of the material, it seems likely that Melville planned *The Piazza Tales* late in 1855, and that he wrote "I and My Chimney" shortly thereafter.

[3] Raymond Weaver, *Herman Melville, Mariner and Mystic* (New York, 1921), p. 308.

ther discussion. The action turns on the affection of its narrator for his beloved old chimney, which he describes in detail, and his lengthy dispute with his wife over her proposals to alter it and later to remove it entirely from the house. Over the protests of her husband, the wife employs an architect and stonemason, Scribe by name, to make a thorough examination of the chimney. Scribe startles the family by suggesting the possible existence of a secret closet within the structure, and the wife and daughters immediately conjure up visions of treasure hidden away by the late builder of the house—the narrator's mysterious kinsman, Captain Julian Dacres. But the husband, to put a stop to such foolishness and to gain a little peace for himself, eventually bribes the not unwilling Scribe to accept fifty dollars in return for a certificate attesting to the entire soundness of the chimney. Fortified with this evidence, which he hangs prominently above the fireplace, the narrator refuses to countenance the slightest alteration to the chimney, but as the story closes he is still facing minor assaults of the opposition and "standing guard over my mossy old chimney; for it is resolved between me and my chimney, that I and my chimney will never surrender."[4]

This rather slight plot has attracted less attention to the story than has its setting, drawn as it is from Melville's surroundings at Arrowhead. Weaver, noting this factual background, states that the farmhouse itself was built in 1780 by a Captain David Bush, but he does not call attention to Bush's transformation by Melville into the narrator's kinsman, Captain Dacres. This is but one example of Melville's free handling of details in the story, which Weaver does not discuss,[5] nor have Melville's other full-length biographers added appreciably to Weaver's treatment of the story. John Freeman remarks only that it is "an example of Melville writing like Hawthorne,"[6] and Lewis Mumford says merely that it is more an essay "in character" than a tale.[7] Yet Mumford himself sees "a glimpse of Melville's own drift of mind" in other prose of this

[4] "I and My Chimney," in *Billy Budd and Other Prose Pieces* (Vol. XIII in the Standard Edition of Melville's works, 16 vols., London, Constable and Co., 1922-24), p. 311. All succeeding references to Melville's works are to volumes of the Constable edition.
[5] Weaver, *Herman Melville, Mariner and Mystic*, pp. 308 ff.
[6] John Freeman, *Herman Melville* (London, 1926), p. 52.
[7] Lewis Mumford, *Herman Melville* (New York, 1929), p. 236.

period,[8] and more recent investigation has found Melville's penchant for symbolism revealed even in one of his most matter-of-fact sketches.[9] With this in mind, the extent of Melville's departures from literal truth in "I and My Chimney" should be carefully considered.

First, as pointed out above, Melville makes the builder of the house a kinsman of the narrator, naming him "Dacres." Secondly, he places in the story a household of four persons: the husband and wife with their two daughters, Anna and Julia. Melville's own daughters were younger than these two characters: Elizabeth was born in 1853 and Frances in 1855, both before the probable time of composition of the story. In addition, the family at Arrowhead included two older sons, Melville's own sisters, and his mother. The presence of Melville's mother is significant because of a notation made by Melville's wife concerning the spouse of the story: "All this about his wife, applied to his mother—who was very vigorous and energetic about the farm, etc."[10] If Mrs. Melville is correct, this represents still another departure from literal truth. The nagging spouse, far from an attractive figure, is scarcely typical of Melville's own wife, whereas according to family tradition his mother was persistently critical. More than one writer toys with the idea that the domineering Mary Glendinning in *Pierre* is based on the character of Maria Gansevoort Melville, and the wife of "I and My Chimney" may be cut from the same pattern. But Mrs. Melville's notation goes still further: "The proposed removal of the chimney," she continues, "is purely mythical." Not only the characters, then, but also the motivation of the plot itself shows Melville's inventive touch—and Melville never invents without purpose. In *Mardi, Moby-Dick,* and *Pierre,* Melville's myth-making is in-

[8] *Ibid.,* p. 238.

[9] E. H. Eby, "Herman Melville's 'Tartarus of Maids,'" *Modern Language Quarterly,* I, 95-100 (March, 1940). Eby holds that here "Melville's main intention is to represent through the medium of the story the biological burdens imposed on women because they bear the children. This is conveyed by symbolism remarkably consistent and detailed" (p. 97).

[10] Weaver prints this notation with the text of the story in the Constable edition, p. 287. He is inaccurate in his accompanying statement that it is taken from the *manuscript* of the story, which has apparently not survived. Mrs. Melville made her notation on a printed copy of the story which, with clippings of other periodical pieces by her husband, she collected in a binder. This volume is now in possession of her granddaughter, Mrs. Henry K. Metcalf, of Cambridge, Massachusetts, who has kindly permitted me to examine it.

tentionally allegorical and symbolic. If the removal of the chimney is "purely mythical," has Melville more to communicate than the mere spinning of a yarn? And why should he write of a chimney?

In *Pierre,* published four years before, Melville had described "the gray and grand old tower" of the Church of the Apostles, "emblem to Pierre of an unshakable fortitude, which, deep-rooted in the heart of the earth, defied all the howls of the air."[11] The chimney in the present story is a similar emblem of fortitude, "for it is resolved between me and my chimney, that I and my chimney will never surrender." Again in *Pierre* Melville writes: "Deep, deep, and still deep and deeper must we go, if we would find out the heart of a man; descending into which is as descending a spiral stair in a shaft, without any end, and where that endlessness is only concealed by the spiralness of the stair, and the blackness of the shaft."[12] So Melville in his writing, like the poet Lombardo in *Mardi,* "got deeper and deeper into himself."[13] It is with the same purpose that in the present story he traces the shaft of the chimney: "Very often I go down into my cellar, and attentively survey that vast square of masonry. I stand long, and ponder over, and wonder at it. It has a druidical look, away down in the umbrageous cellar there, whose numerous vaulted passages, and far glens of gloom, resemble the dark, damp depths of primeval woods."[14] As it would be vain to search for the bottom of the endless shaft described in *Pierre,* so the narrator of "I and My Chimney" digs in vain about the foundation of the chimney. The vast area of this lower part of the structure is emphasized: ". . . large as it appears above the roof," says Scribe, the architect, "I would not have inferred the magnitude of this foundation, sir."[15]

The significance of all this may be summarized briefly: the shaft is the image of "the heart of a man"; the chimney is an emblem of fortitude; what lies at its bottom is hidden in darkness. Like a pyramid in its shape, the chimney is thus discovered to have its greatest area shrouded in mystery. This consistent likening to the pyramids is important: "The architect of the chimney must have had the pyramid of Cheops before him; for after that famous structure it seems modelled. . . ."[16] Had the wife's projected tunnel been

---

[11] *Pierre,* p. 378.
[12] *Ibid.,* p. 402.
[13] *Mardi,* II, 326.
[14] "I and My Chimney," p. 283.
[15] *Ibid.,* p. 295.
[16] *Ibid.,* p. 280.

thrust into the chimney, "some Belzoni or other might have succeeded in future ages in penetrating through the masonry, and
actually emerging into the dining-room. . . ."[17] Belzoni was an
Egyptologist. And again: "We seemed in the pyramids; and I,
with one hand holding my lamp over head, and with the other
pointing out, in the obscurity, the hoar mass of the chimney, seemed
some Arab guide, showing the cobwebbed mausoleum of the great
god Apis."[18] A commentary on this passage is afforded by an
often-quoted sentence in *Pierre*: "By vast pains we mine into the
pyramid; by horrible gropings we come to the central room; with
joy we espy the sarcophagus; but we lift the lid—and no body is
there!—appallingly vacant as vast is the soul of a man!"[19] What
Melville is saying in the story is that in pondering over and wondering at his "chimney" he is introspectively surveying his own
soul—and that introspection is an endless, empty-handed search.

Melville's identification of the chimney with himself is made
certain by the amusing connotations of other passages in the story.
Built around the structure were "the most rambling conceivable"
rooms which (like the organs of the body), "as it were, dovetailed
into each other. They were of all shapes; not one mathematically
square room among them all. . . ."[20] Almost every room "was in
itself an entry, or passageway to other rooms . . . —never was there
so labyrinthine an abode. Guests will tarry with me several weeks,
and every now and then, be anew astonished at some unforeseen
apartment."[21] This jocular anatomizing depicts perfectly the
enigma Herman Melville presented to his acquaintances, who were
anew astonished every now and then by what he said and did.

[17] *Ibid.*, p. 292.

[18] *Ibid.*, p. 295. Apis was "supposed to be the image of the soul of Osiris. . . . He
was also regarded as the reincarnation (or the son) of Ptah—except by Greek writers . . ."
(*Encyclopaedia Britannica*, 14th ed., II, 99).

[19] *Pierre*, p. 397. Note the significance of other references to the pyramids: in a letter
to Hawthorne written in 1851 as printed by Julian Hawthorne, *Nathaniel Hawthorne and
His Wife* (2 vols., Boston, 1885), I, 405 ff.; a passage in "Bartleby the Scrivener," *Piazza
Tales*, p. 64; the profound effect on Melville of the pyramids themselves, described in his
Journal up the Straits, pp. 56-59.

[20] "I and My Chimney," p. 306. For still another physiological connotation, cf. pp.
286 ff.: the "mysterious closet." This passage should be read in the light of Eby's article,
cited above, and with reference to the chronology of Melville's family life in 1855. Those
familiar with E. L. Grant Watson's article, "Melville's *Pierre*," *New England Quarterly*,
III, 195-234 (April, 1930), should also compare the description of Pierre's chambers
(*Pierre*, pp. 413 ff.), noting reference to "the dining room" there as in the present story
(p. 292).   [21] *Ibid.*, pp. 292 ff.

Carrying on the anatomical figure, Melville's narrator exclaims at his wife's proposal "*in toto* to abolish the chimney":

What! . . . abolish the chimney? To take out the backbone of any-thing, wife, is a hazardous affair. Spines out of backs, and chimneys out of houses, are not to be taken like frosted lead-pipes from the ground. Besides, . . . the chimney is the one grand permanence of this abode. If undisturbed by innovators, then in future ages, when all the house shall have crumbled from it, this chimney will still survive—a Bunker Hill monument. No, no, wife, I can't abolish my backbone.[22]

"Backbone," the colloquial term for fortitude, together with the reference to the enduring Bunker Hill monument (like the church tower in *Pierre*), further amplifies the connotation of the chimney. No wonder that to Scribe "this house would appear to have been built simply for the accommodation of your chimney";[23] that "I and my chimney could not be parted";[24] that "it is never out of my house, and never out of my mind";[25] that "I look upon this chim-ney less as a pile of masonry than as a personage."[26] All this is entirely true, for the "chimney" is the heart and soul of Herman Melville.

II

The identification of the chimney with Melville's own personal-ity would constitute nothing more than a piece of subtle ingenuity on the part of both author and reader were it not for the larger implication of "I and My Chimney." This centers in the "purely mythical" proposal to remove the chimney and the subsequent examination made of it by Scribe. Scribe's report of his findings reads in part as follows:

It is my solemn duty to warn you, sir, that there is architectural cause to conjecture that somewhere concealed in your chimney is a reserved space, hermetically closed, in short, a secret chamber, or rather closet. How long it has been there, it is for me impossible to say. What it contains is hid, with itself, in darkness. But probably a secret closet would not have been contrived except for some extraordinary object, whether for the concealment of treasure, or what other purpose, may be left to those better acquainted with the history of the house to guess.[27]

[22] *Ibid.*, p. 294. Cf. the dedication of *Israel Potter* (dated June 17, 1854) to the Bunker Hill monument. [23] *Ibid.*, p. 295.
[24] *Ibid.*, p. 298. [25] *Ibid.*, p. 297.
[26] *Ibid.*, p. 284. [27] *Ibid.*, p. 300.

The wife and daughters, on receipt of this report, immediately conclude that the mysterious kinsman who built the house must have hidden something away—another excuse for probing the chimney:

Although they had never before dreamed of such a revelation as Mr. Scribe's; yet upon the first suggestion they instinctively saw the extreme likelihood of it. In corroboration, they cited first my kinsman, and second, my chimney; alleging that the profound mystery involving the former, and the equally profound masonry involving the latter, though both acknowledged facts, were alike preposterous on any other supposition than the secret closet.[28]

From this point on, the secret closet becomes the central topic of argument: over its possible existence the family quarrel bitterly. The wife argues that "when you think of that old kinsman of yours, you *know* there must be a secret closet in this chimney."[29] The husband, unable to silence his wife by outtalking her, finally resorts to the bribing of Scribe to certify, as "a competent surveyor," that having examined the chimney he "found no reason to believe *any unsoundness; in short, any—any secret closet* in it."[30] This studied phrasing makes the secret closet signify unsoundness, so that the reason for probing the chimney becomes to ferret out its weakness. The likelihood of such "unsoundness," it will be recalled, was corroborated by "first my kinsman, and second, my chimney."

In the story the specific kinship of the highly mysterious Captain Dacres is never disclosed. But in *Pierre* the immediate relatives of the hero are all marked at one time or other by mental unsoundness. Isabel, whom Pierre takes for his half sister, had been kept in a madhouse;[31] Pierre's father had died in delirium,[32] and Pierre's mother also had died insane.[33] "Nor did this remarkable double-doom of [Pierre's] parents wholly fail to impress his mind with presentiments concerning his own fate—his own hereditary liability to madness."[34] And behind this fear in Pierre lay Melville's knowledge of what had befallen one of his own parents. His

---

[28] *Ibid.*, p. 302.
[29] *Ibid.*, p. 304. The ensuing dispute over the ash-hole is a strange passage, dealing with the wife, the cat, and St. Dunstan's devil. Cf. Isabel's mention of the cat in *Pierre*, "softly scratching for some hidden thing among the litter of the abandoned fire-places" (p. 163). [30] *Ibid.*, p. 308. Italics mine.
[31] *Pierre*, pp. 168 ff. [32] *Ibid.*, pp. 96 ff.
[33] *Ibid.*, p. 398. [34] *Ibid.*, p. 400.

mother was still living when *Pierre* was written, but in 1832 his father had died under the cloud of mental derangement. His condition on his deathbed is briefly described in a letter to Lemuel Shaw, Herman Melville's future father-in-law, from Thomas Melville (Herman Melville's uncle): "I found him *very sick*—induced by a variety of causes—under great mental excitement—at times fierce, even *maniacal.*—in short, my dear sir, Hope, is no longer permitted of his recovery, in the opinion of the attending Physicians. . . ."[35]

The pattern of "I and My Chimney" now begins to emerge, becoming more clear as the plot of the story unfolds. Following the bribing of Scribe, the narrator cites the certificate attesting to the chimney's soundness in an effort to put an end to the argument:

Wife, . . . why speak more of that secret closet, when there before you hangs contrary testimony of a master mason, elected by yourself to decide. Besides, even if there were a secret closet, secret it should remain, and secret it shall. Yes, wife, here, for once, I must say my say. *Infinite sad mischief has resulted from the profane bursting open of secret recesses.* Though standing in the *heart* of this house, though hitherto we have all nestled about it, unsuspicious of aught hidden within, this chimney may or may not have a secret closet. *But if it have, it is my kinsman's. To break into that wall, would be to break into his breast.*[36]

The tone of this passage contrasts with the general light tone of the earlier part of the story, as even a casual reading will show. The sudden seriousness here, in speaking of the "profane" meddling with any secrets of the kinsman, is more in keeping with the reverent mood of Pierre in approaching the image of his "sacred father"[37] enshrined in his mind,[38] or in retiring to the "locked, round-windowed closet . . ., *sacred*" to his privacies, where the ambiguous chair-portrait of his father is hung.[39] Though the beloved image is later so tragically shattered, the memory of his father "for right cause or wrong" remains "ever *sacred and inviolate*" to Pierre.[40]

[35] From an unpublished letter dated Albany, January 15, 1832, now in the Melville Collection of the Harvard University Library, printed with permission of Mrs. Eleanor Melville Metcalf and authorities of Harvard University. Peter Gansevoort had touched upon the matter five days earlier in a letter to Thomas Melville, now in the Gansevoort-Lansing Collection of the New York Public Library (Willard Thorp, *Herman Melville: Representative Selections*, New York, 1938, p. xii and n.).
[36] "I and My Chimney," p. 309. Italics mine.
[37] *Pierre*, p. 89.   [38] *Ibid.*, p. 93.
[39] *Ibid.*, p. 98. Italics mine.   [40] *Ibid.*, p. 267. Italics mine.

That such a mood was also Herman Melville's is strikingly indicated by the name given the kinsman in "I and My Chimney," "Dacres" being simply an anagram for *sacred!* This is startling confirmation that both Dacres and Pierre's father are based on memories of the unfortunate Allan Melville.

Besides explaining the first of the two reasons given for the possible unsoundness of the chimney, this analysis is important in an understanding of Melville's intentions in *Pierre*. Many of the details of Pierre's situation, from his surroundings at Saddle Meadows to the torture of his failing eyesight, are unquestionably drawn from Melville's own life. Some critics, cautioned by Melville's distinct warning that "the thoughts we here indite as Pierre's are to be very carefully discriminated from those we indite concerning him,"[41] object to any interpretation of *Pierre* as its author's spiritual autobiography. But from this new evidence it is obvious that a fundamental element in Pierre's situation is taken straight from his creator's experience. When Pierre "dropped his angle into the well of his childhood, to find what fish might be there,"[42] he brought forth dark memories of the unhappy death of his father. And Isabel, supposedly his father's illegitimate daughter, is mysteriously connected with the father's fate just as the chimney in Melville's short story is related to the mysterious kinsman. There is general agreement among recent critics that Isabel, again like the chimney, symbolizes the depths of Melville's mind.[43] As it was impossible to reach the bottom of the endless shaft of the soul, the ultimate foundation of the chimney, so Pierre "renounced all thought of ever having Isabel's dark lantern illuminated to him. Her light was lidded, and the lid was locked." Such is the dark mystery surrounding the girl; though, Melville continues, by interrogating relatives "on his father's side" Pierre "might possibly rake forth some few small grains of *dubious and most unsatisfying things,* which, *were he that way strongly bent,* would only serve

[41] *Ibid.*, p. 233.   [42] *Ibid.*, p. 396.

[43] Note the similarity in terms employed by Lewis Mumford, *Herman Melville*, pp. 220 ff.; E. L. Grant Watson, "Melville's *Pierre*," *New England Quarterly*, III, 201 (April, 1930); George C. Homans, "The Dark Angel: The Tragedy of Herman Melville," *New England Quarterly*, V, 723 (Oct., 1932); William Braswell, "The Satirical Temper of Melville's *Pierre*," *American Literature*, VII, 431 n. (Jan., 1936); Willard Thorp, *Herman Melville: Representative Selections*, p. lxxx.

the more hopelessly *to cripple him in his practical resolves.* He determined *to pry not at all* into this *sacred* problem."[44] So in "I and My Chimney" Melville warns against the profane disturbance of secrets relating to his sacred kinsman.

I interpret this passage as the expression of Melville's own fear that, "were he that way strongly bent," he would experience the same fate as his father's by continued delving into the depths of his mind. His dilemma was something like that of Pierre over the symbolic Isabel: to acknowledge her publicly is impossible without hurting his mother; to vindicate openly her relationship to him means tarnishing his father's honorable memory. Melville's advice to his hero is to "quit Isabel" and to "beg humble pardon of thy mother," but Pierre is unable to free himself so easily from his problem. In the confusion of his soul at these "absurdities" he "would fain have disowned the very *memory* and the *mind* which produced to him such an immense *scandal upon his common sanity.*"[45] This sounds suspiciously like the two reasons offered for the existence of the symbolic secret closet, in "I and My Chimney." At the time of *Pierre* Melville had nevertheless continued his introspection just as Pierre in the novel gave himself over to Isabel. No wonder that he later concluded in "I and My Chimney" that he had been "a little out of my mind, I now think," in trying to lay bare the very *foundation* of the structure which his kinsman had established.[46]

That Melville's family shared his uneasiness is suggested by Mrs. Melville's private account of this portion of her husband's career, from the writing of *Moby-Dick* "under unfavorable circumstances" in 1850 and 1851 until the period now under discussion.[47] "We all felt anxious about the strain on his health in spring of 1853," writes Mrs. Melville: she is confirmed by authentic tradition. At the time of the publication of *Pierre*, Melville, says William Braswell, "had worked himself into so frightful a nervous condition that his family had physicians examine him for insanity. The physicians pronounced him sane and assumed responsibility for his actions; but authoritative tradition survives that tells a pathetic story of his

[44] *Pierre*, p. 199. Italics mine.
[45] *Ibid.*, p. 239. Italics mine.   [46] "I and My Chimney," p. 283.
[47] Weaver prints a lengthy quotation from Mrs. Melville's pocket diary in his Introduction to Melville's *Journal up the Straits*, pp. xv ff.

life during this period." In a note Braswell adds: "I base this statement upon personal talks with Mrs. Eleanor Melville Metcalf [Mel-
ville's granddaughter] and with Professor Raymond Weaver."[48]

Mrs. Metcalf, with whom I have also discussed the entire situation, agrees with me that "I and My Chimney" is an allegorical
version of the circumstances leading to this examination. Melville's
own serious mental condition was the primary cause, made doubly
distressing to his family by the tragic memory of his father's death,
which Melville himself had recalled in *Pierre*. Hence the relation
of the chimney itself and the "kinsman" of the story to the possible
unsoundness of the structure. It is conceivable that Melville's analysis of his own condition in writing *Pierre* played a part in the
decision of the family to have his mind examined. According to
tradition the subtler meanings of his work were a mystery even to
his closest relatives,[49] but the pointed allusion to Pierre's father probably did not escape the notice of those familiar with the facts of
Allan Melville's death—particularly Maria Gansevoort Melville and
Lemuel Shaw. It is significant that Melville's mother is said to be
the original of the character in "I and My Chimney" who instigates
the examination, who is actively hostile to the narrator's "philosophical jabber,"[50] and who even after Scribe's report continues to
tap the wall of the chimney after the manner of a physician examining a man for life insurance.[51]

The possible identification of one other character in the story is
worth considering—that of Scribe, the examiner. Again referring
to Mrs. Melville's journal we find that Melville's physical health
remained poor for several years after the writing of *Pierre*. "In

[48] William Braswell, *Herman Melville and Christianity* (unpublished University of
Chicago dissertation, 1934), p. 166 and n., quoted with permission of the author. A part
of this dissertation (pp. 129-166, 207-211) has been printed in lithotype in a private
edition distributed by the University of Chicago Libraries, 1936. Cf. also Weaver's discussion in his Introduction to Melville's *Journal up the Straits*, pp. xii-xxiv.

[49] Concerning *Mardi* Mrs. Melville had written her mother: "I suppose by this time
you are deep in the 'fogs' of 'Mardi'—if the mist ever does clear away. I should like to
know what it reveals to *you* . . ." (from an unpublished letter dated New York, April 30,
1849, now in the Melville Collection of the Harvard University Library, printed with
permission of Mrs. Eleanor Melville Metcalf and authorities of Harvard University). Melville himself told Mrs. Hawthorne that she was "the only *woman*" who liked *Moby-Dick*,
but that with her "spiritualizing nature" she could "see more things than other people"
(from a letter dated New York, Jan. 8, 1852, printed in part in "An Unpublished Letter
from Herman Melville to Mrs. Hawthorne in Explanation of 'Moby-Dick.'" *American
Art Association—Anderson Galleries Catalogue of Sale*, No. 3911, p. 9 [New York, 1931]).

[50] Cf. "I and My Chimney," pp. 309 ff.   [51] *Ibid.*, p. 308.

Feb 1855 he had his first attack of severe rhumatism [*sic*] in his back—so that he was helpless—and in the following June an attack of sciatica. Our neighbor in Pittsfield Dr. O. W. Holmes attended & prescribed for him."[52] The relation between Holmes and Melville was more than that of doctor and patient. Holmes's "The Last Leaf" was written about Melville's own grandfather, Major Thomas Melville, and interesting records survive of vigorous conversations between the two younger men when both were in residence at Pittsfield.[53] Reviewing these points, we find that the literary doctor was on familiar terms with Melville and had served him in a professional capacity twice during the very year in which "I and My Chimney" was probably written. It has been shown that as the architect found no unsoundness in the chimney, that is, in Melville's mind; so doctors had "pronounced him sane and assumed responsibility for his actions." Is it possible that Holmes had been one of the doctors, and that Melville meant to indicate the fact in the story by giving the examiner there the name of "Scribe," or *writer?* In view of Melville's general procedure in composing the story, this identification is at least not implausible.

The significance of "I and My Chimney" may now be summarized briefly. It is Melville's account of the examination of his mind made a few years before the story was written, at the instigation of his family. This meaning is conveyed in disguised form by the plot itself, with the aid of symbolism parallel to that of *Pierre* though the terms are dissimilar. The examination was made because of anxiety over Melville's nervous condition, represented by the speculation concerning the chimney, and with the knowledge of the tragic circumstances surrounding the death of his father, represented by the mystery concerning the late kinsman of the story. This fear of possible hereditary insanity was alluded to by Melville himself in *Pierre.* The characterization of "I and My Chimney" points to Melville's mother as the person responsible for the consultation of physicians, one of whom may have been Dr. Oliver Wendell

[52] Introduction to *Journal up the Straits,* p. xvi. Note the reference to sciatica in "I and My Chimney," pp. 287 ff.: this may be of some value in confirming the suggested date of the story.

[53] See a letter of Evert A. Duyckinck to his wife dated Pittsfield, August 6, 1850, printed by Luther S. Mansfield, "Glimpses of Herman Melville's Life in Pittsfield, 1850-1851," *American Literature,* IX, 29-31 (March, 1937); M. B. Field, *Memories of Many Men and of Some Women* (New York, 1874), p. 202.

Holmes. The examination revealed that Melville's nervous condition was not a manifestation of insanity, and the subsequent course of his life confirmed the judgment of his examiners.

Of the evidence afforded by records of Melville's career after this time, Forsythe observes that "no one who has any knowledge of Melville in his later years" needs such testimony. "For thinking people, the question ... of Melville's sanity has long since been completely settled."[54] With these words there can be only thorough agreement. In the present study Herman Melville himself has been allowed to explain how the question was first raised: it cannot be too strongly emphasized that any suspicions based on his own nervousness and associated with memories of his father had been entirely groundless. This is not to minimize the seriousness of his condition in 1852-1853, though in a day when a better understanding of nervous disorders prevails than in Melville's own lifetime there is no reason for describing his difficulties in sensational terms. Had modern mental therapeutic knowledge been available to Melville himself, he and his family would doubtless have been spared much of the distress they were forced to endure. More important than misguided amateur psychologizing at this late date, however, is an appreciation of the unexpected extent to which, through employment of symbols, Melville committed his deepest spiritual problems to subtle analysis in print. There is further evidence for this practice in other work of the period of "I and My Chimney," as I plan to discuss in a future publication, but for the present it is sufficient to take leave of him still "standing guard over my mossy old chimney; for it is resolved between me and my chimney, that I and my chimney will never surrender."

[54] Robert S. Forsythe, reviewing Weaver's edition of *Journal up the Straits, American Literature*, VIII, 85 (March, 1936).

Melville's "Sociality"

R. E. Watters

HERMAN MELVILLE lived in an age when most Americans were more concerned that society should not interfere with the individual than that the individual should contribute to the welfare of the social group. In 1837 Emerson, for instance, wrote approvingly of "Everything that tends to insulate the individual,— to surround him with barriers of natural respect, so that each man shall feel the world is his, and man shall treat with man as a sovereign state with a sovereign state."[1] Thirty years later he summarized his generation's development:

The former generations acted under the belief that a shining social prosperity was the beatitude of man, and sacrificed uniformly the citizen to the state. The modern mind believed that the nation existed for the individual, for the guardianship and education of every man. This idea, roughly written in revolutions and national movements, in the mind of the philosopher had far more precision; the individual is the world.[2]

For Emerson, even friendship had its dangers. Although he began his essay on the subject with commendation, he soon found himself battling against any diminution of his independent self-completeness: "Let us feel if we will the absolute insulation of man. . . . Let us even bid our dearest friends farewell, and defy them, saying 'Who are you? Unhand me: I will be dependent no more.' "[3]

It is true that the interrelationships of one man to another and particularly to the Over-Soul are repeatedly mentioned by Emerson; but the self-reliant doctrine of insulated individualism that was more than equally emphasized would seem to have been far more readily accepted by his public, as being more congenial with a spirit dominant in his time. Little heed was taken of Melville's dissenting reminders that man is born, lives, and dies in constant debt to the social community of his fellows. Yet Melville's books

[1] *Complete Works* (Centenary ed., Boston, 1903-1904), I, 113.
[2] *Ibid.*, X, 326.   [3] *Ibid.*, II, 214.

had repeatedly portrayed the distortion of the individual and the destruction of the group which follow upon voluntary repudiation or involuntary neglect of that debt.[4] In his setting up a contrary doctrine of "sociality,"[5] in which the individual is shown to find satisfaction in receptiveness to all the currents of friendliness, sympathy, love, Melville was far closer to Whitman, who once declared:

The common ambition strains for elevations, to become some privileged exclusive. The master sees greatness and health in being part of the mass.... Not that half [of the ideal] only, individualism, which isolates. There is another half, which is adhesiveness or love, that fuses, ties and aggregates, making the races comrades, and fraternizing all. Both are to be vitalized by religion. . . . For I say at the core of democracy, finally, is the religious element.[6]

II

The concept of the commonalty of mankind, past and present, recurs in Melville's works. Several passages voice the thought that "all generations are blended . . . one and all, brothers in essence," because in the beginning "the sons of God did verily wed with our mothers, the irresistible daughters of Eve."[7] In Babbalanja's opinion,[8] "We are full of ghosts and spirits . . . full of buried dead,

[4] See "Melville's 'Isolatoes,'" by the present writer, soon to be published in *PMLA*.

[5] The following paper does not pretend to give an exhaustive discussion of Melville's whole social philosophy. It is believed, however, that the brevity necessary to a short paper entails no essential distortion of the general whole other than, perhaps, the slight overemphasis inseparable from any concentration upon a specific concept. Much more might be said (for instance, about the various complex characters) if all elements of Melville's social philosophy were under discussion.

[6] *Complete Writings* (Camden ed., New York, 1902), V, 80.

[7] *Mardi*, I, 13-14, *Works of Herman Melville* (Standard ed., London, 1922-24). All references are made to this edition.

[8] The danger which exists in attributing to a novelist the opinions voiced by his characters must be faced by all students of Melville, the bulk of whose work is written in the first person and whose practice it undoubtedly was to use his characters as mouthpieces. How much of *Moby-Dick*, for instance—altogether apart from passages spoken or thought specifically by Ishmael or others—may be considered the narrator's (Ishmael's) and how much Melville's? Certainly the narrator sees and knows more than Ishmael, the crewman, could. The safest answer would perhaps be Ishmael-Melville—unless scholarship on the novelist is to cease almost entirely.

The practice followed here is this: all passages spoken by or definitely attributed to the several characters are so indicated, and should be taken as *not necessarily* Melville's own. (Only about one quarter of the passages cited fall into this category.) The other passages are considered to present Melville's opinions, whether or not the work has a supposed narrator. The persistent repetition of the general idea of "sociality" throughout his works from first to last must justify the practice. Would an author repeat a theme constantly in various forms, through various characters, and in nearly all his volumes, written over a period of more than forty years, unless he in general subscribed to it—or (to be overcautious) at least desired to convey it to his readers?

that start to life before us. And all our dead sires, verily, are in us; *that* is their immortality. . . . Every thought's a soul of some past poet, hero, sage. We are fuller than a city."[9] Melville himself reaffirms the general idea of the immanence of mankind in the individual: "I was at the subsiding of the Deluge, and helped swab the ground. . . . With the Israelites, I fainted in the wilderness. . . . I touched Isabella's heart, that she hearkened to Columbus. . . . I, the man in the iron mask; I, Junius."[10] The famous chapter "Dreams" in *Mardi* has been taken as evidence of Melville's leaning toward the transcendental Over-Soul,[11] but if it is read carefully it is found to reveal an identification of self not with an immanent divinity but instead with an immanent humanity: "Many, many souls are in me. . . . In me, many worthies recline, and converse."[12] The apparent identification of self with the universe is the result merely of a more grandiose trope than the one of the frigate which is also used.

The concept of the oneness of the human race, moreover, appears in a review by Melville, published the same month with *Mardi*. To rebuke Parkman's contempt for the Indians in *The Oregon Trail,* Melville reminds the historian that "our own progenitors" were savages:

Who can swear, that among the naked British barbarians sent to Rome to be stared at more than 1500 years ago, the ancestor of Bacon might not have been found? Why, among the very Thugs of India, or the bloody Dyaks of Borneo, exists the germ of all that is intellectually elevated and grand. We are all of us—Anglo-Saxons, Dyaks, and Indians—sprung from one head, and made in one image. And if we regret this brotherhood now, we shall be forced to join hands hereafter.[13]

In *Redburn* Melville opposed the exclusion of immigrants from this country on the ground that "the whole world is the patrimony of the whole world."[14] Immigration had enriched American blood until it has become like "the flood of the Amazon, made up of a thousand noble currents all pouring into one. . . . Our ancestry is

---

[9] *Mardi,* II, 323-324. See also *ibid.,* p. 90.

[10] *Ibid.,* I, 345.

[11] Willard Thorp, *Herman Melville: Representative Selections* (New York, 1938), Introduction, p. xxxviii.

[12] *Mardi,* II, 54.

[13] *Literary World* (March 31, 1849). Quoted by Thorp, *op. cit.,* p. cii.

[14] *Redburn,* p. 378.

lost in the universal paternity; and Caesar and Alfred, St. Paul and Luther, and Homer and Shakespeare are as much ours as George Washington, who is as much the world's as our own. We are the heirs of all time, and with all nations we divide our inheritance."[15]

Part of the individual's inheritance from common humanity was an ethical legacy—a kind of moral common sense. In *Typee* Melville concludes that the idyllic, virtuous life of the natives resulted from

an inherent principle of honesty and charity towards each other. They seemed to be governed by that sort of tacit common-sense law which, say what they will of the inborn lawlessness of the human race, has its precepts graven on every breast. The grand principles of virtue and honour, however they may be distorted by arbitrary codes, are the same all the world over. . . . It is to this indwelling, this universally diffused perception of what is *just* and *noble,* that the integrity of the Marquesans in their intercourse with each other is to be attributed.[16]

In *Mardi* the same doctrine reappears, when Babbalanja quotes Bardianna: "We need not to be told what righteousness is; we were born with the whole Law in our hearts."[17]   Only misanthropes, according to Frank Goodman in *The Confidence Man,* do not or will not "see in man a ruling principle of kindness."[18]

Ethical values to the individual could come in other forms from the human race. Isabel, in *Pierre,* believed herself "saved" by an infant whose innocent and thoughtless confidence in its mother first filled Isabel "with the sweet idea of humanness" and made her aware "of the infinite mercifulness, and tenderness, and beautifulness of humanness."[19] In *Clarel,* Mortmain's physical isolation from his mother and mental isolation from his father were counteracted only by "the vague bond of human kind," which inspired him to philanthropy.[20]   The high value Melville placed upon this "vague bond" is indicated by one of his Civil War poems:

[15] *Ibid.,* pp. 216-217.

[16] *Typee,* pp. 269-270. Melville's doctrine of innate morality should be distinguished from Emerson's. To the transcendentalist, "All things are moral," and every natural process "shall hint or thunder to man the laws of right and wrong" (*op. cit.,* I, 40-41). Emerson's individual inherited his moral principles from Nature and the Over-Soul. To Melville, however, Nature is either evil or indifferent, and the individual derives his principles from humanity (or, in rare passages, the orthodox God; see *Typee,* p. 144).

[17] *Mardi,* II, 303.   [18] *The Confidence Man,* p. 211.

[19] *Pierre,* pp. 171-172.   [20] *Clarel,* I, 187.

Nothing can lift the heart of man
Like manhood in a fellow man.
The thought of heaven's great King afar
But humbles us—too weak to scan;
But manly greatness men can span
And feel the bonds that draw.[21]

Here manliness is asserted to give more sustenance to the human spirit than godliness.

The racial community of mankind, to which the individual owed not only his physical existence but intellectual and ethical values, was always supplemented by the social community in which the individual lived. Sometimes, of course, this society produced evil for individuals, or at least left them dissatisfied. Life on board ship, for instance, could spread moral contagion, since certain evils seem organic in such life.[22] Sailors, often presented unflatteringly by Melville, are what society and their circumstances make them.[23] The tour of the islands in *Mardi* further revealed many social groups in which men inflict misery upon their kind.

But despite all Melville's awareness of the evils and inadequacies of society and civilization, he knew that the individual's physical and spiritual welfare is by no means independent of the social group. The briefest statement of this conviction is found in the sketch "The Two Temples." The narrator, after being rebuffed by the unfriendly atmosphere of a church, was given a ticket to a "genial humane assembly" in a theater. The gift was, he speculates, charity; but, he asks himself, " 'Why these unvanquished scruples? All your life, naught but charity sustains you, and all others in the world. Maternal charity nursed you as a babe; paternal charity fed you as a child; friendly charity got you your profession. . . . You, and all mortals, live but by sufferance of your charitable kind.' "[24] This admission is antipodal to Ahab's boast: "Ahab stands alone among all the millions of the peopled earth, nor gods nor men his neighbors!"[25] Yet Ahab himself recognizes, even while he curses it, "that mortal interdebtedness which will not do away with ledgers. I would be free as air; and I'm down

[21] *Poems*, p. 76.
[22] *White-Jacket*, pp. 473-474.
[23] See *Redburn*, chap. xxix.
[24] *Billy Budd and Other Prose Pieces*, p. 187.
[25] *Moby-Dick*, II, 341.

in the whole world's books. . . ."[26] Despite himself he is forced
to acknowledge indebtedness to others—to the carpenter "for a
bone to stand on" and to his forebears "for the flesh in the tongue
I brag with."[27]

In *Pierre* Melville disguised a fundamental truth in bitter irony
when he reminded his hero of "the perils and miseries thou callest
down on thee, when, even in a virtuous cause, thou steppest aside
from those arbitrary lines of conduct, by which the common world,
however base and dastardly, surrounds thee for thy worldly
good."[28] The community may sometimes impede a man's search
for absolute heavenly virtue, but its regulations do promote his
earthly well being.

Typee society displayed communal life nearly at its best: everybody shared in the fishing, building, worshiping, rejoicing. Although overt political and religious organization was negligible,
the Typees' "unanimity of feeling" (a trait which more than all
else aroused Melville's admiration)[29] produced "that social order
which is the greatest blessing and highest pride of the social
state."[30] "They showed this spirit of unanimity in every action of
life; everything was done in concert and good fellowship."[31]
Heaven itself would not satisfy Melville unless good fellowship
existed there. He once described to Hawthorne their life together
in Paradise, with good talk and good champagne producing friendly joviality.[32] More seriously, in *Mardi* he advocated friendliness
among the peoples of the world because "in heaven, at last, our
good, old, white-haired father Adam will greet us all alike, and
sociality forever prevail."[33]

III

That the individual should recognize and value his indebtedness
to all mankind and to his social group was, then, one of Melville's
recurrent beliefs. But he goes further to show that the individual

[26] *Ibid.,* II, 240.   [27] *Ibid.,* II, 239-240.
[28] *Pierre,* p. 246. Melville, it is true, declares that humanity had failed Pierre during
his wretched hours after he received Isabel's letter, just as divinity failed him even more
wretchedly in the city (pp. 412-413). Yet Pierre is shown as at least partly responsible
for his desertion by man and God.
[29] *Typee,* p. 273.   [30] *Ibid.,* p. 269.
[31] *Ibid.,* p. 273.
[32] Julian Hawthorne, *Nathaniel Hawthorne and His Wife* (Boston, 1885), I, 403.
[33] *Mardi,* I, 14.

is unavoidably caught up in both a cosmic and social context whether or not he recognizes or likes the fact. The cosmic limitation of the individual's self-reliant freedom is a kind of Over-Soul— but an evil one. The social limitation springs from the inescapable bonds of the social fabric.

The present paper is not the place to develop at length Melville's doctrine of cosmic evil and its relation to his views of fate and free will.[34] But enough can be suggested to show that the individual, in Melville's opinion, was to some extent limited by a force similar to Emerson's Over-Soul, but a force which was evil rather than good. It is a curious fact that the characters usually chosen by students of Melville to illustrate his "individualism" (Ahab and Pierre) are the very ones who talk most about being dominated by Fate or some other uncontrollable spiritual force. As soon as Pierre began to enter the labyrinth of his relations with Isabel, he for the first time in his life "felt the irresistible admonitions and intuitions of Fate,"[35] and by the time his life ended he had called himself "the fool of Fate."[36] Moreover, Pierre sometimes had a "vague, fearful feeling" of "a God—a Being positively present everywhere." When he sat down he felt that he "displaced the Spirit." Only the "humanness of Delly" near him relieved his apprehensiveness.[37]

Ahab, even more than Pierre, questions his individual freedom and responsibility, and feels the same kind of evil pantheism:[38]

"Is Ahab, Ahab? Is it I, God, or who, that lifts this arm? But if the great sun move not of himself . . . how then can this one small heart beat; this one small brain think thoughts; unless God does that beating, does that thinking, does that living, and not I? By heaven, man, we are turned round and round in this world, like yonder windlass, and Fate

[34] Some discussion of the subject can be found in the present writer's "Herman Melville's Metaphysics of Evil," *University of Toronto Quarterly*, IX, 170-182 (Jan., 1940).
[35] *Pierre*, p. 85.
[36] *Ibid.*, p. 499.
[37] *Ibid.*, p. 441.
[38] It is worth noting that the transcendentalist Winsome, who seems created in the image of Emerson, confesses his inner desire to be exempt from "knowledge, and conscience, and revel for a while in the care-free, joyous life of a perfectly instinctive, unscrupulous, and irresponsible creature"—like "the rattlesnake!" (*The Confidence Man*, p. 252). Melville is possibly implying that, in Emerson's doctrine of surrender to instincts and spiritual currents of the Over-Soul, creatures like the rattlesnake should not be forgotten.

is the handspike. . . . Look! see yon albicore! who put it into him to chase and fang that flying-fish?"[39]

To the carpenter, Ahab had speculated that a divine presence may be "invisibly and uninterpenetratingly standing precisely where thou now standest."[40]   Starbuck and such lesser men do not have this sense of identifying their wills with God's, nor of fighting the deity for room to stand or sit.   Ahab's fatalistic pantheism may spring either from the desire to disavow his responsibility to the human beings he leads to destruction or to the wish to consider himself identical with God.   The man who deliberately isolates himself, deliberately severs his connection with mankind, may well try desperately to unite himself with God by expanding his ego.   Only such a man will believe that he is "the Fates' lieutenant," because "this whole act's immutably decreed. 'Twas rehearsed by thee and me a billion years before this ocean rolled."[41]   Starbuck and the others deny Ahab's self-identification with God.   "Aye, sir, thou wilt have it so," remarks Starbuck, when Ahab commences the chase on the third day.   And at the eleventh hour, when the white whale breached to expose Fedallah caught in the lines and then began to swim *away* from Ahab and the *Pequod,* Starbuck cries again: "See! Moby-Dick seeks thee not. It is thou, thou, that madly seekest him!"[42]

It is surely significant that, apart from Ahab and Pierre, the characters in Melville's novels who are presented as flotsam in the currents of Fate are usually such men as Jackson, Bland, Radney, Claggart.   Jackson was "spontaneously an atheist and an infidel."[43] Bland was "an organic and irreclaimable scoundrel, who did wicked deeds as the cattle browse the herbage, because wicked deeds seemed the legitimate operation of his whole infernal organization."[44]   Radney was "doomed and made mad," a "predestinated mate."[45]   Claggart, who of all the type is analyzed at greatest length, was born evil—a man with natural depravity,[46] who had "no power to annul the elemental evil in himself . . . apprehending the good, but powerless to be it"; he was "like the scorpion for

[39] *Moby-Dick,* II, 330.
[41] *Ibid.,* II, 352.
[43] *Redburn,* p. 134.
[45] *Moby-Dick,* I, 310, 314.
[40] *Ibid.,* II, 239.
[42] *Ibid.,* II, 361.
[44] *White-Jacket,* p. 235.
[46] *Billy Budd,* pp. 45-46.

which the Creator alone is responsible."[47] In some moods Claggart "could even have loved Billy but for fate and ban."[48] All these
are men whose individualities are limited by the cosmic interference of an evil Over-Soul, or God.

But although spiritual interference, in the form of predestina-
tion or fate, appears chiefly in connection with error in Melville's
"individualists" or evil in his villians, some limitation exists on the
freedom of every man. In *Pierre* Melville says that his hero was
learning "what all mature men, who are Magians, sooner or later
know, and more or less assuredly—that not always in our actions,
are we our own factors."[49] The "not always" leaves some room
for freedom, but not much. In *White-Jacket* Melville had called
fate "not a fiend . . . but . . . an armed neutrality. . . . I have a
voice that helps to shape eternity."[50] And in *Moby-Dick*, Ishmael,
who at first held the "Fates" responsible for his decision to go to
sea, eventually reached the more considered and comfortable opinion of "chance, free will, and necessity—no wise incompatible—
all interweavingly working together."[51]

Just as no man could entirely escape some restrictions upon his
free individuality from these cosmic forces, neither could he escape
restrictions imposed by social forces. Pierre, who felt some compulsion of the supernatural, was perhaps more aware of the com-
pulsions of society, "the myriad alliances and criss-crossings among
mankind, the infinite entanglements of all social things, which for-
bids [*sic*] that one thread should fly the general fabric, on some
new line of duty, without tearing itself and tearing others."[52] Both
Ahab and Pierre reduce their worlds to tatters when they follow
their self-assigned duties. For Ishmael, the chief social limitation
of his will was symbolized in the "monkey-rope" that joined him
to Queequeg. This rope protected Queequeg from falling into the
sea while he worked on the slippery whale moored alongside the
ship; at the same time the rope endangered Ishmael, who could
be pulled overboard unless he took proper care:

[47] *Ibid.*, p. 49. Compare this passage with that about Winsome and the rattlesnake, as
cited in footnote 38 above.
[48] *Ibid.*, p. 60.
[49] *Pierre*, p. 69.
[50] *White-Jacket*, p. 404.
[51] *Moby-Dick*, I, 270.
[52] *Pierre*, p. 267.

I seemed distinctly to perceive that my own individuality was now merged in a joint stock company of two: that my free will had received a mortal wound; and that another's mistake or misfortune might plunge innocent me into unmerited disaster and death. . . . And yet . . . I saw that this situation of mine was the precise situation of every mortal that breathes; only, in most cases, he, one way or other, has this Siamese connexion with a plurality of other mortals. If your banker breaks, you snap; if your apothecary by mistake sends you poison in your pills, you die. . . .[53]

And whatever care Ishmael took, he had the management of only one end of the rope. Ahab, too, had his spiritual "monkey-rope" yoking him with Fedallah,[54] and even a physical one with Starbuck, who guarded the rope which hoisted Ahab aloft to look for the whale.[55] Without the help of Starbuck (and, of course, the crew to sail the ship) Ahab could not look for Moby Dick, just as he could not even stand without the carpenter's help. The social fabric enmeshed Ahab despite himself.

Unrestricted free will has always been attributed to the self-reliant individualist. Emerson, aware though he was of some of the difficulties in the concept of freedom, nevertheless wagered his intellectual wealth upon it. Melville's inability to subscribe to the doctrine without notable qualifications—that cosmic and social forces limited one's free will—refutes those who designate him an extreme individualist. It is true that while finishing *Moby-Dick* he wrote to Hawthorne applauding the man who "declares himself a sovereign nature (in himself) amid the powers of heaven, hell, and earth" and who "insists upon treating with all Powers upon an equal basis."[56] But this famous utterance and possibly one or two similar ones cannot adequately support the contention that Melville celebrated "an individualism whose acceptance required more hardihood than his generation possessed," and which was "founded . . . on the hard doctrine that security is an illusion" and on the rejection of Emerson's belief "that the constitution of the universe is on his [man's] side."[57] That Melville rejected Emer-

[53] *Moby-Dick*, II, 49.
[54] *Ibid.*, II, 320.
[55] *Ibid.*, II, 321.
[56] Julian Hawthorne, *op. cit.*, I, 387.
[57] R. H. Gabriel, *The Course of American Democratic Thought* (New York, 1940), p. 73.

son's optimism about the bias of the universe is true enough; any man who let himself drift with Emerson's "currents of Universal Being" would, in Melville's opinion, soon find himself in the Great Maelstrom. The alternative is not individualism, however, since Melville could believe that although man can not rely upon Nature he may (or must) rely upon mankind.

That Melville did think this reliance necessary would seem indicated by the fates he assigned his principal individualists, Ahab and Pierre and Bartleby the Scrivener. They repudiated their bonds with their social group; all met defeat and death. If Ahab and Pierre can be regarded as tragic heroes in the Shakespearean sense, then it is at least conceivable that Melville intended their scorn of their social debts to be the "tragic flaw" in their characters that encompasses their fall. At the end of *Mardi,* Taji, also, shows himself as an unsubmissive individualist. He refuses to content himself with Serenia, which satisfies his companions. Rejecting the values of sociality, he in effect rejects everything in this life. Turning away with "eternity in his eye," he cries: "Now I am my soul's emperor; and my first act is abdication! Hail! realm of shades!"[58] For some few, who spurn sociality to pursue some phantom value of their own devising, the realm of shades may perhaps be preferable to Serenia; but Melville warns us that the passage thither is "over an endless sea."[59]

Nevertheless, Melville advocated no bemused or heedless anchorage in the harbor of humanity or the social emotions. Though he admired Typee society, he deserted the valley at first chance, since he himself would always be an alien in a Marquesan community. Typee society was not good for a Westerner, just as Western civilization was not good for Typees. Each society had its own internal evils, but the evils were exaggerated when one sought to impose its cultural pattern upon the other. He therefore pitied the Marquesans for extending their trustfulness beyond the confines of their own culture: "Unsophisticated and confiding, they are easily led into every vice . . . by their European civilisers."[60] As Melville shows, there are too many Claggarts, Jacksons, Blands—perhaps even Winsomes—in the world for men to bestow complete

[58] *Mardi,* II, 400.
[59] *Ibid.*
[60] *Typee,* p. 18.

confidence upon everybody and expect generous dealing at all times.   But surely, in urging caution, Melville is being neither cynical nor misanthropic.   Those readers who see in *The Confidence Man* a bitter exposure of confidence, misinterpret the book entirely.   The more careful reader will find no evidence at all that in any of his guises the Confidence Man defrauds anybody.   The men exposed in the book are not the herb-doctors or the Frank Goodmans, but the Charlie Nobles, Mark Winsomes, and Egberts.   The latter are men whose intellectual principles have frozen their hearts.   Each is sufficient unto himself and feels no sympathy or generosity towards the poor and miserable among his fellow travelers.   The unfortunates who turn to humanity for aid and comfort are shrugged off by these men of self-centered intellect, but they can and do find relief from the herb-doctors and Goodmans, who are animated by love of their kind.   But whatever the risk of reproof, the unfortunates must turn to their fellow men rather than to a distant deity, in Melville's opinion, if they are to find help at all.

IV

The psychological quality which Melville believed was chiefly responsible for "insulated" individualism was the excessive development of intellect at the expense of the heart.   Several critics[61] have already remarked upon Melville's concern with the problem of "disequilibrium" between head and heart, between thought (which is relatively solitary) and emotion (which is relatively social).

What seemed to him to be the excessive intellectualism of the transcendentalists chiefly aroused Melville's criticisms.   Writing to Duyckinck in 1849, he remarked that Emerson's dislike of cakes-and-ale geniality was "his misfortune, not his fault. His belly, Sir, is in his chest, and his brains descend down into his neck. . . ."[62] Presumably Emerson simply had no room for heart.   About fourteen years later, in an annotation on Emerson's *Essays,* Melville attributed Emerson's "gross and astonishing errors & illusions" to an "intensely intellectual" "self conceit."   "Another species of Mr.

---

[61] For example, Thorp, *op. cit.,* p. lix; William Braswell, *Melville's Religious Thought* (Durham, N. C., 1943), pp. 22 ff.; F. O. Matthiessen, *American Renaissance: Art and Expression in the Age of Emerson and Whitman* (New York, 1941), *passim.*

[62] Thorp, *op. cit.,* p. 373.

Emerson's errors, or rather blindness, proceeds from a defect in the region of the heart."[63]   Goethe, often linked by Melville with the philosophic ancestors of transcendentalism, is condemned as "the pretentious, heartless part of a man."[64]   Plotinus Plinlimmon, the transcendentalist philosopher in *Pierre,* belied his winning appearance by his characteristic of "non-Benevolence."[65]   From his self-sufficient isolation he detachedly observed Pierre's growing despair.[66]   *The Confidence Man* contains an exposure of the transcendentalists' principles of friendship, which would coldly banish from the world any generous, friendly help in money matters.   It is worth noting also that whenever Melville wished to present human depravity he chose to make his villains—such as Jackson, Bland, Claggart—men of cold objectivity, not hot passion.

The character who mainly illustrates separation of head and heart is, of course, Ahab. As he says of himself: "Gifted with the high perception, I lack the low, enjoying power."[67] In his sleep, the frustrated "living principle or soul" would sometimes rebel against "the characterizing mind." "God help thee, old man. Thy thoughts have created a creature in thee; and he whose intense thinking thus makes him a Prometheus; a vulture feeds upon that heart forever; that vulture the very creature he creates."[68]   In Ahab's "broad madness," we learn, "not one jot of his great natural intellect had perished. That before living agent, now became the living instrument."[69] Ahab himself was aware of this: "All my means are sane, my motive and my object mad."[70] In Ahab, Melville seems to have created his own Ethan Brand to illustrate his comment to Hawthorne on the "frightful poetical creed that the cultivation of the brain eats out the heart."[71] Ahab was, of course, a man of fiery passions, but these were not at all social emotions; rather they served only to fuse other men into instruments for his own egocentric will. Although he has a few moments when he appears to value the help of others,[72] he more characteristically and

---

[63] William Braswell, "Melville as a Critic of Emerson," *American Literature,* IX, 331 (Nov., 1937).

[64] *Pierre,* p. 422.   [65] *Ibid.,* p. 404.
[66] *Ibid.,* pp. 408-409.   [67] *Moby-Dick,* I, 207.
[68] *Ibid.,* I, 252-253.   [69] *Ibid.,* I, 231.
[70] *Ibid.,* I, 232.   [71] Julian Hawthorne, *op. cit.,* I, 404.

[72] Especially in two remarks to Starbuck. First, when Ahab cried, "Close! stand close to me, Starbuck; let me look into a human eye; it is better . . . than to gaze upon God" (II, 329). Secondly, when he supported himself with Starbuck after his whalebone leg

continually hardens his heart not only against the gods but also against the loving Pip, Starbuck, his own remembered wife and child, his crew, and his Nantucket neighbor in search of a lost son. Ahab's specifications for "a complete man after a desirable pattern" would include "no heart at all" but a "brass forehead, and about a quarter of an acre of fine brains."[73] The tyrannical king Abrazza, who lives only for his selfish pleasures no matter the cost in misery to others, would agree with Ahab, since he says: "We kings should be ever indifferent. Nothing like a cold heart; warm ones are ever chafing and getting into trouble."[74]

But although Melville saw clearly the evils that resulted when head was dominant over heart, he was not blind to the dangers of excesses of the heart. Pierre's uncritical heart leads him as surely to suffering and disaster as Ahab's overdeveloped intellect.[75] Pierre's "enthusiastic heart" bursts itself against "the heart-vacancies of the conventional life . . . [the] heartless, proud, ice-gilded world."[76] "The heart! the heart!" cries Pierre; "'tis God's anointed; let me pursue the heart!"[77] In his opinion, "the brains grow maggoty without a heart; but the heart's the preserving salt itself, and can keep sweet without the head."[78]

That was, however, only Pierre's opinion. Mere sweetness, as Melville shows, is not enough. He did not identify himself completely with either Ahab or Pierre. Reviewing Hawthorne's *Mosses,* he maintained that no man who possesses humor and love developed to the point of genius can exist "without also possessing . . . a great deep intellect, which drops down into the universe like a plummet. Or, love and humor are only the eyes through which such an intellect views the world."[79] A year later, in a letter to Hawthorne, he advances as his "*prose* opinion" that "in most cases, in those men who have fine brains and work them well, the heart extends down to hams."[80] It is true that he goes on to add: "I stand for the heart. To the dogs with the head! I had rather be a fool with a heart, than Jupiter Olympus with his head." But this

had been snapped off: "Ay, ay, Starbuck, 'tis sweet to lean sometimes . . . and would old Ahab had leaned oftener than he has" (II, 350). Thus even the individualistic Ahab at times paid tribute to human sociality.

[73] *Moby-Dick*, II, 238.
[74] *Mardi*, II, 341.
[75] See Matthiessen, *op. cit.*, p. 467.
[76] *Pierre*, p. 126.
[77] *Ibid.*, p. 127.
[78] *Ibid.*, p. 445.
[79] Thorp, *op. cit.*, p. 332.
[80] Julian Hawthorne, *op. cit.*, I, 404.

merely emphasizes his general belief that a scientific head could lead a man farther astray than a social heart. Heart alone was better than head alone, but the best endowment is a warm heart directed by a cool (not cold) head—as he was to show in *Billy Budd*.

Clarel (1876) contains much discussion of the head-heart antithesis, as seen for example in the conflict of science and religion. Preference is usually given to the heart, though not uncritically. The suave cleric Derwent, who is portrayed rather unsympathetically, is the chief advocate of the heart. But when he echoes Pierre and cries

> "Behead me—rid me of pride's part
> And let me live but by the heart!"

his enthusiasm is pierced by Mortmain's "Hast proved thy heart? first prove it."[81] Nevertheless, in the Epilogue Melville returns to the heart:

> Then keep thy heart, though yet but ill-resigned—
> Clarel, thy heart, the issues there but mind.[82]

In opposition to the doctrines of intellectualism, Melville set up almost as a religion the social and emotional values of love, companionship, sympathy, beneficence, unselfishness. In *Typee* he had applauded the "instinctive feeling of love" in the breasts of the natives, who among themselves "appeared to form one household, whose members were bound together by the ties of strong affection. The love of kindred . . . seemed blended in the general love."[83] Serenia, in *Mardi,* is another such community. All men are brothers in this Land of Love.[84] The highly intelligent but untranscendental philosopher Babbalanja is finally converted to the doctrines of Alma [Christ], whose "great command is Love." Yet this love is not opposed to thought, since the old Serenian says that if "Right-reason and Alma" were not the same, "Alma, not reason, would we reject."[85] The love Melville perceived at the root of Christ's teachings impelled him to condemn the logic of the Old Testament Jehovah. He once wrote to Hawthorne: "The reason the mass of men fear God, and *at bottom dislike* Him, is because

[81] *Clarel*, II, 29.
[82] *Ibid.*, II, 298.
[83] *Typee*, pp. 33, 275.
[84] *Mardi*, II, 364.
[85] *Ibid.*, II, 370.

they rather distrust His heart, and fancy Him all brain like a watch."[86]   Melville's criticism of religion was aimed at the conventional and institutional encrustations which men had added to the simple, loving doctrines of Christ.[87]   The brain, not the heart, builds systems and regulations.

Billy Budd, Melville's last work, portrays the balance of head and heart.   Captain Vere, who is sympathetically portrayed, has "a marked leaning toward everything intellectual," but he is also full of fatherly affection for Billy.   At the court-martial he warns the officers: ". . . let not warm hearts betray heads that should be cool. . . . The heart is the feminine in man, and . . . must here be ruled out."[88]   But it is ruled out not to further some coldly rational or selfish purpose, but to promote the good of the disciplined community (the Navy) in which both judge and prisoner live, and to serve which both joyfully die, one a felon's death, the other (later) a warrior's.   Because of the love and trust Billy has for Vere, he accepts unrebelliously his role as the sacrificial Isaac offered by Abraham in obedience to higher authority.   Each of them has surrendered some individual good for the good of the community.   Vere, who calls Billy's blow a "divine judgment," surrenders the wish of his heart which would pardon this "angel of God."[89]   He declares that at "the Last Assizes" Billy would be acquitted, but he insists that he and his officers must "proceed under the law of the Mutiny Act."[90]   The bonds of love and sympathy which unite Billy and Vere are strong.   So sure was Vere that Billy would agree with and forgive the military compulsion which made his death necessary that he reveals to Billy all the motives and circumstances which led to the decision.[91]   Billy, who finds "a sort of joy" in Vere's frankness and trust, surrenders his life. His dying words, "God bless Captain Vere!" show that he not only forgave the captain and condoned the judgment, but glorified the whole act, since under his influence the entire crew, as if they were "the vehicles of some vocal current-electric," returned a sympathetic

---

[86] Julian Hawthorne, *op. cit.,* I, 404.

[87] Babbalanja had rejected the religion of Alma on the island of Maramma, where the Church flourished as an elaborate and heartless institution. The Reverend Mr. Falsgrave, because he accepted the established moral code, repulsed Pierre.

[88] *Billy Budd,* p. 87.

[89] *Ibid.,* p. 75.

[90] *Ibid.,* pp. 87-88.

[91] *Ibid.,* p. 91.

echo of the same words.[92]   In short, at the moment of his death Billy healed any breach his execution might have caused in the respect and affection of the crew for the captain. Though the individual may die, the community must live on, whole and sound. Thus Billy submerged his individuality in love for his captain and loyalty to his country. Unlike Ahab, who was dragged down to his death; unlike Pierre, who died in a low dungeon; Billy "ascended; and ascending, took the full rose of the dawn."[93]

Hawthorne as well as Melville had opposed the transcendentalists' approval of solitude and self-reliance by revealing the distortion which accompanied the individual's arrogant separation from his fellows. But in so far as Melville substituted a positive alternative for such isolation, he went beyond Hawthorne's cool observation of a human phenomenon. That alternative sprang from the racial and social community of mankind, with its wealth of social virtues: love, sympathy, gratitude, friendliness, charity, kindness, companionship. Some virtues a man may acquire in solitude—such as, perhaps, self-reliance, truth, benevolent goodness; but he cannot acquire charity, love, beneficent goodness. Babbalanja's longing to prune himself down to "what is unchangeably true"[94] is transformed, after his voyage round the Mardian world, into the flowering of love, nourished by the brotherly community of Serenia: "Love and Alma prevail. . . . Reason no longer domineers; but still doth speak."[95] Captain Vere, unflinchingly exposing the cold truth of Billy's case—innocent under heavenly law, guilty under earthly law—unites that truth with a warm human love which purges it of all its cerebral harshness and redeems its earthly injustice. The two surrender their individualities, but they discover fulfillment in an embracing sociality.

[92] *Ibid.*, p. 102.
[93] *Ibid.*, p. 103.
[94] *Mardi*, I, 80-81.
[95] *Ibid.*, II, 371.

Melville's "The *Town-Ho's* Story"

Sherman Paul

O F THE NINE ENCOUNTERS with whaling ships in *Moby-Dick*, "The *Town-Ho's* Story" is the first on-the-sea report of the white whale. Unlike the other reports this story can stand alone artistically and was actually printed separately in *Harper's* in 1851. R. S. Forsythe says that "since this sailor's yarn is not closely woven into the fabric of the novel, there is no awkwardness in its publication as an independent work; it is complete in itself."[1] This, however, does not mean that the story is not integrally necessary to the deepest understanding of *Moby-Dick*, for "The *Town-Ho's* Story" offers an alternative and variant meaning of the significance of the white whale. It is a tragic but not an unwarrantably pessimistic tale that inspires an awe of, but not an aversion to, the whale; it marks the beginning of that feeling of attraction for the whale which Melville nurses carefully in the seven remaining stories and without which the dramatic focus on Ahab's monomania would be diminished. Furthermore, the themes and characters of the story, and its symbolic techniques, make it Melville's "Ethan Brand," the kind of short story the significance of which, as in the case of Hawthorne and similarly of Melville, penetrates the main body of an author's work.

The story itself, stripped of long digressions for its recital, is told with yarnlike ease at the Golden Inn in Lima, Peru. Its portentous meaning, which, Melville wrote, "seemed obscurely to involve with the whale a certain wondrous, inverted visitation of one of those so-called judgments of God,"[2] arises seemingly from the simple fabric of a sailor's recollection. The audience of entertainment-expecting Dons of "This dull, warm, most lazy and hereditary land" are driven to outbursts of incredulity much as the reader who at this point in *Moby-Dick* first encounters the whale and who must readjust his faculties and shift his expectations for even more "won-

---

[1] "Herman Melville's The Town-Ho's Story," *Notes and Queries*, CLXVIII, 314 (May 4, 1935).

[2] *Moby-Dick* (London, 1922), I, 306.

drous visitations" to come. The scene of the telling of the story in "corrupt" Lima, to men conditioned by Catholic mysteries and yet unbelieving, forms a contrast to the heightened all-pervading religious content of the tale and reaffirms Ishmael's devotion to the mysterious fatalities of life. The humor of their skepticism—for the faith of the land-locked, comfortable, aristocratic wine drinkers who never put to sea is another "tale" in the Holy Evangelists— moves Ishmael to ask for "the largest sized Evangelists," even to swear on the Testament.[3]

"The *Town-Ho's* Story" contains Melville's germ of tragedy and his portrayal of the retributive justice of the whale. In this there is a glimmer of relief from the overwhelming sense of evil that engulfs Ahab. For here the whale carries out a cosmic decree that more nearly accords with our ideas of Christian justice. And there is more: an affirmation of the sanctity of personality and of the kind of democracy that recognizes kings in commoners. As Charles Olson has indicated, "Democracy, to Melville, merely gave man his chance to be just—in politics, society *and* intimate human relations."[4] The idea of the inviolability of man's personality was the key to what Melville called, in his "Hawthorne and His Mosses," "that unshackled, democratic spirit of Christianity in all things."[5] Christian democracy was that democracy in which the laws were more in accord with divine law and the natural dignity of all men. Melville thought that after eighteen hundred years it was democracy that should realize this fundamental Christianity, this unique value of the human being which, when recognized, was manifested by men in bonds of love, sympathy, and charity. Startled by the apathy of mankind toward humanity caught up in poverty and death in the streets of Liverpool, as described in *Redburn,* he went further to protest against the inhumanity of law in *White-Jacket.* Here, he cited Blackstone on the Law of Nature as a moral justification for mutiny[6] and dramatized man's instinctive sense of his own dignity as justification for defiance of authority. When White Jacket was arraigned at the mast to be flogged for no offense by a wilful captain who "would not forgive God Almighty," he

[3] *Ibid.,* p. 330.
[4] "Lear and Moby Dick," *Twice a Year,* I, 188 (Fall-Winter, 1938).
[5] *Billy Budd and Other Prose Pieces* (London, 1924), p. 136.
[6] *White-Jacket* (London, 1922), p. 181.

decided to rush against the captain and pitch him into the sea. In describing White Jacket's justification for this defiance of authority, Melville wrote:

But the thing that swayed me to my purpose was not altogether the thought that Captain Claret was about to degrade me, and that I had taken an oath with my soul that he should not. No, I felt my man's manhood so bottomless within me, that no word, no blow, no scourge of Captain Claret could cut me deep enough for that. I but swung to an instinct in me—the instinct diffused through all animated nature, the same that prompts even a worm to turn under heel. Locking souls with him, I meant to drag Captain Claret from this earthy tribunal of his to that of Jehovah, and let Him decide between us.[7]

The sense of tragedy comes when this essential dignity is abused, whether through the self-willed arbitrary law of a captain or through Ahab's misuse of his own personality. In both it was the God-idea in man—as Starbuck recognized it—which should be used in better ways than revenge on man or animal.

Out of this conflict between the different orders of law and the warrant for the higher law which Melville dramatizes in terms of the dignity of man grows the problem of good and evil. *White-Jacket, Billy Budd,* and "The *Town-Ho's* Story" have this as their basic situation: the instance of Ushant's beard as a symbol of his dignity brings him before the mast in *White-Jacket;* the essential innocence of Billy Budd is at the mercy of human law as executed by the all-knowing, godlike Captain Vere; Radney, the mate of the *Town-Ho,* goes beyond the law of the ship and the divine law and brings down upon himself the force of divine justice.

In Melville's development of this problem, "The *Town-Ho's* Story" stands midway between *White-Jacket* and *Billy Budd.* For White Jacket's intention of letting God decide is fulfilled by the whale in the action between Steelkilt and Radney. Their story is a simple one.[8] When the whaler *Town-Ho* sprang a leak in the Pacific, it became necessary to man the pumps almost continuously. Steelkilt, "a Lakeman and desperado from Buffalo," exhausted by his turn at the pumps, was ordered to sweep down and remove some excrement from the deck. In so ordering, the mate Radney had

[7] *Ibid.,* pp. 352-353.
[8] "The *Town-Ho's* Story," *Moby-Dick,* I, 306-330.

overlooked the rules applying to such duties and had issued a command to Steelkilt only to "sting and insult" him. Radney was moved to do this because he was "ugly" and resented Steelkilt's physical nobility. It was only conventional, Melville points out, "that when a person placed in command over his fellow men finds one of them to be very significantly his superior in general pride of manhood . . . he will pull down and pulverize that subaltern's tower, and make a little heap of dust of it." Steelkilt "instinctively saw all this" but, like a "really valiant" man, refused to give way to passion and so arouse further anger; he merely refused on the grounds that it was not his duty. Again Radney ordered, cursing him, and threatened Steelkilt with a hammer. And when Radney, in defiance of Steelkilt's warnings, grazed him with the hammer, the latter smashed the mate's jaw.

Mutiny followed. Steelkilt and his fellow seamen entrenched themselves and refused to man the pumps until the captain swore not to flog them. In the face of the captain's indecision Steelkilt twice shouted, ". . . treat us decently, and we're your men; but we won't be flogged." When neither party would give in, Steelkilt followed the Captain's orders and allowed himself to be confined with his nine followers in the forecastle. But "The fetid closeness of the air, and a famishing diet . . . constrained" all but three to surrender. Then Steelkilt, "maddened by his long entombment in a place as black as the bowels of despair"—a Melvillean hell—proposed to the two other seamen to break out and take the ship. The other two, however, betrayed him, and all three were bound and hoisted into the rigging for the remainder of the night. On the following morning the captain flogged the two betrayers into lifelessness, but Steelkilt forewarned the captain with a "hiss." (One is reminded here of old Ushant's saying after he was flogged that " 'tis no dishonour when he who would dishonour you, only dishonours himself. . . . My beard is my own.")[9] The captain, apparently recognizing in this defiance Steelkilt's inviolability, ordered him to be cut down, but Radney refused to take heed and personally laid on the punishment.

When the normal life of the ship was resumed, the seamen agreed to Steelkilt's plan of giving up the chase by no longer singing

[9] *White-Jacket*, p. 461.

out for whales, and returning to port to desert ship. Meanwhile Steelkilt planned his revenge—to crush Radney's skull and drop him into the sea. But at the moment of execution, "by a mysterious fatality, Heaven itself seemed to step in to take out of his hands into its own the damning thing he would have done." "Just between daybreak and sunrise," the topwatch spied out Moby-Dick and involuntarily cried, " 'Jesu, what a whale,' " calling out Christ's name instinctively at the critical moment when the whale had come to take from Steelkilt his revenge. In the hunt for Moby-Dick that followed, Radney was tossed into the sea and destroyed when his boat struck the whale. After the crew reached port, they deserted ship and, detaining the captain by the sheer force of Steelkilt's will, "forever got the start on their Captain." In the end, Steelkilt triumphed; God had decided, by means of Moby-Dick, between Steelkilt and Radney.

Melville's handling of the story sharpens this central idea. In the character of Steelkilt he creates another handsome sailor, who, although an inlander, is, like Jack Chase, "wild-ocean born" and "wild-ocean nurtured."[10] He is of the pattern of Billy Budd and Chase in his personal strength and beauty, his seamanship, his qualities of leadership and geniality, and his "off-hand unaffectedness of natural regality."[11] The type of person Melville portrayed in Steelkilt he describes in *Billy Budd* as "an amusing character all but extinct now, but occasionally to be encountered, and in a form yet more amusing than the original, at the tiller of the boats on the tempestuous Erie Canal or, more likely, vapouring in the groggeries along the towpath."[12] And like Jack Chase, who was "a stickler for the rights of man,"[13] the canaller "was the champion [ashore]; afloat the spokesman; on every suitable occasion always foremost."[14] Steelkilt became the embodiment of the American savage, the natural man, a being free from civilized hypocrisy. Melville describes him fondly as the fulfilment of his idea of the democratic hero, sharing that "democratic dignity which, on all hands, radiates without end from God . . . our divine equality!"[15]

---

[10] *Moby-Dick*, I, 309.
[11] *Billy Budd and Other Prose Pieces*, p. 5.
[12] *Ibid.*, p. 6.   [13] *White-Jacket*, p. 19.
[14] *Billy Budd and Other Prose Pieces*, p. 6.
[15] *Moby-Dick*, I, 144.

"Steelkilt was a tall and noble animal with a head like a Roman, and a flowing golden beard like the tasseled housings of your last viceroy's snorting charger; and a brain, and a heart, and a soul in him, gentlemen, which had made Steelkilt Charlemagne, had he been born son to Charlemagne's father."[16] He would have fitted Melville's description of the canaller as "the young Alexander curbing the fiery Bucephalus."[17]

One can hardly fail to see the physical mold of Steelkilt. What goes unemphasized in this characterization, only to rise foremost in that of Billy Budd, is Melville's corollary that "The moral nature was seldom out of keeping with the physical make."[18] Steelkilt, like Melville's cherished friend Jack Chase and "peacemaker" Billy Budd, whom all his fellows "love," maintains throughout the story a certain passiveness, intensified and dramatized by the exceptional strength and violence of the man. Except when threatened with flogging and abused by Radney, he follows orders. He has a sense of duty which Melville points up by having Steelkilt save the crew by cutting the line holding their boat fast to the whale (which in this instance, though fulfilling justice in the destruction of Radney, is still the symbol of universal physical force that gives the whale an almost Old Testament significance as the bearer of both wrath and justice). It is Steelkilt, also, who meets his captain with Christ's words, "I come in peace,"[19] and who seeks revenge only when "maddened" by the hell of confinement and stung by flogging to "the ventricles of his heart."[20] Again, the heart as symbol of feeling and of man's innate dignity contrasts with the cold intellectuality of a Radney, Claggart, Bland, or Jackson. Each of them partakes of that depravity which "towards the accomplishment of an aim which in wantonness of malignity would seem to partake of the insane, he will direct a cool judgment sagacious and sound."[21] Against this background, Ahab's tragedy comes to mean the same thing as Radney's: Ahab's violation of his own personality or heart by his will makes him proudly assert that other men are his hands and feet, thereby violating them and the natural law:

[16] *Ibid.*, p. 311.
[17] *Billy Budd and Other Prose Pieces*, p. 6.
[18] *Ibid.*, p. 6.   [19] *Moby-Dick*, I, 329.
[20] *Ibid.*, p. 324.
[21] *Billy Budd and Other Prose Pieces*, p. 46.

and this is reflected in his consequent inability to feel, to sympathize, and to look into man's eyes. His tragedy is a self-wrought loneliness arising from the separation of men from men by the separation of mind and heart. For Radney destruction came about through his own rash ignorance; for Ahab, through his acceptance of fate as a rationalization for his wilfulness.

Against this formula for monomania, Melville indirectly builds up Steelkilt's moral nature by creating in him a Christ-indwelling figure. Radney's offense had insulted Steelkilt "as though Radney had spat in his face."[22] And this action, symbolic of striking the godhead in man, is reminiscent of a similar incident of the individual versus authority in Matthew 27:30, where the soldiers spit on Christ. And there are other more marked symbolic Christian referents in Steelkilt's passivity, his betrayal "at midnight," his coming from the depths of the forecastle, and the stringing of the three seamen in the rigging. Probably the three mutineers are intended to remind one of Christ's crucifixion, for after the beating of the two betrayers Melville compares their lifelessness to "the two crucified thieves."[23] This is enough to suggest the Christian insight that Melville wished to provide in his characterization of Steelkilt. For Melville, befriended by Jack Chase, the humanity of helping "a poor stranger in a strait" was a Christlike thing, and even for a man of violence, a redeeming quality.[24]

Melville merely sketches the figure of Radney as a symbol of evil. He describes him as "brutal," "overbearing," "fearless," "ugly," "hardy," and "malicious." He provoked Steelkilt by failing to show him "that common decency of human recognition which is the meanest slave's right."[25] Where Ahab has strength of purpose and a tragic perception of his willingness to fulfil fate, Radney has only maliciousness. But Radney, too, had his saving part—like Jackson and Claggart, to whom he is more nearly akin, and whom Melville pities as men of sorrows. He is said to have "some good-hearted traits," just as Ahab had his "humanities." What these were in Radney's case the story never reveals, unless in his widow's grief we recognize the one bond of love that tied him to humanity. Coming at the very end of the tale, it bears the weight of final verity, the one redeeming feeling and value of this cosmic struggle.

[22] *Moby-Dick*, I, 313.　　　　　[23] *Ibid.*, p. 322.
[24] *Ibid.*, p. 317.　　　　　　　 [25] *Ibid.*, pp. 309-310.

But there seems to be more to Radney's tragedy than this. A forecast of doom can be sensed in the symbolic details of the story: the leak that compels the action that follows is never found because it is too far below the ship's water line; submerged in evil, in mystery, it is beyond man's probing. The leak widens mysteriously, and only Radney feels apprehensive over making port. The self-contained ship is somehow rent, and the sea-evil enters, and from this moment Radney "was doomed and made mad."[26] Melville says that Radney was moved by a "cozening fiend," was "predestined," was "branded for the slaughter by the gods."[27] In fact, "a strange fatality pervades the whole career of these events, as if verily mapped out before the world itself was charted."[28] This can be seen in the symbolic merger of the white-bandaged Radney and the white whale, where the whale again takes on an evil significance, and evil blends with evil, at the same time that this judgment of God gives Steelkilt his salvation.[29] That the smallest event should be so ordered was the sign of fatality; the ways of necessity, as Babbalanja observed in *Mardi,* left more to man—the choice of evil and a self-imposed and self-willed fate.

There are two modes by which Melville further illumines what he means by Christian democracy: the moral contrast of the tale with the scene of its recital, and explanations in the story of references to America. The Peruvian backdrop of decadent Christianity and the ship-symbol serve to bring into focus the struggle for faith in America. The land of the Dons has no more autos-da-fé, but Don Pedro thought "that at your temperate North the generations were as cold and holy as the hills."[30] In explaining this Melville re-creates the savage-civilized life of the American interior by imaginatively developing its parallels to the antipodal societies he himself has found in the world—the primitive life of *Typee* and the regimentation of a frigate. The interior is a world in itself; its great lakes are oceans with romantic Polynesian isles like the great oceans and bordered by a variety of life as ancient and barbaric, as new and civilized as any provided by history. It has its "paved capitals of Buffalo and Cleveland," its "ancient and unentered

[26] *Ibid.,* p. 310. [27] *Ibid.,* pp. 312, 314, 315.
[28] *Ibid.,* p. 327. [29] *Ibid.,* p. 327.
[30] *Ibid.,* p. 317.

forests." The link between this "Christian corn-field" and the "barbaric seas" is the Erie Canal, whose "one continual stream of Vene-
tianly corrupt and often lawless life" flows "by rows of snow white
chapels, whose spires stand almost like milestones." To the corn-
field of churches the water-borne evil of the canal brings the old
and new corruptions, the wicked "Mark Antony" of a canaller, and
the challenge of its commerce and vulgarity. But it is not the canaller whom Melville despises; rather, it is the American pagan "under
the long-flung shadow, and snug patronizing lee of churches" which
serve as mileposts along the way. This disunity and cross-purpose,
represented by the canal which separates as well as connects, is Melville's picture of the outrunning of the religious support of democracy and of the ever-grasping, ever-extending rapaciousness of
American life.[31]

This apparent failure in the basis of American democracy has
its counterpart in the mutiny that takes place on the *Town-Ho*. The
ship-as-society or world-in-itself is a recurrent symbol in Melville's
work and in "The *Town-Ho's* Story" becomes a stage on which is
acted one possible failure in human institutions. The captain, "believing that rare good luck awaited him in those latitudes," little
heeds the sea-evil, relies wholly on his pumps and stout men. But
the evil reaches deeper and brings on a mutiny by enlarging the
sense of separation that had taken place between Steelkilt and
Radney or, symbolically, between those who rule and those who
obey. Melville suggests that all would have been well if Radney
had only recognized that portion of the right of manhood in Steelkilt which was due even a slave—but Radney "did not love Steelkilt."
Law, to have religious sanction, must be tempered with love,
Christian love and compassion, and for this fundamental right, like
the French in 1848, the "sea-Parisians"[32] patrolled their barricades.
More was at stake than the ship *Town-Ho;* it was a matter of the
humane basis of society, of Christian democracy.

The vindication of mutiny in the name of personality and the
retributive role of the whale are the secret parts of the story that
Ahab never hears. Ahab, as one who himself felt oppressed, might

[31] *Ibid.*, pp. 308-309, 315-317.
[32] *Ibid.*, p. 318.

have responded to Steelkilt's rebellion on the grounds of personality. For in his soliloquy on fire Ahab proclaims his inviolate part, "the queenly personality" that "lives in me, and feels her royal rights."[33] But as oppressor, intent on shaping the world to his monomaniac vision of it, he had seen the cosmic evil, but could not hearken to his humanities and give love its redemptive place. The central meaning of "The *Town-Ho's* Story" is the reaffirmation of the heart with which Melville arms his reader for the greater tragedy to come.

[33] *Moby-Dick*, II, 282.

Melville's " 'Soiled' Fish of the Sea"

John W. Nichol

IN CHAPTER XCII of *White-Jacket,* Melville describes his fall into the sea from the yardarm of the U. S. frigate *Neversink.* F. O. Matthiessen selects this passage to illustrate the manner in which Melville, the artist, worked.[1] His discussion is an excellent example of judicial and appreciative critical comment, but on one important point Mr. Matthiessen is the victim of a rather unlucky error. After setting forth the series of trancelike moods which Melville employs in describing his experience of falling, Matthiessen quotes, evidently from the Constable Standard Edition of Melville's *Works,* the following passage in which Melville relates his feelings while still under the water:

I wondered whether I was yet dead or still dying. But of a sudden some fashionless form brushed my side—some inert, soiled fish of the sea; the thrill of being alive again tingled in my nerves, and the strong shunning of death shocked me through.[2]

Commenting on these lines, Matthiessen says:

But then this second trance is shattered by a twist of imagery of the sort that was to become peculiarly Melville's. He is startled back into the sense of being alive by grazing an inert form; hardly anyone but Melville could have created the shudder that results from calling this frightening vagueness some *"soiled* fish of the sea." The *discordia concors,* the unexpected linking of the medium of cleanliness with filth, could only have sprung from an imagination that had apprehended the terrors of the deep, of the immaterial deep as well as the physical.[3]

The unlucky error of all this lies in the fact that Melville in all probability used the adjective *coiled* rather than *soiled* in describing his "fish of the sea," and that it was some unknown typesetter,

[1] *American Renaissance: Art and Expression in the Age of Emerson and Whitman* (London and New York [1941]), pp. 390-395.
[2] *The Works of Herman Melville* (London, 1922-1924), VI, 497.
[3] *American Renaissance,* p. 392.

rather, who accounted for the "shudder" and the *"discordia concors"* of the "unexpected linking." If, as is probable, Constable made up the *Works* from first editions, then the word "soiled," which Matthiessen quotes correctly from his source, is really a misprint for Melville's "coiled," for both the American and English first editions of *White-Jacket* printed the latter word.[4] It is interesting to note that the change in this case does not invalidate the general critical position arrived at by Matthiessen; it merely weakens his specific example. However, such a textual slip could, in the proper context, have promulgated an entirely false conception.

[4] I am indebted to Dr. Howard P. Vincent for checking a copy of the English first edition.

Melville on Homer

R. W. B. Lewis

T HE WORKS of the great poets have never yet been read by mankind," Thoreau wrote, indulging in paradox and exaggeration to make a very good point; "for only great poets can read them." Melville's reading of the *Iliad* and the *Odyssey* provides a unique illustration of at least the second half of that statement; and we are fortunate in being able to watch the process at work: the process, that is, by which a great book and a great reader can affect each other by mutual impact. Melville first looked into Chapman's Homer in November, 1858, when George Duyckinck sent him the two epics in four volumes; he had already read Pope's translation and found the earlier one incomparably better.[1] The line pencilings he made in those volumes indicate the most penetrating, thorough, and comprehensive reading of the poems; they are flashes illuminating the book and the reader and, more significantly, the human experience both were involved in. There is a measure of happy surprise in this for the student who remembers the temper of the age: since, to hear them talk, one might assume that Americans of creative strength had quite decided to abandon those old sources and to be nourished purely and simply by the immediate and actual and the national landscape. And yet even Emerson, who had the odd habit of announcing the break with the past by a hundred allusions to books that came out of it, had written in an essay called "Spiritual Laws":

[1] Chapman's version, Melville wrote Duyckinck in a letter of thanks, would send Pope's "off shrieking, like the bankrupt deities in Milton's hymn." He wrote in the margin Pope's translation of half a dozen passages, and underlined the sentences in the editor's (Richard Hooper's) introduction comparing the two versions—unfavorably to Pope.

Houghton Library at Harvard contains the Chapman volumes (London, 1857), along with Homer's *Batrachomyomachia, Hymns and Epigrams* (London, 1858), also by Chapman and also marked by Melville. A complete "Checklist of Books Owned and Borrowed by Melville," by Merton M. Sealts, Jr., began in the Spring, 1948, issue of the *Harvard Library Bulletin*. A slightly outdated list of "Books in the Harvard College Library Once Owned by Herman Melville" appears in the bibliography of F. Barron Freeman (ed.), *Melville's Billy Budd* (Cambridge, Mass., 1948).

We are always reasoning from the seen to the unseen. Hence the perfect intelligence that subsists between wise men of remote ages. A man cannot bury his meanings so deep in his book, but time and like-minded men will find them. Plato had a secret doctrine, had he? What secret can he conceal from the eyes of a Bacon? of Montaigne? of Kant? Therefore, Aristotle said of his works, "they are published and not published."

When he read that passage in 1862, Melville knew at once what Emerson was talking about: "Bully for Emerson," he wrote; "good." (He disagreed violently with other Emersonian effusions in the same essay.) Homer's secret, if he had any, was not long concealed from Herman Melville.

But "secret" is probably not as apt a sign of what Melville discovered in the epics as "pattern" or "figure" (to make use of Henry James's term). The most rewarding aspect of Melville's markings, here as elsewhere in his editions of Shakespeare and Hawthorne, is that they do form patterns; rarely casual or isolated, they fall usually on the essential threads, forcing the poems to yield the figure woven within them. They are not of course the only figures we can trace in Homer; they have indeed, especially the *Odyssey,* a queer new look about them, for Melville was not a passive reader.[2] His response to great literature was often baffling. But the mystery about it is resolved when we accept the fact that poems like the *Iliad* and *King Lear* defy metaphysical laws; they are animate; they have souls of their own and are always growing. This growth is most conspicuous when they are confronted by an imagination as active and creative as Melville's.

It is the "figures" which Melville's markings bring sharply into the foreground that I wish particularly to consider here. Occasionally he marked details for their mere vividness: in the *Iliad* (III, 232), he was struck by the observation that, though the son of Atreus was the tallest member of the Greek council when it stood, "Yet *set,* Ulysses did *exceed,* and bred more reverence." Images caught his fancy, and a careful exploration of them would heighten our perception of the tone and rhythm of Melville's style.[3] But the great

2 Since "The Poet" was the essay of Emerson he most heavily annotated, Melville probably shared the conception elaborated there of the dynamic interrelation of poet, poem, reader, and object: all working together, co-operating in the creation of newer and higher forms.

3 E.g., the description of Thetis appearing to comfort the weeping Achilles (I, 360): "Up from the grey sea like a cloud." This reminded Melville of one of the most effective similes in *Paradise Lost*. He wrote: "Exhalation. Milton—'rose like an exhalation'—the Pandemonium Palace."

majority of the passages Melville checked or underlined have thematic interrelations; they are worth examining.[4]

II

The *Iliad,* under Melville's inspection, emerges as a tragedy: a
dark portrait of a world at war, a world in which lonely, grieving
men are caught up in vast, indefinable forces and move without hope
to meet the violence and death that awaits them, under the rule of
implacable divinities. If this appears to be a somewhat conventional
view of the poem, we should recall the peculiar comment of Emerson
only a year or two before: "True bards have ever been noted for their
firm and cheerful temper. Homer lies in the sunshine; Chaucer is
glad and erect." Emerson's reading was almost exclusively an index
to his own mind; as he thought it ought to be: "Nature and books
belong to the eyes that see them." But in Melville, discovery and
projection intermingled, and he could discover little sunshine penetrating the clouds which lay thickly over the siege of Troy. The atmosphere he sensed emanated rather from passages he underlined
like the following:

> Evermore worst matters put down best. (I, 557)
>   because his power is most,
> He will destroy most. (II, 101)
> But Jove hath order'd I should grieve, and to that end hath
>   cast
> My life into debates past end. (II, 330)

Death—sudden, violent, irresistible—is the identifying feature of human experience in such a world. Melville rarely failed to mark the
moments of abrupt collision, the language imaging the swift and
utter finality of the clanging blow, the instant plunge into Hades.
The effect of so-to-speak italicizing these passages (e.g., IV, 556; V,

---

[4] I am not concerned with "literary influence." However, the relation between the
Homeric epics and *Moby-Dick* ought perhaps to be sketched here. The reading of Chapman
is irrelevant, since it followed *Moby-Dick* by at least seven years; the problem turns on the
date of Melville's reading of the Pope translation. The facts, as I quote them from a letter
recently received from Merton M. Sealts, Jr., seem to be as follows: "On 19 March 1848,
HM was charged with '1 Classical Library, 37 v. ($) 12.23.' . . . This is Harper's series . . .
and Pope's Homer constitutes three of the volumes, nos. 32-34, containing a biographical
sketch plus the Iliad and Odyssey. . . . No one knows what's become of any of these
books. . . . Also at some time after 1856 . . . he acquired The Poetical Works of Alexander Pope, with a Life, by Rev. Alexander Dyco, Boston, Little, Brown, 1856. 3 v." The
apparently Homeric overtones to some of the language and incidents in *Moby-Dick* were
touched on by F. O. Matthiessen in *American Renaissance* (pp. 460-463).

63, 83; 161; VI, 13) is to draw the outlines of a crowded and compressed world animated chiefly by pure force. A tragic awareness by the warriors through whom the deadly current flowed did not escape Melville: his marking of the crash of heroes extended to the clear and disturbingly passionless comments of their killers (e.g., Diomede, Achilles) on the inevitability of the stroke of death in human life as they had learned to suffer it.

But as the last quotation above suggests, Melville saw in the *Iliad* an ambiguity of power, an obscurity affecting and affected by the relation between man and the gods. He brought to the passages about the gods the imagination which had spoken in *Moby-Dick* seven years earlier: "There can be no hearts above the snow-line. Oh! ye frozen heavens!" This becomes the spirit of the *Iliad* too, as Melville's pencil bears down on comparable passages in it, slighting a little certain others which might have softened the pervasive grimness. An active reader tends to select and order in a novel way. Melville selected passages like these:

> He pray'd; Jove heard him not, but made more plentiful the birth
> Of his sad toils.   (II, 366)
> The race of Gods is far above men creeping here below.   (IV, 426)

The pattern which forms under these markings and literally dozens more like them is almost Puritan in its contours. The bustling intrusion of the gods on either side of the battle is largely forgotten, and we are left with a remote and hostile race, quick to anger, harshly indifferent to the fate of man, interfering only to blast his tenuous hopes. Human will and freedom count for little; an impression rises from the marked pages of men accomplishing their own destruction in the midst of forces they can neither identify nor control. Melville found no cause for complaint against Homer, if the epic vision was ultimately obscure. He recognized a mystery, and in the mystery he felt he had probed to the meaning. Chapman's comment, in the discussion following Book XIV, was heavily underlined; he spoke of the "plebeian opinion that a man is bound to write to every vulgar reader's understanding." Homer, Chapman said, wrote "darkly." The author of *Pierre* knew about that.

One source of relief could yet be found amid so much darkness and pain: love of family, love of friends. An intense preoccupation with the value and need of friendship had allowed Melville to trace a compelling theme even in so slight a performance as *The Two Gentlemen of Verona;* in the *Iliad,* he could pause over Diomede's plea for a companion on the secret mission in Book X (ll. 196 *et seq.*): "Two may together see," Diomede explained. But the most sustained marking in the entire poem occurs in Book VI, from line 440 to the end: the parting of Hector from his wife and child. The framework of Melville's other patterns (violent death, hostile deities) lends a peculiar sense of compassion to this long passage. It has something of the effect produced on a smaller scale by the friendship of Queequeg and Ishmael in *Moby-Dick:* "I felt a melting in me. No more my splintered heart and maddened hand were turned against the wolfish world." The heroes of the *Iliad,* and especially Achilles, appear in Melville's edition as terribly alone; Melville found a portion of what he brought to the book, the sense of isolation which had gone into the projection of Ahab. Fighting alone after the death of Patroclus, Achilles has only his magic armor to sustain him; as Ahab, cut off from human companionship, has only the great harpoon. The making of the armor (XVIII, 422-501), a turning-point so comparable in significance and power to the forging of the harpoon, is marked over nearly a hundred lines.

III

The impact of Melville on the *Odyssey* led it to take the form of a *Bildungsroman* in which the relation between the characters and the sequence of the events stands for growth of insight into the heart of reality. The metaphysical term is intended since, to judge from the markings, Melville read the *Odyssey* on a more symbolic level than he did the *Iliad.* In the latter, his pencil was attracted principally to actions and to the forces which directed them; he stayed with the concrete embodiment; his reading was dramatic. But the passages he noted in the *Odyssey* (which he apparently read somewhere in the Pacific in 1860) move in the direction of interpretation. There are signs of immense enjoyment in the adventures themselves—the Lotophagi, the Laestrygonians, the visit to Hades, the conquest of Ithaca, and the slaying of the wooers—but Melville was primarily interested in meaning.

The meaning he seems to have found borrows much of its force from the unusual emphasis Melville laid on the sorrows and hardships of Ulysses and the generalizations about human evil which they gave rise to: to the point where a rich and spacious poem looks surprisingly gloomier than we have normally regarded it. There are undoubtedly sorrows enough in the *Odyssey;* but they stand forward in a new way under Melville's gaze; for that itself showed a tendency towards gloom in those days. Melville noted the recurring description of Ulysses and his dwindling crew sailing on stricken at heart after some frightful encounter; and he made much of Ulysses's somewhat artful sigh to Nausicaä, that he was the victim of "a cruel habit of calamity" (VI, 257). The author of *The Confidence-Man* may have taken a bitter personal relish in the disclaimer of Telemachus which he marked:

> Not by any means
> If Hope should prompt me or *blind confidence*
> (*The God of fools*) or ever deity
> Should will it, for 'tis past my destiny.   (III, 309)

The gods have become no more benevolent than they had been in the *Iliad*. Both of Nestor's remarks (III) are checked:

> Not with ease
> The eternal Gods are turned from what they please.
> I know God studied misery
> To hurl against us.

Passages touching the power of the gods are regularly scored (e.g., V, 222; VI, 283). The grief of the central characters and the severity of the gods join to develop the perception of a wolfish world, when marked passages like the following are added: the reaction of Telemachus to the dishonor shown his father:

> No more let any sceptre-bearing man
> Benevolent, or mild, or human be,
> Nor in his mind form acts of piety,
> But ever feed on blood.   (II, 348)

I am deliberately trying to indicate the special nature of Melville's response to the *Odyssey,* for if you put together lines and passages like those quoted (and they are typical of thirty-odd more) you begin to create a vision of terror and evil which casts a deep shadow over the beauty and fluid grace which the poem could otherwise be seen to reflect, and its sustained sense of impending triumph. But the passages are there, integral parts of the poem as it stands, invented by Homer and Chapman and not by Melville; and I can never read the *Odyssey* again without being sharply conscious of their presence. The *Odyssey* moves perceptibly, shifts and re-forms, as Melville's imagination engages it (as it does under the impact of Joyce's legend of Leopold Bloom). For if he dims some of the brightness in the poem, he does so by unfolding a pattern whose theme is education, the motion of the human spirit from appearance to reality; a painful process in Melville's and very likely in Homer's view. It is a reading which brings the *Odyssey* effectively close to *Moby-Dick*.

A sign of Melville's attitude is the particular value he apparently attached to the Telemachiad, the first four books. Melville's consistent fascination with the subject of children may have been personal and domestic, but it was not unique in the age. Emerson found "a certain tenderness" towards children the symbol of the period, when he looked back at it in 1867; Thoreau reverted again and again to the theme of children as natural poets whose imaginations might yet be spared the deadening effects of characteristic adulthood. Melville missed hardly a single allusion to any aspect of childhood in the plays of Shakespeare; and a continuing preoccupation is suggested by his double-check in the *Odyssey* of such relatively trivial remarks as the one comparing the ages of Telemachus and the son of Nestor: "His years seem short of yours" (III, 71). The historic impulse to most of this was probably the prevailing concern with a fresh awakening of consciousness emerging from the contemporary tension between tradition and freedom. The transition from youth to manhood could serve both as image and illustration; and this Melville could find in the *Odyssey*.

The departure of Telemachus for sandy Pylos assumes an inescapably symbolic quality when Melville's pencil relates passages like these:

> If fits not you so young
> To suffer so much by the aged seas
> And err in such a wayless wilderness.
>   (Eurycleia to Telemachus)   (II, 545)
> Why left my son his mother?   Why refused
> His wit the solid shore to try the seas
> And put in ships the trust of his distress
> That are at sea to man unbridled horse,
> And run past rule?   (Penelope) (IV, 942)

The enterprise of going to sea as an image of the growing-up process in its varied dimensions has long been central for Melville; he even marked a particularly fine use of it by Hawthorne in *The House of the Seven Gables*. In the first of the pair of quotations above, Melville underlined the adjectives whose contrast deepens the significance of the entire passage: young and aged. It is tempting indeed, contemplating the two passages together, to find a proto-Jungian interpretation in Melville's mind; for the crucial motion towards the archaic unconscious which Jung elaborated was reflected everywhere (he believed) in the twin images of shore-and-sea and horse-and-rider—images combined in the question of Penelope.

But we do not need to go so far afield to follow Melville's notion of the education-theme in the *Odyssey*. Going to sea was a way of doing what Thoreau could do by settling down along a tiny lake: he went, Thoreau said, in order "to front . . . the essential facts of life." For Melville this was fundamentally an intellectual, indeed a metaphysical, venture; and if not more difficult, it was a good deal more harrowing than it had been for Thoreau, since malice and evil were among the facts to be fronted. Both the nature and the peril of the undertaking were suggested in the advice Proteus gave Menelaus, along the margin of which Melville ran a strong penciled line:

> Cease
> To ask so far. It fits thee not to be
> So cunning in thine own calamity.
> Nor seek to learn what learned thou shouldst forget.
> Men's knowledges have proper limits set
> And should not prease into the mind of God.   (IV, 657)

The echo of Eurycleia's admonition carried by the impersonal verb ("it fits not") must have been intended; for the old nurse and the old man of the sea are saying very much the same thing. Both are remarking on the danger, the rashness, the inappropriateness of attempting to probe too deeply into what Melville called elsewhere "the very axis of reality." All of Melville's heroes, like Telemachus and Ulysses, aware of their rashness, take the plunge nevertheless. Melville noted some of the results, as Ulysses (to whom his interest of course shifts, along with Homer's) struggles ashore on the island of Nausicaä:

> The sea had soak'd his heart through.   (V, 612)
>   The hard pass
> He had at sea stuck by him.   (VI, 198)

Both lines are underscored.

If the poem is some sort of allegory describing the quest of the mind for truth, a prying beyond natural limits into the mind of God, what answer does it offer? What can be learned by braving the sea, by meeting the challenge of the sea-god—who, as Melville noted in I, 33, "divine Ulysses ever did *envy?*"[5] What is gained in exchange for the buffets, the soaking, the hard pass that stays by one? Ulysses's experience is contained in the tales he told the court of Antinoüs, the incidents of which Melville marked heavily. But all that the wanderer will ever tell are adventure stories embodying human suffering; and most of them will be lies. He knew it would be fatal to do otherwise. One of the heaviest markings in the poem, three emphatic lines in the margin, greets the action of Ulysses when he arrives in Ithaca:

> Therefore he bestowed
> A veil on truth; for evermore did wind
> About his bosom a most crafty mind.   (XIII, 370)

That scene, in which Ulysses's impromptu fabrications are affectionately exposed by Athena, can be read as high comedy; a cheerful temperament will normally read it so. But in the framework Melville had built it deepens the tragic tone; it has the quality of the fool's speech in the tragedy of Lear: "Truth's a dog must to kennel." When he marked that in 1850 Melville still felt the possibility as well as the compulsion to speak forth what he saw and knew: the sermon he wrote for Father Mapple in *Moby-Dick* concluded with the injunction to "preach the Truth to the face of Falsehood." But the response to his books convinced him of the impossibility of writing this way; and write the other way, he could not, as he told Hawthorne. By the time he read the *Odyssey* in the Pacific Ocean he had himself "bestowed a veil on truth"; he had withdrawn into that privacy which none of his biographers has ever fully invaded.[6]

---

[5] "Envy" carried the connotation of "malice" for Melville; he so used it in *Billy Budd*, and he noted the footnote to his edition of *Julius Caesar* which explained the proximity of the nouns for the Elizabethan.

[6] F. Barron Freeman (op cit.) may be an exception; his careful and sensible account of Melville's last years and the writing of *Billy Budd* can help modify opinions like my own. However, even Freeman finds the following quotation from Arnold, underlined by Melville,

Athena's response to the elaborate lie of Ulysses is a wondering exclamation:

> Not secure thy state
> Without these wiles, though on thy native shore
> Thou settest safe footing?

Triple-checking and underlining those lines, Melville may have felt he knew the answer, knew it was negative. Ulysses had suffered too much at sea; he had discovered the abundance of evil in the heart of reality. However Homer resolved his narrative, in Melville's *Odyssey* the education of the hero ends in fables or silence.

---

the most apt summary of Melville's final attitude: "There is more power and beauty in the well-kept secrets of one's self and one's thoughts than in the display of a whole heaven that one may have inside one" ("Maurice de Guerin").

Some Notes on the Structure of *The Confidence-Man*

John G. Cawelti

O NE OF THE significant phenomena of recent Melville criticism has been an awakening of interest in *The Confidence-Man.*[1] The book has been, until the last ten years or so, the least appreciated of Melville's longer works, for it is a most enigmatic novel and the range of disagreement over its meaning has been extreme.[2] Little attention has been given to the book's structure, however, and in this article I shall develop a structural analysis that appears to illuminate some of the novel's important themes and the way in which the author relates them.

Melville, himself, provides the best clue to his intention in three short chapters, spaced throughout the novel, in which he leaves the narrative thread in brief quasi-philosophical digression. This type of philosophical interlude is familiar. We recall such chapters as "The Whiteness of the Whale" in *Moby-Dick* and the digression on horologicals and chronometricals in *Pierre,* both crucial to the meaning of those works. In *The Confidence-Man,* these three breaks not only develop and expand the meaning of the narrative but have the important structural function of emphasizing significant episodes: the first stresses a sudden revelation by one of the characters; the second emphasizes the most enigmatic of the many anecdotes woven into the narrative; and the third prepares the reader for the novel's conclusion.

Chapter XIV ("Worth the consideration of those to whom it may prove worth considering") ostensibly explains why one of the characters approached by the confidence-man has suddenly burst out with the desperate cry:

---

[1] I would like to express my appreciation to Prof. John C. Gerber for encouragement in the preparation of this paper.

[2] Scholarship and criticism are discussed in *The Confidence-Man: His Masquerade,* ed. Elizabeth S. Foster (New York, 1954), pp. xxxiii-xlvii. All citations are to this edition.

"Ah, wine is good, and confidence is good; but can wine or confidence percolate down through all the stony strata of hard considerations, and drop warmly and ruddily into the cold cave of truth? Truth will *not* be comforted. Led by dear charity, lured by sweet hope, fond fancy essays this feat; but in vain; mere dreams and ideals, they explode in your hand, leaving naught but the scorching behind!"[3]

This statement might stand as a summary of one aspect of the novel's moral content. Yet, it is presented in this peculiar way: a character whom the reader has no occasion for thinking to be other than a good-natured, simple, easily duped country merchant, without insight into the nature of things, suddenly, after a few glasses of wine, breaks forth with it. Immediately after he has spoken, he subsides into confusion, not at all understanding what he has said. Chided by the confidence-man, he can only stammer apologies and retire: "So saying, the merchant rose, and making his adieus, left the table with the air of one, mortified at having been tempted by his own honest goodness, accidentally stimulated into making mad disclosures—to himself as to another—of the queer, unaccountable caprices of his natural heart."[4]

Chapter XIV takes up at this point. Admitting that this sudden reversal of character is an inconsistency, Melville defends himself on the ground that this sort of inconsistency is more characteristic of real life than the false consistency imposed by most writers of fiction on their material. The reader insists that fiction be based on reality, but is it not a fact, he asks, that in real life a consistent character is a *rara avis*? Where the lesser author presents only sections or parts of life, eliminating the inconsistencies for the sake of clarity and comprehension, the truly great writer will draw life with all its complexities. He concludes:

Upon the whole, it might rather be thought that he, who, in view of its inconsistencies, says of human nature the same that, in view of its contrasts, is said of the divine nature, that it is past finding out, thereby evinces a better appreciation of it than he who, by always representing it in a clear light, leaves it to be inferred that he clearly knows all about it.[5]

It seems that, for Melville, reality is ultimately inscrutable; the things man experiences are only a glittering surface over impene-

[3] *The Confidence-Man*, p. 74.   [4] *Ibid.*, p. 75.
[5] *Ibid.*, p. 77.

trably dark depths. Yet, at certain times a hint of the depths comes boiling up to the surface, like a great fish, breaking the water, shattering the calm and scattering men and boats. The representation of such a moment is, for him, the ultimate goal of art. Roberts's sudden outburst is such a moment, though, like everything in *The Confidence-Man,* in a minor key. To be presented with its full shock, it must be wholly inconsistent with everything that has been and will be. It must be a reversal, sudden and startling, of character, action, and tone, for only in this way can it represent the moment at which the mask gives way to the face behind.

And yet it leads to nothing definite. The insightless, slightly bewildered character, the glittering surface action, the inanely jocular tone, are immediately resumed. So, with Melville, it must always be, for reality remains unattainable; the moment of seeming truth may be only another mask, the sudden inconsistency only another delusion. We are left with ambiguity at the heart of things.

The second philosophical digression can be found in Chapter XXXIII ("which may pass for whatever it may prove to be worth"). Here Melville rouses himself to reply to "a certain voice," presumably the reader, who exclaims: "How unreal all this is! Who did ever dress or act like your cosmopolitan?"[6] His answer to this charge is particularly striking in the light of the disquisition in the chapter we have just discussed. There he defended an inconsistency by claiming that real life has this characteristic, and that the serious writer should strive above all to represent real life. Here he responds:

Strange, that in a work of amusement, this severe fidelity to real life should be exacted by any one, who, by taking up such a work, sufficiently shows that he is not unwilling to drop real life, and turn, for a time, to something different. Yes, it is, indeed, strange that anyone should clamor for the thing he is weary of; that any one, who, for any cause, finds real life dull, should yet demand of him who is to divert his attention from it, that he should be true to that dullness.[7]

He goes on to give a brief rationale of romanticism. Fiction should be real life heightened, nature "unfettered, exhilarated, in effect, transformed." In this way it can present even more reality

[6] *Ibid.,* p. 206.
[7] *Ibid.*

than real life can show.   The concept is quite close to Hawthorne's as expressed in the prefaces to *The Scarlet Letter* and *The House of the Seven Gables*.   That Melville has the former in mind is suggested by his allusion to "the same old crowd around the custom-house counter."

But Melville has, in effect, reversed himself.   In Chapter XIV, he argued that the serious writer of fiction should attend faithfully to such characteristics of real life as inconsistency.   Here he insists that fidelity to real life is not the proper course.   The writer should heighten real life, should present another world than this one.   By implication he is in both chapters discussing his own practice so that the reader is left wondering just what his fiction is supposed to be. Is he dealing with reality in the sense of real life, with the intention of telling us something about it, or is he dealing with reality as real life transformed, seeking to ". . . minister to what, as he understands it, is the implied wish of the more indulgent lovers of entertainment, before whom harlequin can never appear in a coat too particolored, or cut capers too fantastic."[8]   No matter how carefully we read, we never find a sure answer to this question.

What Melville has done in these two chapters is the same thing we find him doing on every level in *The Confidence-Man*.   He presents something for the reader to hold onto and then snatches it away by presenting its contrary.   The result is that the reader is confronted with a vast maze of conflicting clues to the meaning of the novel.   But I do not think this is just a perverted attempt to bedevil the reader.   It arises from a serious view of reality as ultimately inscrutable and ambiguous and leads to a dynamic search for some way to structure and represent this reality.

The third and last of the reflective interludes gives us a good example of the way in which Melville carefully develops his representation of an unattainable reality.   Chapter XLIV ("In which the last three words of the last chapter are made the text of discourse, which will be sure of receiving more or less attention from those readers who do not skip it") is a discussion of the aptness of the phrase "quite an original" as a description of the cosmopolitan, the final incarnation of the confidence-man.   We might expect to discover from such a disquisition some hint of the author's attitude toward his protagonist, as we might have anticipated some statement

[8] *Ibid.*, p. 207.

of his attitude toward the relationship between his fiction and reality
in the two earlier chapters. As the interlude begins the author is
ruminating on the subject of original characters in fiction. He
stresses the rarity of such characters, mentioning as examples Hamlet, Don Quixote, and Milton's Satan, and insists that originality
is more than being novel, singular, striking, or captivating. Then,
after asserting that the novelist picks up his characters from life and
not out of his imagination (we recall the argument of Chapter XIV)
he comes to his crucial point: the truly original character ". . . is
like a revolving Drummond light, raying away from itself all
around it—everything is lit by it, everything starts up to it (mark
how it is with Hamlet), so that, in certain minds, there follows
upon the adequate conception of such a character, an effect, in its
way, akin to that which in Genesis attends upon the beginning of
things."[9]

The confidence-man is such a "revolving Drummond light" in
that every event in the novel is contingent on him; everything starts
up to him and no character or occurrence has any significance
or existence apart from its relationship to him. In his terrifying,
enigmatic, and ambiguous nature he would be a superb embodiment
of the Melvillean universe. Yet, for Melville, even this is saying
too much about reality, which must remain, despite all hints and
counter-hints, past finding out. In the concluding paragraph of the
chapter, the author suddenly gives the lie to the implication he has
built up:

In the endeavor to show, if possible, the impropriety of the phrase, *Quite
an Original,* as applied by the barber's friends, we have, at unawares,
been led into a dissertation bordering upon the prosy, perhaps upon the
smoky. If so, the best use the smoke can be turned to, will be, by retiring
under cover of it, in good trim as may be, to the story.[10]

These three philosophical interludes are of utmost significance
to the novel as a whole: they provide a frame of ambiguity within
which the enigmatic action of the narrative takes place; and they
furnish the key to the structural representation of a dark reality
that is, by definition, past finding out. That key is what we might
call the incomplete reversal: something is presented, a character, an
incident, an idea, anything which might give the reader some clue

[9] *Ibid.,* p. 271.   [10] *Ibid.*

to the interpretation of the represented reality; then a counter incident or idea appears, powerful enough to destroy the usefulness of the first clue, but insufficient to provide a foundation for a new interpretation of what has been presented. We are left in the air with no way of resolving two mutually exclusive possibilities.

II

The Confidence-Man is structured around incomplete reversals at every level. The book's two main divisions provide a good illustration. In the first section, Chapters I-XXIII, the confidence-man appears in a series of six major disguises (not including the Mute who will be discussed later, and the elderly Quaker who appears only briefly): Black Guinea, the man with the weed, the man with the gray coat and white tie, the man with the book, the herb-doctor, and the man from the Philosophical Intelligence Office. In each of these disguises he bilks one or more of his fellow passengers of varying sums of money. In the second section, Chapters XXIV-XLV, the confidence-man appears in only one mask, the cosmopolitan, and, in this section, his role is reversed. He is not the purveyor of false stocks, the false cripple, or the dispenser of Omnibalsamic Reinvigorator, but the seeker of friendship and brotherhood. Instead of succeeding as the earlier confidence-men do, each time he makes his appeal he is rebuffed by distrust, suspicion, indifference, and hostility. In the first part of the second section, the drinking scene with Charlie Noble (Chapters XXV-XXXV), the reader is even temporarily led to believe that Charlie is the confidence-man, and so Mark Winsome later judges him. But again the reversal is incomplete, and in the scene with the barber, (Chapters XLI-XLIII), the confidence-man is again up to his old tricks, bilking the barber out of the price of a shave. This prepares us for the terrifyingly ambiguous conclusion; when the cosmopolitan turns out the light and "kindly" leads the old man away, it is almost overpowering, for we are completely unable to evaluate the meaning of this obviously symbolic act. We see the two possibilities: the cosmopolitan is truly kind and is charitably assisting the old man as he had "kindly" purchased a poem from a seedy poet,[11] or he is a devil malevolently leading the old man out on the deck where he can rob and murder him. Yet, to attach either meaning con-

---

[11] *Ibid.*, p. 219. The word "kind" is actually employed.

clusively would require ignoring one set of the clues given earlier in the novel.

An analysis of the secondary divisions of the novel discloses that some kind of reversal takes place in almost every one. Generally these reversals occur on three levels: there are reversals of roles, e.g., the pursuer becomes pursued,[12] the suspicious, confiding;[13] reversals of ideas, e.g., lying becomes truth,[14] charity becomes villainy,[15] and fiction, reality;[16] and reversals of the reader's expectations and interpretations, e.g., villains become heroes;[17] philosophers, practical;[18] philanthropists, surly, and misanthropes, genial;[19] and comedy, tragedy.[20]

III

A detailed examination of the many scenes in the novel is beyond the compass of this paper, but an analysis of two of the crucial episodes will demonstrate, I think, how carefully Melville has employed the reversal throughout *The Confidence-Man.*

Take, for example, the novel's first scene: the appearance of a mute on the *Fidèle.* The first description given of this character stresses his innocence, weakness, and isolation, but hardly has he stepped onto the boat when he comes to a placard ". . . offering a reward for the capture of a mysterious imposter, supposed to have recently arrived from the East. . . ."[21] The connection between the mute and the mysterious imposter, though hardly sure, is suggestive, and the suggestion is strengthened by the superb bit of irony which immediately follows. The author, commenting on the bandits who had once infested the region, compares them to wolves whose ex-

[12] As when the collegian, who has been pursued by the man with the weed, becomes the pursuer of the man with the book, *ibid.,* chap. v and ix.

[13] As when the crippled and misanthropic "Soldier of Fortune" suddenly confides his true story to the herb-doctor, *ibid.,* chap. xix.

[14] Cf. the story of Charlemont, a fiction told as a truth, then claimed as a fiction, but actually a truth about life, *ibid.,* chaps. xxxiv and xxxv.

[15] Cf. the fictitious Seminole widows' and orphans' home, a charity employed by the confidence-man to bilk his fellow passengers.

[16] The novel itself as brought out in *ibid.,* chaps. xiv, xxiii and xliv.

[17] As in the Noble-Goodman scene, *ibid.,* chaps. xxv-xxxv, when the cosmopolitan-confidence-man, a kind of villain to this point, becomes a hero of sorts by his bearding of the even more hypocritical and deceitful Charlie Noble.

[18] Cf. the character of Egbert, disciple of the philosopher Mark Winsome in *ibid.,* chaps. xxxvii-xli.

[19] *Ibid.,* pp. 200-201.

[20] Cf. *ibid.,* chap. xlv, the conclusion of the novel.

[21] *Ibid.,* p. 1.

termination ". . . would seem cause for unalloyed gratulation, and is such to all except those who think that in new countries, where the wolves are killed off, the foxes increase."[22]

By this time, the mute has begun inscribing on his slate the Pauline quotations on charity. This, combined with the rough treatment he receives from the other passengers, stresses again his innocence and weakness, arousing the sympathy of the reader. This second reversal of the mute's character and significance reaches its climax in the final description accorded him before he disappears from sight:

His aspect was at once gentle and jaded, and from the moment of seating himself, increasing in tired abstraction and dreaminess. Gradually overtaken by slumber, his flaxen head drooped, his whole lamb-like figure relaxed, and, half reclining against the ladder's foot, lay motionless, as some sugar-snow in March, which, softly stealing down over night, with its white placidity startles the brown farmer peering out from his threshold at daybreak.[23]

However, the reversal is again incomplete, and the earlier suspicion lingers. We are left with the insoluble question of whether the mute is what he seems, or another mask for the confidence-man.

This first chapter provides important preparation for the rest of the book, particularly for the second half, which, as we have seen, is a reversal of the first. It announces the two basic idea-complexes of confidence and distrust around which the book centers, and the mystery of the mute foreshadows the later, more complex ambiguity of the cosmopolitan. The barber with his "NO TRUST" sign not only prepares us for his reappearance at the end of the book, but is a prototype of the distrustful and hypocritical characters the cosmopolitan will encounter: Charlie Noble, Mark Winsome, Egbert, and then the barber, himself. And the final ambiguity of the mute with the reference to the book of Genesis (Jacob's ladder) sets the stage for the terrifying enigma of the last chapter with its references to Revelation.

Another example, the Charlie Noble-Frank Goodman episode, occurs at the center of the book. Frank Goodman, the cosmopolitan, has appeared one chapter earlier. He has first encountered the surly Pitch, by whom he is rebuffed, and then he himself has

[22] *Ibid.*, p. 2.   [23] *Ibid.*, p. 5.

been accosted by Charlie Noble, who, it turns out, is another Mississippi operator. Charlie invites Frank to join him for a drink and the next ten chapters (XXV-XXXV) retail the ensuing discussion. The episode is shot through with reversals and ambiguities. First of all, the roles of confidence-man and victim are exchanged. At the beginning of the episode it seems apparent that the cosmopolitan is the confidence-man, but Charlie's behavior is suspicious enough that he soon has the cosmopolitan suggesting that he is the confidence-man. At this point, the cosmopolitan, hitherto the apostle of confidence, becomes distrustful. Then the roles are reversed again; when the cosmopolitan asks for a loan, Charlie, who to this point had been playing the innocent by eulogizing the virtues of trust in one's fellow men, is suddenly filled with hissing suspicion. He becomes snakelike; later the cosmopolitan takes on some of the attributes of the snake in similar fashion, in his conversation with Mark Winsome.

Several idea reversals take place in the Noble-Goodman scene, the most important centering around the antitheses of confidence-suspicion, isolation-sociability, love-hate, and philanthropy-misanthropy. We see, in the actions of both the cosmopolitan and Charlie, a professed confidence and geniality become the most profound mutual suspicion and dislike. In the story of Charlemont, the gentleman madman, we see sociability suddenly succeeded by, and indeed the cause of, intense isolation, while in the anecdote of Col. Moredock, the Indian-hater, the two extremes of sociability and isolation are combined in the same person. The story of the Indian-hater is also an examination of the love-hate polarity, illustrating the growth of hate out of love, and then the co-existence of the two in the same personality. These thematic ideas are brought together in the extended discussion of philanthropy which is the focal center of the Goodman-Noble episode. In Melville's world the philanthropist is bound to be surly and isolated from other men, for his love of his fellows makes his expectations too high. Being cut off from society, however, he is cut off from life. On the other hand, the misanthrope, hating his fellows, can at least accept them and be sociable. Neither the surly philanthropist nor the genial misanthrope has a particularly desirable role, but perhaps there is none other for the honest man. We sense that Melville, himself, feels that he has passed through the stage of surly philanthropy and has

reached a kind of passive acceptance of things in the role of the
genial misanthrope, that man described by the cosmopolitan's un-
named friend in the parable of the wine-drinker:

"He said that it illustrated, as in a parable, how that a man of disposition
ungovernably good-natured might still familiarly associate with men,
though, at the same time, he believed the greater part of men false-
hearted—accounting society so sweet a thing that even the spurious sort
was better than none at all. And if the Rochefoucaultites urge that, by
this course, he will sooner or later be undermined in security, he answers,
'And do you think I don't know that? But security without society I
hold a bore; and society, even of the spurious sort, has its price, which
I am willing to pay.' "[24]

IV

The Confidence-Man, then, is not a random collection of episodes; it is not the bitter polemic of a despairing man; it is not
merely a philosophical leg-pull, but a serious, carefully planned attempt to present one man's vision of reality. As the vision sees ambiguity at the heart of things, so the basic structural principle is one
that leaves the reader alone with an enigma. One cannot deny,
I think, that Melville prepared for this result painstakingly and
skilfully.

We find in this novel an attempt to grasp and structure human
experience; to represent man's involvement in an inscrutable cosmos,
where life is only a shimmering surface masking the impenetrable
depths of ultimate reality. And man is masked; he changes suddenly, meaninglessly, from one role to another, his purposes and
motivations always obscure. If there is any wisdom in such a universe it can only be that of seeing that there are at least two
opposing sides to everything. This wisdom may not make man any
happier or more successful, but it may help him avoid the dismal
fate of China Aster, the subject of the novel's last anecdote:

FOR HE WAS RUINED BY ALLOWING HIMSELF TO BE PERSUADED/ AGAINST HIS
BETTER SENSE,/ INTO THE FREE INDULGENCE OF CONFIDENCE,/ AND/ AN ARDENT-
LY BRIGHT VIEW OF LIFE,/ TO THE EXCLUSION/ OF/ THAT COUNSEL WHICH
COMES BY HEEDING/ THE/ OPPOSITE VIEW.[25]

[24] *Ibid.*, p. 184.
[25] *Ibid.*, p. 248.

Is there anything conclusive in the novel: a hidden moral sense or a "true map" for navigating the world? There is, I think, none. Melville is less interested, at this point, in solving the world's problems than in presenting a paradigm of reality as he envisages it. The confidence-man, enigmatic, ambiguous, inscrutable, and vaguely terrifying, is such a paradigm. He is also man, many faced, confronting a many-masked world and headed for a destiny that is past finding out.

Hawthorne, Melville, and "Blackness"

Hubert H. Hoeltje

T HE GROWTH OF THE REPUTATION of Herman Melville as a writer
of fiction, once so astonishing, has become a commonplace in
contemporary commentary on American literature. The interest in
Melville as a critic, and more specifically as a critic of Hawthorne,
is, however, a fairly recent and, to some of us, a startling phenomenon. For instance, thirteen years after the appearance of R. M.
Weaver's pioneering *Herman Melville, Mariner and Mystic* in 1921,
a scholarly selection of Hawthorne's writings, with introduction,
bibliography, and notes, and having a wide currency among our
colleges and universities, made no reference whatever, either in the
introduction or in the bibliography, to Melville's "Hawthorne and
His Mosses."[1]

Today the picture is different. Now we have been assured that
the so-called "blackness" which Melville thought he found in Hawthorne's fiction has emerged as "Hawthorne's trademark," so impressed by the significance of Melville's criticism has one of our
contemporaries become. Indeed, so impressed has this critic been
by Melville's comment that he apparently finds this "blackness"
even more characteristic of Hawthorne than of Melville himself.[2]
Perhaps a veteran reader of Hawthorne might be inclined to dis-
miss such judgments as evidence of an unrestrained enthusiasm
did these views not seem to be supported by the remark of a
distinguished Hawthorne scholar that "'Hawthorne and His
Mosses' is one of the great critical essays of the nineteenth century. . . ."[3] Melville, it appears, has now been adjudged a great critic
as well as a great novelist—or, at least, a great critic of Hawthorne.

Before this seeming tide of opinion quite oversweeps discretion,

[1] Austin Warren, ed., *Nathaniel Hawthorne: Representative Selections, with Introduction, Bibliography, and Notes* (New York, 1934).
[2] Harry Levin, *The Power of Blackness: Hawthorne, Poe, Melville* (New York, 1958),
p. 26.
[3] Randall Stewart, review of *Inward Sky, the Mind and Heart of Nathaniel Hawthorne*,
by Hubert H. Hoeltje, Durham, N. C., 1962, *American Literature*, XXXIV, 577-578 (Jan.,
1963).

it might be well to do what appears not yet to have been done—
namely, to examine Melville's essay on Hawthorne's *Mosses* in some
detail and to determine whether it represents a sound criticism supported by irrefutable evidence or whether it reveals a mistaken view
which, in our day, has turned much of the comment on Hawthorne
into a quagmire of erroneous interpretation.

One need not quarrel with Melville's ardor for the prospects for
American literature, especially since one can now be confident that
our literature has established itself among the literatures of the
world. Nor need one quarrel in its general nature with Melville's
high regard for the fiction of Hawthorne, since that fiction with-
stood the debunkers of several decades and has maintained its standing through the re-evaluations of recent years. As mature criticism,
however, Melville's essay may seem to lose some of its force when
one becomes aware that the young man who rather cavalierly takes
to task the "endless commentators and critics" of Shakespeare[4] had
himself discovered Shakespeare only a little more than a year
before,[5] and could therefore hardly have read very widely in the
critics. And what can one say of Melville's assertion that " 'The
Mosses from an Old Manse' will be ultimately accounted [Haw-
thorne's] masterpiece,"[6] except to reply that apparently the prophecy
after one hundred years has not yet been fulfilled? Even more
disturbing, what scholarly charity can accept such a judgment when
the prophet has apparently only a very slight acquaintance with any
other book by Hawthorne, and so bases his prophecy and makes all
his allegations regarding "blackness" as a dominating trait in Hawthorne after reading only one book?[7] Surely even the most gentle
reader who judges Melville's commentary with his eyes open must
have some doubts regarding the validity of the essay as a whole.

I

Before examining Melville's major theme, that is, the "blackness"
which he is assured he has personally discovered in Hawthorne's
writing, it may not be amiss briefly to scan Melville's approach to his

[4] Willard Thorp, ed., *Herman Melville: Representative Selections, with Introduction,
Bibliography, and Notes* (New York, 1938), p. 334.

[5] *Ibid.*, p. 370.

[6] *Ibid.*, p. 345.

[7] *Ibid.*, p. 385. In a letter to Duyckinck, Melville, now having read *Twice-Told
Tales*, says that they "far exceed the Mosses"!

concluding thought. It is a gradual approach, skilfully made, leading the reader from commonly accepted views to the view which Melville offers climactically as deeper and truer than any ever offered before. Early in his essay he speaks of the "noon-day repose of Hawthorne's spell," and then, presently, of the melancholy which rests like an Indian summer all over Hawthorne. But these qualities, he says, are only the least part of the genius of Hawthorne which has attracted admiration. In spite of "the Indian-summer sunlight on the hither side of Hawthorne's soul," the other side, he now asserts, "is shrouded in blackness, ten times black." Whether this blackness is only an artistic device or evidence of a Puritanic gloom in Hawthorne himself, Melville at this point is not ready to say, though within the limits of the same paragraph he is ready to say that "the world is mistaken in this Nathaniel Hawthorne." Then, with an apparently cautious reserve, he approaches the heart of his argument: "Perhaps he does not give us a ray of his light for every shade of his dark." Having made this advance, he at once qualifies and reasserts his position by saying that the reader need not fix upon the blackness in Hawthorne, nor will all readers discern it, though it will be evident to those best qualified to understand it—a remark surely calculated to encourage the reader to wish to be among the discerning ones.

Now, too, Melville dissolves the doubt whether Hawthorne treats his subject matter as mere material for art, or whether it represents the man himself, for, like "all true, candid men," Hawthorne, in Melville's eyes, is "a seeker, not a finder yet." Furthermore, in the second part of his essay, after the lapse of the twenty-four hours during which he has read more of the tales in *Mosses,* and during which he has discovered "Young Goodman Brown," Melville seemingly throws all qualification to the winds by offering that celebrated story as a "strong positive illustration of that blackness in Hawthorne, which I had assumed from the mere occasional shadows of it, as revealed in several other sketches."

In short, when the essay comes to an end, "blackness," which has earlier been offered as "the very axis of reality," has become, so Melville is convinced, the basic quality in Hawthorne's writing, a quality inherent in the constitution of the man Hawthorne, and not a mere device of artistry. And if any doubt may hover in the mind of the reader regarding the meaning of "blackness" as the word is used by Melville, that doubt is dispelled by Melville's letter written to Hawthorne subsequent to his reading of *The House of the Seven Gables,* a letter appearing less than a year after the essay: "There is the grand truth about Nathaniel Hawthorne. He says NO! in thunder; but the devil himself cannot make him say *yes.* For all men who say *yes,* lie . . . ."[8] The remark is obviously a caustic reference to Carlyle's exulting "Everlasting Yea" in *Sartor Resartus,* and, though more literary in flavor, is no less to the point than a later blunt pronouncement by Mark Twain—namely, "the man who *isn't* a pessimist is a d——d fool."[9]

If, then, Melville stamps the brand of pessimism on Hawthorne, it will be interesting to examine the major tales and sketches in the one book which Melville has read and to which he alludes. He has, for instance, read the introductory essay, "The Old Manse," as well as "Buds and Bird Voices," in which he finds the "noon-day repose" of Hawthorne's spell, and the delicious apples of the "thoughts and fancies of this sweet man of Mosses," remarks sufficiently appreciative. But since these qualities, though granted and shortly to be spoken of as "the least part" of Hawthorne's genius, presumably discernible even to the "superficial skimmer of pages," it may be well to point out in particular some aspects of these essays to which Melville makes no specific reference but which may have more bearing upon Hawthorne's ultimate thought than Melville has seen or admitted. For instance, in "The Old Manse," is it truly only the least part of his genius that is to be found in Hawthorne's remark, after a wild day on the Concord with Ellery Channing, "how sweet was it to return within the system of human society"? Is Hawthorne not truly serious when he returns to the Old Manse and home with the prayer "that the upper influences might long protect the institutions that had grown out of the human heart"? Is he expressing only a soothing pleasantry, and not a deep conviction near "the very axis of reality," when, reclining on the withered autumn grass, he whispers to himself, "O perfect day! O beautiful world! O beneficent God!" Is he writing only for the

---

[8] Julian Hawthorne, *Nathaniel Hawthorne and His Wife* (Boston, 1885), I, 388. Leslie A. Fiedler, in *No! in Thunder* (Boston, 1960), p. 6, quotes Melville's comment on Hawthorne's *The House of the Seven Gables* as the most explicit of all expressions of the "Modern Muse," which Fiedler characterizes as "demonic, terrible and negative."

[9] Albert B. Paine, *Mark Twain, a Biography* (New York, 1912), III, 1508.

"superficial skimmer of pages" when he says, in "Buds and Bird Voices," "But who can estimate the power of gentle influences"? Or, "There is no decay. Each human soul is the first created inhabitant in its own Eden"?

One may feel sympathetic with Melville's finding, in "The Old Apple Dealer," "the subtlest spirit of sadness," but the use of this sketch as an example of the "melancholy" which rests all over Hawthorne—the melancholy which Melville employs as a transition to the "blackness" which he is about to introduce—needs the careful examination for which Melville himself has pleaded. If there is melancholy in this sketch, it is not the melancholy of despair. The climactic sentences in the character sketch of the old apple dealer Melville seems not to have observed: "the soundless depths of the human soul and of eternity have an opening through your breast. . . . There is a spiritual essence in this gray old shape that shall flit upward too." Shall one say that this Christian hope of immortality is not honestly expressed, or that it is the least part of Hawthorne's genius? This sketch, if it is representative of Hawthorne, is representative, not of a melancholy tinged with "blackness," but of his idealism and his high hopes for even the humblest of men.

It is, however, when Melville enters the body of his essay that he becomes most convinced that he has found the true Hawthorne who is pervaded by blackness "through and through." "How profund, nay appalling, is the moral evolved by 'Earth's Holocaust'. . . ." What is so appalling, one might ask. The poor deceived girl, who would throw herself into the conflagration, is advised by the good man: "Be patient, and abide Heaven's will. So long as you possess a living soul, all may be restored to its first freshness. These things of matter and creations of human fantasy are fit for nothing but to be burned when once they have had their day; but your day is eternity." Is it so appalling to be assured that "Our faith can well afford to lose all the drapery that even the holiest men have thrown around it, and be only the more sublime in its simplicity," or that "Not a truth is destroyed nor buried so deep among the ashes but it will be raked up at last"?

Of course it is the last paragraph of "Earth's Holocaust" that Melville finds most appalling: "The heart, the heart. . . . Purify that inward sphere, and the many shapes of evil that haunt the outward, and which now seem almost our only realities, will turn to shadowy phantoms and vanish of their own accord; but if we go no deeper than the intellect, and strive, with merely that feeble instrument, to discern and rectify what is wrong, our whole accomplishment will be but a dream. . . ." Are these sentiments so very different from those of one of Hawthorne's contemporaries?

The problem of restoring to the world original and eternal beauty is solved by the redemption of the soul. . . . Love is as much its demand as perception . . . when a faithful thinker, resolute to detach every object from personal relations and see it in the light of thought, shall, at the same time, kindle science with the fire of holiest affections, then will God go forth anew into the creation. . . . Build therefore your own world. As fast as you conform your life to the pure idea in your mind, that will unfold its great proportions. A correspondent revolution in things will attend the influx of spirit . . . until evil is no more seen.

Do not both passages emphasize love or the heart and the need for the redemption of the soul, and the weakness of the intellect as the sole instrument of that redemption, a redemption following which the many shapes of evil which haunt us shall vanish? Are we to say, therefore, that Emerson's *Nature,* too, ends in an appalling moral?

If the nature of the human heart seemed appalling to Melville, it did not seem so to Hawthorne. In the very period at the Old Manse when he was planning "Earth's Holocaust," Hawthorne was contemplating another sketch, the plans for which show how completely Melville misunderstood him:

The human heart to be allegorized as a cavern; at the entrance there is sunshine, and flowers growing about it. You step within, but a short distance, and begin to find yourself surrounded with a terrible gloom, and monsters of divers kinds; it seems like Hell itself. You are bewildered, and wander long without hope. At last a light strikes upon you. You peep towards it and find yourself in a region that seems, in some sort, to reproduce the flowers and sunny beauty of the entrance, but all perfect. These are the depths of the heart, or of human nature, bright and peaceful; the gloom and terror may lie deep; but deeper still is the eternal beauty.[10]

[10] Randall Stewart, ed., *The American Notebooks by Nathaniel Hawthorne* (New Haven, 1932), p. 98.

It is in reference to "The Christmas Banquet" and "The Bosom Serpent" that Melville finds the "other side" of Hawthorne's soul "shrouded in blackness, ten times black." Why so? The former is patently an indirect plea for the preciousness of the human affections, a recurring theme in Hawthorne's writing; and as for the latter, could Melville have read its conclusion? "Rosina had emerged from the arbor and was bending over [Roderick Elliston] with the shadow of his anguish reflected in her countenance, yet so mingled with hope and unselfish love that all anguish seemed but an earthly shadow and a dream." And when the question is asked, "Can a breast where jealousy has dwelt so long, be purified?" Rosina replies, "O yes. . . . The serpent was but a dark fantasy, and what it typified was as shadowy as itself. The past, dismal as it seems, shall fling no gloom upon the future. To give it its due importance we must think of it but as an anecdote in our Eternity." Hope, love, forgiveness, Eternity. Do the ideas encompassed in these words suggest "blackness"? Melville's inversion of meanings is here surely beyond the bounds of rational thought.

It is in "Young Goodman Brown," however, that Melville sees "such a strong positive illustration" of blackness in Hawthorne—presumably because he sees in it "that Calvinistic sense of Innate Depravity and Original Sin" to which he had earlier attributed the "Puritanic gloom" in Hawthorne. That Hawthorne was dramatizing the repulsive elements of Puritanism is a thought that seems not to have occurred to Melville in his hasty two-day reading.

II

If these remarks seem unfair to Melville, perhaps the reactions of Hawthorne himself and those of his wife Sophia,[11] may throw some light on the accuracy of Melville's interpretations, for both read Melville's reviews when neither as yet knew who was their author. That Hawthorne was pleased by Melville's generous appreciation of his book is clear enough from his letter to Evert Duyckinck, though he protests that with his wife's admiration he should do very well without any other. What may not be apparent at first reading is the fact that Hawthorne limits his remarks to Melville's praise (not all of which he necessarily accepts), and that he says not one word about Melville's interpretation of his tales and

[11] Both letters are quoted in Thorp, p. 423.

sketches. Sophia in her letter to Duyckinck is of course happy over
such an enthusiastic review of her husband's writing, as she is in
her letter on the same subject to her mother. In the latter, however,
Sophia indicates clearly enough that Melville has misinterpreted
her husband's thought: "But it is funny to see how he [the anony-
mous writer, Melville] does not know how this heart and this
intellect are enshrined."[12] Like her husband, she had said nothing,
in her letter to Duyckinck, to approve of Melville's interpretation.
In her letter to her mother she had not hesitated to qualify her
pleasure in Melville's review.

What Hawthorne thought of Melville's interpretation of his
writing after he probably knew that Melville was the author, may
be clearly indicated by his remarks on a general review of all his
writings by Henry T. Tuckerman in the *Southern Literary Messenger* following the publication of *The House of the Seven Gables*.
When Tuckerman's essay was republished in *Littell's Living Age*
on June 11, 1864, shortly after Hawthorne's death, it was preceded
by a letter to Tuckerman from Hawthorne written at Lenox, Massachusetts, and dated June 20, 1851, a letter which, with the accompanying essay by Tuckerman, will place Melville's review in proper
perspective.

I have received the *Southern Literary Messenger*, and have read your
beautiful article on my, I fear, unworthy self. It gave me, I must confess,
the pleasantest sensation I have ever experienced, from any cause connected with literature; not so much for the praise as because I felt that you
saw into my books and understood what I meant. I cannot thank you
enough for it.

It is obvious that this letter is quite different from the one that
Hawthorne wrote to Duyckinck. In his comment on Melville's review, Hawthorne had spoken of his pleasure in Melville's praise, not
of Melville's understanding of his writing. In his letter to Tuckerman he minimizes the praise and emphasizes Tuckerman's understanding. That Hawthorne valued Tuckerman's comment much
more than he did Melville's is clearly implied. Hence, though
Tuckerman's excellent essay is too long even to be outlined here,
some of its more salient aspects are offered as pertinent to a criticism
of Melville's enthusiastic but faulty commentary.

[12] Rose Hawthorne Lathrop, *Memories of Hawthorne* (Boston, 1897), p. 173.

In the first place, Tuckerman had done what Melville should have done before he undertook to make such broad and sweeping generalizations—that is, Tuckerman had read thoroughly all of Hawthorne's writing, and hence did not superficially base his judgment on one solitary volume. Consequently, Tuckerman's review possesses, among other things, a balance quite lacking in what Melville had to say. It is apparent, too, that Tuckerman had a width of experience in reading, and certainly in reviewing, unknown to Melville. He was aware that the first duty of a good critic is to see what an author has to say, and not merely to express the reviewer's predilections. Melville's essay, however revelatory of Melville, is much less satisfactory than Tuckerman's for the simple reason that Melville ignored this first principle of criticism.

More specifically, the balance present in Tuckerman's review and absent from Melville's is indicated by Tuckerman's awareness of the variety in Hawthorne's writing. Instead of reducing all to melancholy and "blackness," Tuckerman sees not only the variety of subject matter, but also the variety of tone. The tragic element and the comic element, the cheerfulness and the solemnity, the tactful humor and the grave undertone, the "alternating melancholy and brightness which is born of a genuine moral life," all receive due recognition; hence there emerges not the emaciated author whom Melville's imperfect vision had imagined, but the healthy and affirmative man and author that Hawthorne really was. Furthermore, though Tuckerman gives but a nod of recognition to "Young Goodman Brown," which to Melville seems to have been such a positive illustration of the Puritanic gloom in Hawthorne, he fully disposes of the question of such gloom in his comment on *The Scarlet Letter,* which Melville had not read when he rushed into his broad generalizations. Beneath "the picturesque details and intense characterization" of *The Scarlet Letter,* said Tuckerman, "there lurks a profound satire. The want of soul, the predominance of judgment over mercy, the tyranny of public opinion, the look [lack?] of genuine charity, the asceticism of the Puritan theology, the absence of all recognition of natural laws, and the fanatic substitution of the letter for the spirit, which darken and harden the spirit of the pilgrims to the soul of a poet are shadowed forth with keen, stern, and eloquent, yet indirect emphasis that haunts us like 'the cry of the human.' " The profound satire and the indirectness which Tuckerman correctly perceived in *The Scarlet Letter,* and which are present with equal subtlety in "Young Goodman Brown," have, of course, escaped the observation of many a "superficial skimmer of pages."

But it is among his concluding remarks on *The House of the Seven Gables* that Tuckerman focuses the final and true aim and accomplishment of Hawthorne as man and author. In reading this statement, one should remember that it had Hawthorne's own approbation as what he meant to do in his writing, though that writing itself, to the careful reader, is ample evidence of Tuckerman's judgment.

Thus narrowly, yet with reverence, does Hawthorne analyze the delicate traits of human sentiment and character; and opens vistas into that beautiful and unexplored world of love and thought that exists in every human being, though overshadowed by material circumstance and technical duty. This . . . is his great service.[13]

"Reverence . . . human sentiment and character . . . love and thought. . . ." In the recognition of these ultimates, what must one think of the "blackness ten times black" which Melville, in holding a mirror up to himself, saw pervading Hawthorne "through and through"? What now of the hectic assertion, "There is the grand truth about Nathaniel Hawthorne. He says NO! in thunder; but the devil himself cannot make him say *yes.* For all men who say *yes,* lie. . . ." Coolly appraised, these remarks of Melville are sophomoric distortions. Sympathetically viewed, they are the words of an unhappy, lonely man who longs for the understanding of a kindred pessimistic spirit—one whom he quite mistakenly supposes he has found in Hawthorne.[14]

As for our contemporary who has convinced himself that "blackness" is "a virtual obsession with Hawthorne," and that "it became Hawthorne's trademark after Melville had pointed it out"—well, one should perhaps be willing to forgive what may only be a tender susceptibility to the maladies current in our present-day critical

[13] Tuckerman's essay deserves to be reprinted because it won such high approval from Hawthorne and because of its inherent excellence.

[14] The story of the friendship of Hawthorne and Melville I have told in some detail in *Inward Sky,* mentioned earlier in these notes. It was a true friendship in spite of limitations, respected and valued by both men.

climate. That Melville's "Hawthorne and His Mosses" is an interesting essay as revealing somewhat of the literary hope of the time,
and much more interesting as disclosing the mind of Herman Melville ("a seeker, not a finder yet"), may readily be granted; but
as an interpretation of Nathaniel Hawthorne it is certainly not "one
of the great critical essays of the nineteenth century" for the one
overpowering reason that it lacks a necessary ingredient of greatness
—namely, Truth.

The Domestic Adventurer in Melville's Tales

Judith Slater

IT HAS BEEN RECOGNIZED that the philosophical development which can be traced through Melville's novels has important ramifications in the tales as well. Six of the tales in particular become more meaningful if viewed as a group and as an extension of one of the major philosophical preoccupations of the novels. "Cock-a-Doodle-Doo!," "The Lightning-Rod Man," "I and My Chimney," "Jimmy Rose," "The Apple-Tree Table," and "The Piazza" all treat what might be called the "Ishmael" theme. After the wild defiance of the quest and after what we are led to believe is the acceptance of moral ambiguity which saves him, what is the future of Ishmael? That is to say, how can such an individual without sacrificing his complexity of vision adjust himself, as he must, to "home"? Melville answers that question indirectly in these particular tales by creating a series of domestic adventurers, widely different in personality, each of whom stands in a more or less mature relationship to his environment.[1]

The tales have several common denominators. The most conspicuous is domesticity as it is embodied in wives and children, hearths, attics, cellars, rambling country homes, pastoral vistas, and old age. The narrators share certain important characteristics: like Ishmael, they come to terms with reality without denying its ambiguity. Like him, their orientation is humanistic—they share a reverence for the past, a love of meditation, a feeling of kinship with nature and divinity, and an enjoyment of friendship and mirth. In some way, these narrator-protagonists are all forced to defend their values against an encroaching modernism which threatens the spaciousness of their experience; but aside from this outside threat, the narrators are notably secure. The agonizing introspection, the search for the "phantom of life" which dominates the novels, is conspicuously absent from these tales.

---

[1] "Cock-a-Doodle-Doo!" is a burlesque variation on the theme and must be exempted from the following generalizations.

The acceptance of the narrators must not be confused with defeat, however; for while they admittedly lead tame lives, they are still, in a special sense, adventurers. They have not abandoned the quest but, whether consciously or not, have accepted limits on it. Ishmael foreshadows this development in his figure of the Catskill eagle in the mountain gorge: still pursuing the knowledge of "darkness," the eagle does so within the protective enclosure of a gorge and thus avoids the abyss and the "woe that is madness." Similarly, these narrators are insulated from the mad quest of the ego; they do not assault the universe but are content to live in "low" houses and to seek symbolic adventure in contemplation.

I

"Cock-a-Doodle-Doo!" enjoys a special status within the domestic adventurer group. Whereas the other tales are concerned with the manifestation or development of dual vision in a single character, "Cock-a-Doodle-Doo!" dramatizes the failure of partial vision in two characters. Its method is a less ambitious version of that of *Moby-Dick*: the characters are deployed around a central symbol—the cock—which is ambiguous. Both Merrymusk and the narrator choose to interpret the cock solely in terms of one of its aspects. Their distortions, though opposites, are equally destructive.

The narrator's sin is optimistic excess. His "transformation" comes as no surprise to the reader, for from the beginning he displays a childish self-indulgence. His peevish mood, we soon discover, is occasioned as much by his inability to rid himself of a dun as by the death of a close friend. Then, the triumphant crow rings out and the narrator leaps from one emotional extreme to the other: self-pity becomes self-exaltation; the train, just previously a murdering Moloch coming through the woods like the "Asiatic cholera," is suddenly "white cars, flashing through the trees like a vein of silver"; and as for the dun—"I'll club him, by Jove, if he duns me this day," crows the narrator in high spirits.

Once he has yielded to the cock's illusion, the narrator ceases to be merely foolish and becomes a fool. One critic has said that he loses his sense of proportion, renounces social responsibility, and gives himself over to hedonistic self-indulgence.[2] While this is

[2] William B. Stein, "Melville Roasts Thoreau's Cock," *Modern Language Notes*, LXXIV, 219 (March, 1959).

generally true, it is doubtful that the narrator ever had a sense of proportion, and we suspect that he yields to the illusion with a fairly clear perception of what is to be gained: it affords, after all, a rather fancy, if not philosophical, justification for a life of indolence and pleasure. As the story develops we see more and more clearly that it is the narrator who is transforming the cock into an alter ego. He fancies that the cock crows solely for his benefit, to encourage and to compliment him. Even his praises of the cock are a form of self-flattery ("It was...the crow of a cock who knew a thing or two; the crow of a cock who had fought the world and got the better of it").

It is not surprising that the narrator admires the cock's "solitary scorn and independence," for he too lives solely "on his own account." His life is a merry round of loafing, gormandizing, and joking, the latter at the expense of the unfortunate dun who, despite a sober manner and lean appearance bespeaking conscientiousness and honest need, receives from the narrator only ridicule and physical punishment.

Merrymusk too is under the cock's spell, but his delusion is expressed in the "woe that is madness." From his first appearance, as the narrator's wood sawyer, he gives evidence of an unbalanced personality: he has "a long saddish face, yet somehow a latently joyous eye, which [offers] the strangest contrast." He saws steadily all day without speaking and even while sharing the narrator's dinner maintains a "sullen silence." The narrator learns from the villagers that Merrymusk in his youth had been a man of extremes, that in the ten years since his marriage he has led a sober and industrious existence but has fallen victim to extreme misfortune. Just as there was psychological motivation for the narrator's transformation, these details prepare us for Merrymusk's madness.

When the narrator visits Merrymusk in his wretched cottage, the latter flaunts his despair, scornfully aware that the narrator will not perceive the truth of the situation. (It is, in some respects, a Benito-Delano relationship, for the narrator is all but blind to the signs of Merrymusk's distress.) When he is questioned about the cock, Merrymusk hurls back the narrator's own sentiments, but steeped in such bitter irony that they echo like a curse. The narrator asks if the sick family *really* likes the crowing: "Don't *you*

like it? Don't it do *you* good? Ain't it inspiring? don't it impart
pluck? give stuff against despair?" The narrator comments that it
must be a doleful life for the Merrymusks: "Haven't I Trumpet?
He's the cheerer ... crows at the darkest; Glory to God in the
highest! continually he crows it." The narrator expresses his
amazement at Merrymusk's owning the cock:

Poor man like *me?* Why call *me* poor? Don't the cock I own glorify
this otherwise inglorious, lean, lantern-jawed land? Didn't *my* cock
encourage *you?* And *I* give you all this glorification away gratis. I am
a great philanthropist. I am a rich man—a very rich man, and a very
happy one.

For Merrymusk, the cock's "glory to God" is derisive and
blasphemous, and yet he is under the bird's spell more inexorably
than is the narrator. Merrymusk's madness is his refusal to sell
the cock, his masochistic insistence on steeping himself in his own
despair and yielding to the maniacal vision which is only one aspect
of the cock. This madness culminates in the diseased ecstasy of
his death, which appalls even the narrator, as well it should. But
if Merrymusk has succumbed to a distorted vision, no less so has
the narrator who, recovering from his fear and yielding again to
the cock's spell, perceives the death scene as one of transfiguration
and triumph, sanctified by the cock's "Bravo! Hurrah! Three-times-
three!" The ending of this "comic" spectacle is uncompromisingly
bleak. Both men are grotesque; both have sacrificed their humanity in indulging in opposite, yet equally devastating, emotional
extremes.

In contrast, "The Lightning-Rod Man" centers on a narrator
whose perspective is balanced and in harmony with his world.
In emphasizing the satiric aspects of this tale, critics have slighted
the stature of the narrator who, although he fails to rout the lightning-rod salesman from his neighbors' property, achieves a personal
triumph over that "false negotiator." Against the salesman's invo-
cation of fear, the narrator invokes his "faith": "In thunder as in
sunshine, I stand at ease in the hands of my God. False negotiator,
away! ... I read in the rainbow, that the Deity will not, of purpose,
make war on man's earth."[3]

[3] Several critics have suggested that the character of the salesman may have been
inspired by Cotton Mather's chapter on thunder in *Magnalia Christi Americana*: see

There may appear slight similarity between the narrator's Christian view of a sacramental universe and the complicated perspective of an Ishmael, but there is more to the narrator than his final affirmation. Like Ishmael, he combines aspects of the empirical and the imaginative. In response to the salesman's attempts to arouse his fear, he calmly insists: "The reasons, if you please." His first instinctive response to the stranger, however, has been warm and fanciful: "Sir ... have I the honor of a visit from that illustrious god, Jupiter Tonans?"

The parallel should not be overdrawn, for the boldly speculative aspect of Ishmael is absent from this portrait. While Ishmael undoubtedly would have viewed the lightning as a profoundly ambiguous force, the narrator's "faith" prevents his so doing, although there are suggestions that he has at least considered the malign possibilities of lightning ("Did you hear of the event at Montreal last year? A servant girl struck at her bed-side with a rosary in her hand; the beads being metal. Does your beat extend into the Canadas?"). The narrator's strength derives essentially from his acceptance of the universe and from his humble humanity: his house is a "low" one on top of a mountain, and the symbols with which he identifies are humble—his hearthstone and his rush-bottomed chair. For him, the quest is not to perceive the nature of reality but to sustain his vision of it. His adventure is the contemplation of the majestic in nature and the attempt at communion between "clay and sky." (What excites him about the "returning stroke" of lightning is its suggestion of a direct response of earth to divinity.)

While this man lacks the full dimensions of Ishmael, his proportions are nevertheless grand. In his refusal to be lured away from his fireplace and into the center of the room—that is, to relinquish his breadth of vision—he looks ahead to the more com-

---

especially Leon Howard, *Herman Melville* (Berkeley, 1951), p. 216, and Jay Leyda, ed., *The Complete Stories of Herman Melville* (New York, 1949), p. xxvii. It seems more likely, though, that if Melville used "Ceraunius," it was as a basis for the characterization of the narrator, since the predominant message of the chapter is the magnificence and beneficence of God as manifested in the voice of His thunder.

An even closer analogue to the characterization of the narrator is found in Jonathan Edwards's "Personal Narrative." Edwards recalls how he "felt God" at the first approach of a thunder storm and "used to take the opportunity, at such times, to fix [himself] in order to view the clouds, and see the lightnings play, and hear the majestic and awful voice of God's thunder."

plicated narrator in "I and My Chimney" (hereafter referred to as "I").

"I" too lives in a "low," but "wide," old house, and in the "Chimney" sketch houses are explicit metaphors for approaches to reality: for want of abundant space, the narrator explains, town houses are narrower than country houses; town people, to compensate, vie with one another in the height of their houses. "Such folks, it seems to me, need mountains for neighbors, to take this emulous conceit of soaring out of them." The wife is, of course, the human embodiment of the town house spirit; her narrow progressivism which insists on an egotistic, unchecked soaring is most vehemently expressed in her open rebellion against the chimney.

As Stuart C. Woodruff has shown, the chimney which dominates the house and "I"'s perspective seems in its broadest sense to represent the entire historical and creative process. To accept the "sober, substantial fact" of the chimney is to accept a temporal framework and thereby gain a sense of identity. The wife's perversion is her inability to accept anything but newness; in her defiance of the chimney she not only exhibits her own moral deformity, but she also threatens that which makes man most fully human —his ties with humanity and his rich hoard of experience, the past.[4]

The conflict over the chimney comes to a head in the dispute over the "secret closet." "I" tells his wife that "infinite sad mischief has resulted from the profane bursting open of secret recesses." To be sure, upon first hearing of the closet from Scribe, he himself had been tempted to break in, just as once earlier, a little out of his mind, he had begun to dig at the foundations of the chimney. But despite these temptations, he has learned that to purchase peace of mind one must govern the overweening curiosity of the ego. To protect his sanity, the eagle stays within the gorge; to maintain *his* equilibrium, "I" accepts the inscrutability of the universe, just as he has come to accept in "a comfortable sort of not unwelcome . . . way" the fact of mortality.

But whatever "I" may sacrifice in height (he neither soars nor plummets into the abyss), he more than gains in breadth. Just as the country provides ample space for the construction of roomy houses, so his way of life is the vehicle for personal growth. De-

[4] See "Melville and His Chimney," *PMLA*, LXXV, 285 (June, 1960).

spite the loneliness of his domestic situation, "I" lives as full a life
as most "real" adventurers. His chimney is his "open sesame" to
the realms of human experience and human fellowship. "I" has
often been cited as an important development in the theme of the
search for self-knowledge which runs through Melville's novels.
At the very least we can say that in this sketch Melville dramatizes
in a quiet domestic context one method of existing in a hostile environment without sacrificing one's personal development or happiness.

"Jimmy Rose" uses some of the same materials as "My Chimney," although its focus is quite different. The characters are nearly
identical: both stories have a conservative, sentimental old narrator
whose "progressive" wife and daughters are intent on remodeling
an old house. The more important thematic similarity has not been
noticed, however, because most analyses of "Jimmy Rose" pass
over the narrator to concentrate on Jimmy's story, which is generally treated as a charming and compassionate study of a failure who
triumphs over his adversity. James W. Gargano takes exception
to such a reading; he insists that "Jimmy Rose" is the story of a
man whose adjustment to failure is made without any moral growth,
told by a narrator who, although sentimental and compassionate,
manages to suggest the truth about Jimmy's pride which keeps him,
even on his deathbed, from self-knowledge.[5]

Mr. Gargano's analysis is, in the main, soundly convincing, although his treatment of the narrator as an experimental refinement
is not entirely satisfactory. If we say that the narrator is simply a
device for heightening the realism and the subtlety of the narration,
then we have to admit that the fairly lengthy account of the narrator's relationship to his house is digressive and delays Jimmy's
story unjustifiably, and that the rich symbolism of that prologue is
equally irrelevant. It seems scarcely possible that such an artistic
flaw should occur in a story otherwise so subtly constructed. The
shape of "Jimmy Rose" is more satisfactorily accounted for if the
narrator is viewed as part of the thematic pattern—as a moral yard-
stick for Rose and his society.

The narrator is an old man, heir to a "great old house" whose
roots are in the past. Like the chimney, the house has been sub-

[5] "Melville's 'Jimmy Rose,'" *Western Humanities Review*, XVI, 276-280 (Summer,
1962).

jected to various attempts at modernization: its romantic shutters and its "fine old pulpit-like porch" have been removed. Like the "wax nose" on the chimney, the "graft of modernness" on the house presents an incongruous aspect; but just as the essential dimensions of the chimney had been preserved, so too the house in its essence (its inside) has not been altered.

There is one room in particular which attracts the narrator— "the parlor of the peacocks."[6] Here a small leak in the eaves has, over a period of time, "sadly dimmed" the wallpaper on the north wall. And yet in the bedraggled peacocks on that wall, the narrator finds a curious pleasure:

Yet so patiently and so pleasantly, nay, here and there so ruddily did they seem to bide their bitter doom, so much of real elegance still lingered in their shapes, and so full, too, seemed they of a sweet engaging pensiveness, meditating all day long, for years and years, among their faded bowers, that though my family repeatedly adjured me (especially my wife, who, I fear, was too young for me) to destroy the whole hen-roost, . . . I could not be prevailed upon, however submissive in other things.

Both "I" and this narrator, then, stand firm against their families' attempts to alter the essence of things. Both, in identifying themselves within a temporal dimension, have arrived at a cheerful acceptance of mortality, presenting a sharp contrast to their wives who are unable to accept the "north" side—the fact of death and decay. ("I"'s wife, it will be remembered, persisted in planting flower beds on the north side where they could not live.) Both have the habit of meditation: just as "I" enjoys the meditative companionship of his chimney and pipe, this narrator chooses as his favorite companions the elegant, pensive peacocks. The humanity of both narrators, then, derives from a more or less philosophical acceptance of things and people as they are.

To be sure, the narrator in "Jimmy Rose" has decided limitations: his sentimentality and kindness cloud his perceptions about Jimmy. Occasionally he skirts the truth, as for example when he indirectly suggests that Jimmy's flaw was a "weak love of vain display," but he can go only so far and the final ironies must be perceived by the reader.

[6] Although, like "I," he too is fond of his huge, mysterious cellar, rich in ruin.

It is, however, the moral presence of the narrator in the tale that heightens those ironies; he provides a continual contrast. For example, Jimmy's story is framed by the quiet meditative atmosphere of the parlor of the peacocks, an atmosphere which opposes itself sharply to the environment of Jimmy; his society had no roots in the past, no habit of meditation, no capacity for feeling—in short, no inner life. Jimmy, who must be judged both as a child and victim of his society, cannot escape comparison with the narrator who refuses to judge him; we see Jimmy as a shrunken, pitiful, yet repulsive creature. Unlike the narrator, he is unable to adjust himself to change or to accept the ravages of time. (Whereas the narrator feels an affinity for the bedraggled peacocks, Jimmy preserves artificially the roses in his cheeks.) It is thus the narrator who unconsciously gives the portrait of Jimmy's moral degeneracy its final poignancy, for despite his limitations he represents an approach to old age which is truly dignified: he is the real coin and Rose's society the counterfeit medal.

The domineering, "modernistic" wife and the hubsand submissive in all but one particular reappear in "The Apple-Tree Table." This sketch is a farcical treatment of the domestic conflict which figures in "My Chimney" and, to a lesser extent, in "Jimmy Rose." But more interesting, "The Apple-Tree Table" traces an individual's progress toward a mature perspective, records, so to speak, the birth of a domestic adventurer.

The symbolic center of the story is the ambiguous attic which contains elements of the grotesque and the beautiful: it is insect-infested but also festooned with cobwebs which shine "like Bagdad tissues and gauzes"; it is a graveyard of human accumulations and yet it contains the "pulpit-like platform" which leads to the scuttle opening into "living greenness" (perceived by the narrator in terms of resurrection). Like cellars in the other tales, the attic reaches far back into a mysterious past; in this case, the mystery is given more definite outlines: the narrator discovers in the attic a document resembling "the original bond that Doctor Faust gave to Mephistopheles," a broken telescope, and a staved-in celestial globe—all suggestive of the vanity of the search for knowledge. In one of its aspects, then, the attic represents the realm of forbidden knowledge, the secret closet whose recesses it is profane to search. But, on the other hand, the attic leads to "living greenness" and out of it comes the beautiful bug.

The attic, like the whale and like the cock, is a fusion of the demonic and the divine. Its repulsive, deathly aspect warns of the danger of spending too much time there, but its exotic mystery and its associations with resurrection suggest that not to know the attic is to be somehow impoverished. It is significantly the narrator, the only person in the story capable of moral and intellectual growth, who visits the attic. The wife is scornful of all that is old and "unfashionable" and the daughters fearful of experience which would contradict their roseate vision of life.

Whereas the narrators in "My Chimney" and "The Lightning-Rod Man" were a serious blend of pragmatism and imagination, this narrator, at first, is an obviously comic blend, a perpetual contest between "panic and philosophy": "In a strange and not unpleasing way, I gently oscillated between Democritus and Cotton Mather."

The absurdity of being "all Democritus" is illustrated by the wife. Upon first hearing the ticking in the table, she wants to cure it speedily with an application of roach powder or a sound whipping. In rejecting her "cures" the husband gently reminds her that there is a mystery about the table which they ought to respect: "It's a queer table, wife; there's no blinking it." (We are reminded of "I"'s admonition to his wife about the "fact" of the chimney.) Wildly impatient, the wife later proposes cutting into the wood with a knife. But again her husband prevails upon her to wait, for he is now imaginatively involved with the portending event and is anxious to see what all the "warm nursing" is about to hatch.

The cryptic ending of the sketch suggests that the narrator, unlike his wife and daughters, has recognized in the event an ambiguity which he has not yet fully digested. He accepts neither the factual explanation of the scientist nor the simple-minded, rapturous belief of Julia (for the bug did die the next day).[7] There is little doubt that the narrator has gained from the experience. His refusal to accept a simple or easy explanation is a significant step beyond his earlier comic oscillations; it is the refusal to deny

[7] See Richard Harter Fogle, *Melville's Shorter Tales* (Norman, Okla., 1960), p. 84, who similarly contends that the last word lies with "the introspective and finally uncommitted narrator [who] ... does not choose to speak it."

complexity characteristic of a balanced view. This dawn of a new perspective is also evident in the playful irony with which the narrator takes his leave of the reader: unbelievers, he suggests, should come to view the exact spots where the bugs emerged, which his daughters have marked in somewhat the same way as the spots "where the cannon balls struck Brattle Street Church." As if the casual observer could "know" the bug without the imaginative experience of it!

The last of this group of stories, "The Piazza," in several ways epitomizes the theme of the domestic imaginative adventure. This sketch has the familiar setting and symbolic motifs: a wide, old-fashioned country house, its stone quarried from "the heart of the Hearth Stone Hills," set amidst the splendor of Greylock and his surrounding hills. Again, the narrator is contemplative and conservative in his reverence for a tranquillity and constancy which he associates with the past. As soon as he has occupied his new home, he decides that a piazza must be built. The significance of the covered porch is made explicit in his contrast of spiritual adventurers of the past and those of his own day:

For though, of old, when reverence was in vogue, and indolence was not, the devotees of Nature, doubtless, used to stand and adore—just as, in the cathedrals of those ages, the worshipers of a higher Power did—yet, in these times of failing faith and feeble knees, we have the piazza and the pew.

Later, he compares his experiences on the deck of the piazza to those of a sea adventurer on his ship's deck. Taken together, these two comparisons are an explicit formulation of the motif underlying the stories I have discussed: the transmutation of the grand quest into a tamer mode of adventure.

Like the other narrators, this one is determined to be an adventurer, however feeble his knees. Just as "I" recognizes his chimney as the central fact of his existence, so this narrator in building his piazza to the north yields to the overwhelming presence of Greylock. (He is derided for his "winter piazza" much as the narrator in "Jimmy Rose" is abused for defending his north wall.) But although the narrator is an intelligent and imaginative man, he has yet to realize the full significance of his choice of exposures. The burden of the sketch, as one critic has remarked, is his "progress from immaturity to maturity."[8]

Recovering from an illness, the narrator experiences a revulsion against his Chinese creeper after discovering worms among its leaves: "millions of strange, cankerous worms, which, feeding upon those blossoms, so shared their blessed hue, as to make it unblessed evermore—worms, whose germs had doubtless lurked in the very bulb which, so hopefully, I had planted." His mood is close to that of Ishmael at the conclusion of "The Whiteness of the Whale." For him, as for Ishmael, it is the suggestion of evil at the very core of existence which appalls. The thought is so overwhelming as to upset temporarily the emotional equilibrium of both men, but while Ishmael's reaction is to identify himself with Ahab's resolve to destroy the emblem of the evil, this narrator's reaction is less heroic: he seeks an escape in fantasy from the ambiguity suggested by the cankered flower and accordingly sets out to discover the fairy ring which sparkles on the mountain.

With the discovery comes the inevitable disillusion: the fairy window is fly-specked; the sun that gilds the cottage also burns and blinds its human tenant; the fairy lore proves to be that of suffering and isolation. Resolved to be done with "real" adventure, the narrator returns to his piazza where the scenery is "magical— the illusion so complete" and he can forget the weary face behind the golden window. The knowledge of woe, however, has left its indelible mark: "But, every night, when the curtain falls, truth comes in with darkness. . . . To and fro I walk the piazza deck, haunted by Marianna's face, and many as real a story."

As critics have pointed out, the experience does broaden the narrator's perspective. He learns to accept the dark truth of the north exposure, but he is still able to enjoy the illusion of beauty. Yet, there is something distinctly unsatisfactory about the resolution. Doubtless the narrator suffers sincerely, but there is an artificiality about enjoying illusion by day and wrestling with truth by night and within the protective enclosure of a piazza. Certainly he is wise to insulate himself from the "woe that is madness," but he falls short of the truly comprehensive perspective which can look

[8] Darwin T. Turner, "A View of Melville's 'Piazza,'" *College Language Association Journal*, VII, 57 (Sept., 1963). Both Mr. Turner and Mr. Fogle interpret the narrator's inability to delight in his Chinese creeper as symptomatic of a limited perspective.

steadily on a universe in which good and evil live side by side day
and night. The narrator lives in a divided realm and suffers from
his inability to reconcile the halves.

II

Although none of the narrators, with the possible exception of
"I," measures up to Ishmael, nearly all of them possess to some
degree a doubleness of vision which was foreshadowed in Ishmael's
development. The stories suggest Melville's continuing concern
with the relation of the individual to an ambiguous universe, but
they show him consciously adapting that theme to what Richard
Chase has called "lower, but more stable levels of being."[9]

These domestic adventurers, despite their naïveté and other
limitations, have something essential to tell us about Melville's
thinking during that period of personal crisis in the fifties in which
the tales were written. The protagonists in some way all illustrate
the importance of accepting certain limitations to the search for
self-knowledge and for knowledge of the universe. (Conversely,
the "villains" in these tales illustrate the danger of creating personal
versions of reality which, of necessity, will involve distortion and
will end up by warping their creators.) The protagonists who adjust most successfully are those who acknowledge the "forbidden
enclosures," who, unlike the gander in "My Chimney," wear their
"collar of the Order of the Garotte" *willingly*. Self-strangulation,
Melville seems to be saying, is the price of insatiate curiosity. The
true intellectual and emotional development is not a soaring upward or plunging downward, but a gradual broadening process—a
creative act whereby the individual honestly and yet modestly confronts the complexity of experience and assimilates it.

[9] *Herman Melville: A Critical Study* (New York, 1949), p. 143.

Redburn and the Failure of Mythic Criticism

James Schroeter

T HE USUAL CRITICAL OPINION OF *Redburn* is that it is a gloomy book. Some recent critics, including William Gilman and Edward Rosenberry, have pointed out comic elements in it, and when the book first appeared it was praised mainly for its "freshness" and "humor." But ever since the Melville revival of the twenties, the critics, perhaps because they were trying to stress that the book ought to be taken seriously, have been calling it a "dark" book, a "bitter" book, a self-pitying book, a tragedy of some kind, or a reflection of Melville's own misery.[1] Commenting on the period when Melville was composing it, Lewis Mumford observes:

Now, for the first time, Melville is conscious of the black maggot within him, deposited as a mere egg in his youth, and growing day by day, nourished by his later disappointments, sorrows, frustrations. Things have begun to go badly: he thinks back without difficulty to times when they were even worse. The physical misery of those early years, the patched clothes, the bad food, the rough treatment of the sailors, the feeling of homelessness, the consciousness of being an Ishmael—all these experiences tallied point by point with the world outside, its cruelty, its misery, its sordidness and vice.[2]

Similarly, F. O. Matthiessen says that both *Redburn* and *White-jacket* "reveal that the actual sufferings of mankind had been so impressed upon [Melville's] consciousness that none of the optimistic palliatives or compensations of his age could ever explain them away. As was the case with Keats, the miseries of this world became misery for him, and would not let him rest."[3] Newton Arvin writes: "Blows and hard words are mostly Redburn's lot on the

[1] Edward H. Rosenberry, *Melville and the Comic Spirit* (Cambridge, Mass., 1955). William Gilman, *Melville's Early Life and Redburn* (New York, 1951), pp. 227-230. A summary of the early reviewers and their comments on the humor is contained in Gilman, Appendix D, "The Reputation of *Redburn*," pp. 274-281.

[2] Lewis Mumford, *Herman Melville: A Study of His Life and Vision*, rev. ed. (New York, 1962), p. 72. (The book originally appeared in 1929.)

[3] F. O. Matthiessen, *American Renaissance: Art and Expression in the Age of Emerson and Whitman* (New York, 1941), p. 396.

Highlander, yet he suffers not only from the inhumanity of men but from the spectacle of their depravity generally."[4]

<h1 style="text-align:center">I</h1>

Despite the general stress on the gloomy tone of the book, there have been two critical methods of interpreting it, two radically different frameworks into which critics have tried to fit it. The first, which might be called the biographical framework, is most clearly represented in the books on Melville written in the twenties by Raymond Weaver, John Freeman, and Lewis Mumford. "In *Redburn,* Melville went back to his youth and traced his feelings about life and his experience up to his eighteenth year," says Mumford. "The book is autobiography, with only the faintest disguises: Bleecker Street becomes Greenwich Street, and the other changes are of a similar order."[5]

The last major reading of *Redburn* as autobiography was William Gilman's *Melville's Early Life and* Redburn (1951), which delivered, or was intended to deliver, the death blow to the biographical school by demonstrating painstakingly that the book is not "autobiography, with only the faintest disguises." But in any event the biographical mode of reading *Redburn* was already dying at the time Gilman's book appeared, a victim of widespread changes in the fashions of literary criticism and of a shift away from the biographical method of reading Melville. By about 1950, a second method, which might be called the "mythic" method, had already taken root, the most influential instance of it being an interpretation in Newton Arvin's *Herman Melville.*

Arvin's main point is his statement of what he takes to be *Redburn's* "inward subject":

The outward subject of the book is a young boy's first voyage as a sailor before the mast; its inward subject is the initiation of innocence into evil—the opening of the guileless spirit to the discovery of "the wrong," as James would say, "to the knowledge of it, to the crude experience of it." The subject is a permanent one for literature, of course, but it has also a peculiarly American dimension, and in just this sense, not in any other, *Redburn* looks backward to a book like Brockden Brown's *Ormond* as well as forward to *The Marble Faun* and to so much of James himself.

[4] Newton Arvin, *Herman Melville* (New York, 1950), p. 104.
[5] Mumford, p. 71.

Wellingborough Redburn sets out from his mother's house in a state of innocence like that before the Fall, a state like that of Brown's Constantia Dudley or James's Maisie Farange, but he has hardly gone a mile from home before the world's wickedness and hardness begin to strip themselves before him. Man, Redburn quickly finds, is a wolf to man.[6]

The point that *Redburn* is concerned in some way with "the initiation of innocence into evil" is too fundamental to have escaped detection. For instance Matthiessen had noted in 1941 that "the account of Redburn's first voyage is a study of disillusion, of innocence confronted with the world, of ideals shattered by facts."[7] But Arvin was the first critic who attempted in a unified way to substitute the "initiation" theme for the autobiographical one as a broad pattern into which details of character, incident, and symbol could be fitted.

Arvin does this by selecting a number of more or less vivid details for symbolic interpretation—the character Jackson, "the first of Melville's full-length studies of 'depravity according to nature,'" and a figure on whom, according to Arvin, all the "accumulated evil . . . is focused so concentratedly" as to "raise him to something like heroic stature"; Melville's "wonderful series of Hogarthian evocations" of Liverpool, which Arvin takes to be Melville's "symbol of human iniquity"; the London chapter concerned with "Aladdin's Palace," which Arvin identifies as "the opulent counterpart of the 'reeking' and 'Sodom-like' dens in Liverpool, where Redburn's shipmates indulge their squalid vices"; the imagery of "disease, disaster and death," especially the dead sailor who is thrown overboard and the suicide of the drunken sailor, which Arvin takes to be part of the "metaphor of death and rebirth, of the passage from childhood and innocence"; a series of humble "antiromantic" or "shrunken" symbols—the glass ship, the guidebook to Liverpool, Redburn's moleskin shooting jacket; and the shipboard epidemic among the immigrants, which Arvin calls "the symbolism of plague and pestilence that had been or was to prove so expressive for a long series of writers from Defoe and Poe to Thomas Mann."[8] The point, in other words, that Arvin seems to be striving

[6] Arvin, p. 103.
[7] Matthiessen, p. 396.
[8] Arvin, pp. 104-109.

to make is that practically the whole of Redburn's experience with the outside world is with various guises of horror, death, and depravity.

Although clearly Arvin selected the features and stressed the symbolic horror in the way he did, even at the risk of appearing to strain and exaggerate slightly, because he wanted to lend substance to his "initiation" theory, his points seem to have been a guide to subsequent critics. For instance, Ronald Mason, whose study of Melville appeared the year after Arvin's, takes up the guidebook, the glass ship, the violent deaths, the Liverpool slums, and Jackson, whom he describes as "personified iniquity."[9] R. W. B. Lewis takes up the epidemic, the guidebook, Jackson—who "reveals to Redburn the power of the scabrous," and Liverpool and its "stench of corruption."[10] Harry Levin, in *The Power of Blackness,* confines himself mainly to Jackson and Liverpool.[11] But the important point is that Arvin's central idea, that the real subject of *Redburn* is the "initiation of innocence into evil," has formed a main tenet—perhaps *the* main tenet—of *Redburn* criticism since about 1950. Two independent studies, James E. Miller's *"Redburn and Whitejacket:* Initiation and Baptism" (1959) and Heinz Kosok's "A Sadder and a Wiser Boy: Herman Melville's *Redburn* as a Novel of Initiation" (1965), adopt the initiation idea as a framework; and much of the incidental comment on *Redburn* either explicitly or implicitly accepts the initiation idea in much the way earlier critics once accepted the idea that *Redburn* was autobiography.[12] "In *Redburn* (1849), the Adamic coloration of the experience which most interested Melville became explicit," according to R. W. B. Lewis. "This has been remarked by Melville's best commentator, Newton Arvin, who observes that the boy-hero of the novel 'sets out from his mother's house in a state of innocence like that before the fall'; and the voyage to Liver-

[9] Ronald Mason, *The Spirit Above the Dust: A Study of Herman Melville* (London, 1951), pp. 71-78.
[10] R. W. B. Lewis, *The American Adam* (Chicago, 1953), pp. 136-138.
[11] Harry Levin, *The Power of Blackness* (New York, 1958), pp. 178-180.
[12] James E. Miller, *"Redburn and Whitejacket:* Initiation and Baptism," *Nineteenth Century Fiction,* XIII, 273-293 (March, 1959). Heinz Kosok, " 'A Sadder and a Wiser Boy': Herman Melville's *Redburn* as Novel of Initiation," *Jahrbuch für Amerikastudien,* X, 126-152 (1965). Other critics who refer to *Redburn* as a novel of "initiation" include Robert Spiller, Merlin Bowen, Ronald Mason, and R. W. B. Lewis.

pool and back comprises for young Redburn 'the initiation of innocence into evil.' "[13]

The "mythic" interpretation of *Redburn* first appeared about the
time that a wave of books which either argued for, or explicitly
applied, a mythic method to the interpretation of American literature was gathering strength—for instance, Richard Chase's *Herman
Melville* (1949), Chase's *Quest for Myth* (1949), and Henry Nash
Smith's *Virgin Land: The American West as Symbol and Myth*
(1950). These were followed by R. W. B. Lewis's *The American
Adam* (1955), and after that a deluge of studies which reinterpreted
Irving, Cooper, Hawthorne, Twain, James, Faulkner, and Heming-
way in the light of mythic quests and patterns. In other words the
reinterpretation of *Redburn* which has been going on for the past
fifteen years must be seen in the context of a broad critical movement and as a contribution to the movement, much in the way that
the biographical books on Melville by Weaver, Freeman, and
Mumford were a contribution to the biographical method of the
twenties—the style represented by Van Wyck Brooks's *The Ordeal
of Mark Twain* or Joseph Wood Krutch's book on Poe. But the
difficulty with the mythic method, certainly as applied to *Redburn,*
is that, like the biographical method, it does not hold up—that
it is contradicted repeatedly by some of the most important tonal
and structural features of the novel.

II

Melville's tone, the peculiar quality of Redburn's narrative voice,
presents the most obvious barrier to the "tragic fall" theory, especially Redburn's voice in the passages which are most clearly
"initiatory," and in which Redburn is most obviously "innocent."
This, for instance, is Redburn's response when he is first initiated
into shipboard blasphemy:

At that time I did not know what to make of these sailors; but this much
I thought, that when they were boys they could never have gone to the
Sunday School; for they swore so, it made my ears tingle, and used words
that I never could hear without a dreadful loathing.[14]

Later, the Greenlander sailor urges Redburn to drink Jamaica
spirits, and Redburn reflects:

[13] Lewis, p. 136.
[14] Herman Melville, *Redburn: His First Voyage* (New York, 1957), pp. 31-32.

But I felt very little like doing as I was bid, for I had some scruples about drinking spirits; and to tell the plain truth, for I am not ashamed of it, I was a member of a society in the village where my mother lived, called the Juvenile Total Abstinence Association, of which my friend, Tom Legare, was president, secretary and treasurer, and kept the funds in a little purse that his cousin knit for him. There was three and six-pence on hand, I believe, the last time he brought in his accounts.[15]

A few pages later, there is a smoking party, and a sailor named Ned offers Redburn a cigar. Redburn reflects:

But I was a member of an Anti-Smoking Society that has been organized in our village by the Principal of the Sunday School there, in conjunction with the Temperance Association. So I did not smoke any then, though I did afterward upon the voyage, I am sorry to say.[16]

Redburn's response to the trio of conventional sailor's vices— smoking, drinking, swearing—depends for the effectiveness of its comedy not only on Redburn's absurdly naïve Sunday school morality but upon the ironic tone, which in turn depends on the separation Melville maintains between himself and his narrator. Clemens was later to handle this device for humor in a more controlled manner in *Huckleberry Finn,* in which the vices of men are also reflected with comic irony through the eyes of a naïve boy, but *Redburn* shows the first sustained use of the device in the American novel.

It can be seen in a more important way in Redburn's initiation into the ship's hierarchy, brought out in his abortive attempts to establish friendly relations first with the men, then with the mates, and finally with the captain:

Thinking to make friends with the second mate, I took out an old tortoise-shell snuff-box of my father's, in which I had put a piece of Cavendish tobacco, to look sailor-like, and offered the box to him very politely. He stared at me a moment, and then exclaimed, "Do you think we take snuff aboard here, youngster? no, no, no time for snuff-taking at sea; don't let the 'old man' see that snuff-box; take my advice and pitch it overboard as quick as you can."

I told him it was not snuff, but tobacco; when he said, he had plenty of tobacco of his own, and never carried any such nonsense about him as

[15] *Ibid.,* p. 40.
[16] *Ibid.,* p. 44.

a tobacco-box. With that, he went off about his business, and left me feeling foolish enough.[17]

One entire chapter, "He Contemplates Making a Social Call on the Captain in His Cabin," is devoted to Redburn's attempt to establish friendship with the captain. It begins with his naïve speculations about the captain:

I had thought him a fine, funny gentleman, full of mirth and good humor, and good will to seamen, and one who could not fail to appreciate the difference between me and the rude sailors among whom I was thrown. Indeed, I had made no doubt that he would in some special manner take me under his protection, and prove a kind friend and benefactor to me; as I had heard that some sea-captains are. . . . Yes, I thought that Captain Riga would be attentive and considerate to me, and strive to cheer me up and comfort me in my lonesomeness.[18]

To prepare himself for making "the first advances," he gets himself up in what he thinks is fitting dress. "I put on a white shirt in place of my red one, and got into a pair of cloth trowsers instead of my duck ones, and put on my new pumps, and then carefully brushing my shooting jacket, I put that on over all, so that upon the whole, I made quite a genteel figure." His hands are stained deep yellow from tar, and thinking "it would never do to present myself before a gentleman in that way," he slips on a pair of woolen mittens his mother has knitted for him. Dressed in that fashion, he plans to "drop into the captain's cabin" to pay his respects.[19]

What is most interesting about the chapter devoted to the social call is that it never takes place. The chief mate collars Redburn on his way to the cabin, and "shoved me forward, roaring out I know not what," while the sailors, standing around the windlass, look aft "mightily tickled." Instead, Melville focuses on Redburn's dreams of the treatment he will receive from the captain—"that he would invite me down into the cabin of a pleasant night, to ask me questions concerning my parents, and prospects in life, besides obtaining from me some anecdotes touching my great-uncle, the illustrious senator; or give me a slate and pencil, and teach me problems in navigation; or perhaps engage me at a game of chess"; on

[17] *Ibid.*, p. 25.
[18] *Ibid.*, p. 65.
[19] *Ibid.*, pp. 65-67.

Redburn's elaborate attempts to get himself up in genteel costume; and the merriment of the crew. Possibly Melville aborted the actual scene because his imagination boggled at the prospect of a boy such as Redburn, dressed in shooting jacket, pumps, and woolen mittens, "dropping in" on the captain. But what is more likely is that Melville softened the climax, deliberately substituting an anticlimax, because, despite all that critics have had to say about the "cruelty" and "hardship" of Redburn's lot on the *Highlander,* Melville sees clearly enough that showing Redburn as the butt of the most crushing and serious humiliations and insults does not fit the larger purposes of the novel.

The imaginative situation of a human, personal confrontation between captain and "boy," between captain and crewman, or in general between superior and inferior was to be touched on with complexity and power in the later Melville—in *Moby-Dick,* "Bartleby," "Benito Cereno," and *Billy Budd.* Such a scene, passed over reverently, forms the crux of *Billy Budd*—the scene between Captain Vere and Billy, which Melville likens to the scene between Abraham and Isaac. In such passages in the later Melville—between Pip and Ahab, between the lawyer and Bartleby, or in quite a different way between the aristocratic Benito Cereno and the slave Babo—Melville suggests that the conventional barrier society interposes between men of differing social stations is in some way terrible, ludicrous, irrational—but capable of being overstepped. The conventional hierarchical arrangement breaks down, much as in Tolstoy's "Master and Man," into an elemental love-hate relationship between two human beings. The "mastery" is subtly reversed, translated by hate in the Benito-Babo relationship, or love in the Pip-Ahab relationship. No transformation of this kind takes place in *Redburn,* partly because Melville is as much concerned with holding up to view the absurdity of Redburn's ignorance of conventional usage as the absurdity of the convention.

The passages in which Melville's ironically comic tone is perhaps most beautifully modulated are the ones concerning Redburn's clothing. A number of critics—Newton Arvin, James Miller—have commented on the fact that Melville raises the clothing, especially the shooting jacket, to poetic or symbolic status. But Arvin's comment that "old, cheap and ill-fitting clothes" are a "natural metaphor" for the "insulted and injured," or that "Redburn's shooting jacket puts one in mind of that other shabby garment, the old clerk's overcoat in Gogol's famous tale," seems—much like Lewis Mumford's sentimental comment about Melville-Redburn's "patched clothes" and "bad food"—wholly to miss the dignity and complexity of Melville's comedy.[20]

Melville focuses mainly on three "patched" or "maimed" items of clothing—Redburn's boots, his pantaloons, and his shooting jacket. The boots are described as follows:

Nor must I forget my boots, which were almost new when I left home. They had been my Sunday boots, and fitted me to a charm. I never had had a pair of boots that I liked better; I used to turn my toes out when I walked in them, unless it was night time, when no one could see me, and I had something else to think of; and I used to keep looking at them during church; so that I lost a good deal of the sermon. In a word, they were a beautiful pair of boots. But all this only unfitted them the more for sea-service; as I soon discovered. They had very high heels, which were all the time tripping me in the rigging, and several times came near pitching me overboard; and the salt water made them shrink in such a manner, that they pinched me terribly about the instep; and I was obliged to gash them cruelly, which went to my very heart. The legs were quite long, coming a good way up towards the knees, and the edges were mounted with red morocco. The sailors used to call them my "gaff-topsail-boots." And sometimes they used to call me "Boots" and sometimes "Buttons" on account of the ornaments. . . .

At last I took their advice and "razeed" them, as they phrased it. That is, I amputated the legs, and shaved off the heels to the bare soles, which, however did not much improve them, for it made my feet feel flat as flounders, and besides, brought me down in the world. . . .[21]

Redburn's magnificent moleskin hunting jacket is also "altered" or "maimed" in a similar way:

Every day it grew smaller and smaller, particularly after a rain, until at last I thought it would completely exhale, and leave nothing but the bare seams, by way of a skeleton, on my back. It became unspeakably unpleasant when we got into rather cold weather, crossing the Banks of Newfoundland, when the only way I had to keep warm during the night was to pull on my waistcoat and my roundabout, and then clap the

[20] Arvin, p. 109.
[21] *Redburn*, pp. 71-72.

shooting-jacket over all. This made it pinch me under the arms, and it vexed and irritated and tormented me every way; and used to incommode my arms seriously when I was pulling the ropes; so much so, that the mate asked me once if I had the cramp.[22]

Redburn focuses mainly, however, on the most maimed item, the pantaloons:

I had them made to order by our village tailor, a little fat man, very thin in the legs, who used to say he imported the latest fashions direct from Paris, though all the fashion plates in his shop were very dirty with fly-marks.

Well, this tailor made the pantaloons I speak of, and while he had them in hand, I used to call and see him two or three times a day to try them on, and hurry him forward; for he was an old man with large round spectacles, and could not see very well, and had no one to help him but a sick wife, with five grandchildren to take care of. . . . Now, this old tailor had shown me the pattern, after which he intended to make my pantaloons; but I improved upon it, and bade him make a slit on the outside of each leg, at the foot, to button up with a row of six brass bell buttons; for a grown-up cousin of mine, who was a great sportsman used to wear a beautiful pair of pantaloons, made precisely in that way.

And these were the very pair I now had at sea; the sailors made a great deal of fun of them, and were all the time calling on each other to "twig" them; and they would ask me to lend them a button or two, by way of a joke; and then they would ask me if I was not a soldier. Showing very plainly that they had no idea that my pantaloons were a very genteel pair, made in the height of the sporting fashion, and copied from my cousin's, who was a young man of fortune and drove a tilbury.[23]

This is Redburn's account of how these beautiful and elegant pantaloons come to be patched and maimed:

When I went aloft, at my yard-arm gymnastics, my pantaloons were all the time ripping and splitting in every direction, particularly about the seams, owing to their not being cut sailor-fashion, with low waistbands, and to wear without suspenders. So that I was often placed in most unpleasant predicaments, straddling the rigging, sometimes in plain sight of the cabin, with my table linen exposed in the most inelegant and ungentlemanly manner possible.[24]

[22] Ibid., p. 72.
[23] Ibid., pp. 70-71.
[24] Ibid., p. 70.

The point of producing these passages is not merely to show that gloomy *Redburn* has its comedy—although this point alone seems in need of being stressed as much as possible. The point is rather to show *why* there is comedy—that it is not simply an element Melville added here and there for relieving the gloom, or, as William Gilman concludes, for "offsetting the prevailing tone of somberness." Instead, the comic tone seems to stem from the structure of the book, and to be a necessary part of the conception. The passages in which Redburn is introduced to smoking, drinking, and swearing seem to be based on Melville's analysis of the conventional sailor's vices. The passages in which Redburn tries to make friends first with the men, then with the mates, and finally the captain stem from Melville's analysis of the ship's social hierarchy. Similarly, the other "initiatory" passages—in which Redburn is introduced to shipboard language, shipboard eating habits, clothing, use of leisure, manners, superstitions—are arranged in a series, as though Melville had worked from an outline in which he divided shipboard language from shipboard customs, and then subdivided these into finer, discrete parts. This technique, which is a general characteristic of Melville's writing, was noted in the thirties by R. P. Blackmur, who observed that Melville tended to work from an intellectual scheme rather than from a dramatic or story conception, and who aptly dubbed this the "technique of putative statement." Melville's presentation of shipboard and English life in *Redburn* is organized, in other words, much as the materials are organized in *Typee* or *Omoo,* in which the novelist devotes so many passages to Polynesian religion, language, social habits, use of leisure; or, in *Moby-Dick,* in the "cetological" portions, or the chapters dealing with the social hierarchy of a whaler.

The vividness of these "putative" sections of *Redburn* are based on the sharpness of the incongruity between Melville's scenes and Melville's narrator—between Redburn's genteel dress, language, customs, and expectations, and those of the people he comes in contact with. But the irony, complexity, and comedy depend on the fact that Melville himself takes a quite independent and detached stance in portraying the conflict, especially when he is working most successfully, removed on the one hand from the narrow gentility of his narrator and on the other from the crudities of shipboard life.

The "Adamic" pattern into which modern critics have rather clumsily been trying to fit *Redburn* requires a prelapsarian hero like Billy Budd or Hawthorne's Donatello—a "natural" man who is uncontaminated by society and its institutions. But the humor in *Redburn* depends on the fact that the hero is not a "guileless spirit," certainly not a Billy Budd or Donatello. His mother's village, with its Sunday School, Anti-Smoking Society, Juvenile Total Temperance Association, and cousin who drives a tilbury, is not an Eden nor a Monte Beni. Nor does Redburn "set out from his mother's house in a state of innocence like that before the Fall," as Arvin and Lewis claim. On the contrary, he sets out from his mother's house as a "Son-of-a-Gentleman," with the catalogue of social attitudes, prejudices, and minor vices that this estate implies—snobbery, exaggerated piety, smugness, priggishness, narrowness. Most important, the mythic Adamic pattern is a tragic pattern; it is a "Fall." But Melville does everything in his power to make clear that Redburn's transition from "Son-of-a-Gentleman" to "Sailor Boy" is not a "fall"—that the gentleman's estate is less rather than more blessed than the deracinated estate of the classless voyager at which Redburn, after completing his initiation, finally arrives.

The fall of Adam might be called an archetypal myth, "archetypal" in the grand sense used by Northrop Frye and other mid-twentieth-century critics who suppose that such archetypes have always secretly but powerfully influenced the imagination; yet it is doubtful whether Melville was writing myth in even the local sense of "myth" which obviously influenced the nineteenth-century storyteller. Many novels of "initiation" had appeared in the years before Melville wrote *Redburn*—stories about genteel or aristocratic young heroes who undergo a change from one class into a lower one. For the most part, these fall into one of two opposite categories. The least common and more modern variety is the democratic romance—the story of the ennobling consequences of hard work or the common lot on the privileged or coddled, the story of the snob who is made into a man. Richard Dana had touched on this theme in *Two Years Before the Mast,* as did Hawthorne in quite a different way in "My Kinsman, Major Molineux"; but it was not until considerably later—in Dickens's *Great Expectations* or, more obviously, in Kipling's *Captains Courageous*—that the theme found full romantic expression. The earlier and more common variety is the bourgeois tragedy—the story of fineness, beauty, and distinction trampled underfoot by the commonplace, or the theme of gentility in adversity that Dickens uses in *Oliver Twist* or *David Copperfield*. Melville had both kinds of myths available to him when he wrote *Redburn,* especially the second; but the point is that he rejects them, carefully steering a middle course between—and this is perhaps the strongest evidence that Melville, rather than relying on myth of any kind, was consciously trying to stay independent of it.

The second alternative, the myth of the fallen aristocrat, was probably the more dangerous temptation for Melville. Those qualities of "bitterness," "misery," and "self-pity" which so many critics have noted in *Redburn,* and which some feel mar the book, may be due to the fact that Melville fails wholly to avoid the temptation. Yet the function of Melville's ironic comedy, which most of the critics who think *Redburn* is full of self-pity ignore, is to reject the myth—to reject genteel pretension of merely any sort.

Another American novel about gentility fallen on hard times written at the same time as *Redburn,* Hawthorne's *The House of the Seven Gables,* has been to some extent recognized as a democratic rejection of aristocratic values. Critics have observed, for instance, that Hawthorne portrays the aristocratic and genteel Pyncheon inheritance from the past as not only useless or chimerical but actually sickly, cumbersome, disadvantageous, harmful: the Pyncheon family claim to vast tracts of land is a harmful chimera; the aristocratic Pyncheon roses sicken while the plebeian Maule beans flourish; Hepzibah's aristocratic name and blood is not only useless but disadvantageous in running a penny shop. But Melville's rejection in *Redburn,* although equally important to the scheme and worked out in more circumstantial detail, seems to have been ignored: that the manners Redburn acquired, which dictate his offering the mate tobacco out of a "tortoise-shell" box, result in the ridicule of the mate; that his attempts to dress in mittens and pay the captain a social call result in the ridicule of the crew; that the more genteel and fashionable his clothes, the more useless they are at sea—that the beautiful moleskin jacket must "shrink," that the elegant pantaloons must rip and be patched before they are useful, that the

fashionable boots must have their high heels removed so that Redburn can "come down in the world"; that Redburn's notions of
"proper" table manners and his ignorance of the way food is served
and eaten by a ship's crew result in the crew's regarding him as
unmannerly and in his going hungry; that the genteel recommendation Mr. Jones gives the captain, the sort of recommendation that
would be given of a young gentleman about to start a career in
banking, result in his advance wages being withheld; that his
father's guidebook, a relic of genteel prosperity, misleads him;
and the elegant glass ship imported from France gives him a dam-
agingly false view of the world of ships.

There has already been too great, or at least too sentimental,
a stress on the terrible hardships Redburn undergoes—the vicious-
ness of Jackson, the cruelty of the captain and crew, the bad clothes
and bad food, the hideous impact of the Liverpool slums. But these
elements are also important. There is a tough-minded realism in
Melville's rejection of gentility and the past, coupled with a democratic dislike of class distinction; but at the same time Melville goes
at least as far in the opposite direction by refusing to romanticize
the common lot or the salubrity of menial labor.

Hawthorne ends his romance by uniting Maule and Pyncheon in
a marriage which implies an acceptance of both the plebeian and
aristocratic myths. But Melville ends his with the phrase, "yet, I,
Wellingborough Redburn, chance to survive"—the expression of a
proud and lonely Ishmael, who has rejected both plebeian and genteel society as opposite but connected parts of a total social order.

III

The strongest evidence of Melville's rejection is provided by the
main structural feature of *Redburn*. Characteristically, Melville
builds the deeper meanings of his stories and novels on the basis
of parallels and contrasts that he draws between characters who
represent certain complex abstractions—for instance, Billy Budd
as a representative of Good, Claggart of Evil; Ahab as a representative of Defiance, Ishmael of Acceptance. Melville uses the same kind
of structure in *Redburn* in the parallels and contrasts he draws between Harry Bolton, the gentlemanly Englishman who sails back
on the *Highlander*, and Jackson, the ruffianly American sailor.

A great deal of attention has been paid to Melville's picture of

Jackson; but except for Merlin Bowen, in his study "Redburn and the Angle of Vision," relatively little comment has been devoted to Harry Bolton, who is as important as Jackson, and who, if Bowen is correct in his guess that Melville would have enlarged the figure had he been less hasty in drawing his book to a conclusion, played a larger role in Melville's conception.

Bowen notes a parallel between Harry Bolton and Redburn, which he claims is "carried out in such detail as to cause one to wonder that it has not been more commonly noted":

Both, to begin with, are more than ordinarily well born and come from a relatively sheltered background. Both are "Ishmaels," driven by hard times and misfortune too soon into the world. They are alike, too, in their romantic and distorted views of the world: the Canaan to which each aspires is the Egypt, from which the other would escape. The illusions of each are at first encouraged by the captain's "sympathetic concern" and later shattered by the cruelty of both officers and crew. Both are inexperienced as sailors, and both exacerbate the contempt this brings upon them by their incongruous dress and by their pretensions to refinement and high social status.

Several incidents of the homeward voyage, moreover, appear as counterparts (occurring in the same order and at roughly similar intervals) of experiences encountered by Redburn on the passage out. The discovery of the burning corpse in the bunk is in effect a repetition of the frenzied suicide that took place on the first night out from New York. Harry's humiliating first trip aloft is a vivid reminder of Redburn's earlier success in meeting the same challenge. . . . Arriving in America, Bolton meets with much the same exclusion and indifference that Redburn had encountered in England. And the last sentence of the book reinforces the parallel with the narrator's expression of wonder that, though Harry has died, he himself has "chance[d] to survive."[25]

Certainly these parallels between Redburn and Harry exist, and are striking enough; but Bowen fails to notice that an equally striking parallel can be made between Harry and Jackson: (1) like Redburn, both are lonely or in some way isolated figures; (2) unlike Redburn, both are exceptionally scornful of proprieties, and override social or conventional restraints; (3) both are careless about their own preservation, Harry by wasting his property and Jackson

[25] Merlin Bowen, "*Redburn* and the Angle of Vision," *Modern Philology*, LII, 107-108 (Nov., 1954).

by wasting his health; (4) both exercise a strange fascination or attraction for Redburn; (5) both, for a time, are able to tyrannize over, and control, Redburn; (6) both lose their control, and become objects of pity to Redburn; (7) both are older than Redburn and his superior in terms of experience and knowledge; and most important (8) both meet their deaths, and in a similarly dramatic way —at sea, without proper burial.

There are, more obviously, differences. Harry's recklessness seems to stem from his having too much money; Jackson's from having nothing. Jackson exercises his control at sea or in sailor-haunts; Harry, on his home ground. Jackson and Redburn are drawn by hate; Harry and Redburn by love. Most important, Jackson represents the lowest, hardest, coarsest element aboard the *Highlander*; Harry—with his finery, girlish beauty, and voice "like a bird"—represents the highest, softest, finest. The contrasts and similarities are such as to suggest that Melville was deliberately drawing in Harry and Jackson two extreme models, both counterparts of Redburn, both representing a kind of experience, but an opposite kind; and both experiences representing certain attractions but also dangers which Redburn, if he is to survive, must avoid. The figures are orbits, either one of which Redburn might have been drawn into with disastrous consequences—and the two orbits are much like the "aristocratic" and "plebeian" commitments which Melville avoids in narrating the book.

H. Bruce Franklin, the most recent commentator on *Redburn*, seems to believe that if Redburn had properly protected and befriended Harry when the two arrived in New York, Harry would not have drowned at sea. He maintains as the main point of his article that Redburn is responsible for Harry's death.[26] But surely Melville, who draws faults and weaknesses in Harry almost from the moment he is introduced more than sufficient to lay the groundwork for his destruction, makes it clear that it is not Redburn's fault but Harry's.

The most vivid instance is the scene in which Redburn, to his astonishment, sees Harry, who has shipped as a common sailor, "on deck in a brocaded dressing gown, embroidered slippers and a tasseled smoking cap, to stand his morning watch":

[26] H. Bruce Franklin, "Redburn's Wicked End," *Nineteenth Century Fiction*, XX, pp. 190-194 (Sept., 1965).

As soon as I came behind him thus arrayed, a suspicion, which had previously crossed my mind, again recurred, and I almost vowed to myself that spite his protestations, Harry Bolton never could have been at sea before, even as a Guinea-pig in an Indiaman; for the slightest acquaintance with the sea-life and sailors, should have prevented him, it would seem, from enacting this folly.

"Who's that Chinese mandarin?" cried the mate, who had made voyages to Canton. "Look you, my fine fellow, douse that mainsail now, and furl it in a trice."

"Sir?" said Harry, starting back. "Is not this the morning watch, and is not mine a morning gown?"

Redburn finally persuades Harry to take off his outlandish costume, and Harry exclaims:

"It's too bad! I meant to lounge away the watch in that gown until coffee time;—and I suppose your Hottentot of a mate won't permit a gentleman to smoke his Turkish pipe of a morning; but by Gad, I'll wear straps to my pantaloons to spite him!"[27]

This passage, with its exaggeratedly farcical humor, combines in a short space several themes developed in a more leisurely way in the first half of the book when Redburn, rather than Harry, appeared in a shooting jacket, high-heeled boots, and gentlemanly pantaloons; and when, like Harry, he showed a comic ignorance of sea language, sea usage, and the relationship between officers and men. But Harry is in every respect more extreme: his dress more absurdly refined and unsuited to sea duty; his ignorance of sea language still wilder. Most important, his response to the seaman's tasks he is given marks a crucial difference. As Newton Arvin has pointed out, Redburn had been desperately afraid of "falling—falling—falling" when he was sent up to loosen the skysail. But he loosens it, and later "Begins to Hop About in the Rigging Like a Saint Jago's Monkey." Harry never does. He makes one desperate attempt, "but no; he stopped short, and looked down from the top. Fatal glance! it unstrung his every fiber; and I saw him reel and clutch the shrouds." From that moment, "he never put foot in rattlin; never mounted above the bulwarks."[28]

[27] *Redburn*, p. 245.
[28] *Ibid.*, p. 248.

Jackson's catastrophic end comes not because he is too little of a sailor but because in a sense he is too much of one. He is hard enough, experienced enough, and cruel enough to survive any voyage; but he is wasted by his strengths—by his hardness, hatred, brutality, and debauchery. But Harry, the girlish youth, seems to perish for the opposite reasons—from being too soft, gentle, refined, genteel. It is perhaps symbolically significant that Harry, besides failing to climb the rigging, fails to jettison his gentlemanly baggage—his "collection of silks, velvets, broad cloths and satins," which he brings aboard in a special chest.

Newton Arvin observes:

Despite the underlying gravity of the symbolism generally, *Redburn* is anything but a lugubrious book as a whole: the current of animation and vivacity on which it is sustained is purely inspiriting. Melville's feeling . . . for light and shade did not fail him in the writing of *Redburn*. . . . There is the familiar ballast of prosaic information—the chapter, for example, on the furniture of the quarter-deck—and there is a good deal of Melville's characteristically smiling and low-toned humor. . . . In its richness of emotion and variety of tone, *Redburn* is generally the most likable of Melville's secondary books.[29]

This concluding statement, which Arvin seems to have added as a needed corrective to his main position, is a triumph of good sense over critical method; and one finds fault with it only in its failure to connect the "feeling for light and shade," the "variety of tone," the "current of animation," with the actual details of Melville's tone and structure—and in the failure to see that this tone and structure runs directly contrary to the view of *Redburn* as a novel of "tragic initiation."

Redburn's rejection of Bolton and Jackson, and Melville's rejection of the genteel and "Jacksonian" viewpoints seem both to stem from Melville-Redburn's striving for balance and independence. Melville projected the striving into a unique artistic technique in *Moby-Dick*—in, for example, the balance between the lyricism of "The Symphony," and the realism of "The Try-Works"; between the rhythms of stasis and of motion; or in the balancing figures of Ahab and Ishmael, who represent far better than Jackson and Harry

[29] Arvin, p. 109.

Bolton what Melville grew to see as the two main responses to life. But if the balances are less complex and less successfully worked out in *Redburn*, they are of a similar kind; and they represent a more nearly unique and independent artistic achievement than any of the critics who have been trying to fit *Redburn* into an auto-biographical or mythic pattern have given Melville credit for.

"Cock-A-Doodle-Doo!" and Some Legends in Melville Scholarship

Sidney P. Moss

I N THIS ESSAY I WISH TO NEUTRALIZE certain legends that distort Melville scholarship. One of them is that Melville was anti-Transcendentalist and especially anti-Emersonian, a mistake that has led to biased interpretations of his later novels, particularly of *Pierre* and *The Confidence-Man*. A second is that Melville's emotional and intellectual temperament was attuned to Hawthorne's, a notion that prevents us from seeing why Melville's fiction is more dynamic than his "mentor's." A third legend is that Melville's "Cock-A-Doodle-Doo!" is a satire, whether of Thoreau, Emerson, Wordsworth, or Transcendentalism in general, a misreading that has made this tale, though the happiest in the Melville canon and one of the most exultant in literature, badly neglected indeed.[1] To accomplish these ends, I shall use "Cock-A-Doodle-Doo!" as my Ariadne's thread into the labyrinth of Melville scholarship, with the prime object of rescuing the tale from the Minotaur.

I

The legend that "Cock-A-Doodle-Doo!" is a satire and that its object of satire is "buoyant transcendental principles"—more particularly, a "brief passage" in *A Week on the Concord and Merrimack Rivers*—seems to have originated with Egbert S. Oliver.[2] Oliver's assumption that the tale is satirical and his adducing of parallel passages from Thoreau and Melville to support that assump-

---

[1] Apart from collections of Melville's fiction, only two anthologies contain the tale—oddly enough, Kenneth S. Lynn's *The Comic Tradition in America: An Anthology* (New York, 1958) and Brom Weber's *Anthology of American Humor* (New York, 1962), as if the story were comic (or, as Lynn says, "comic satire") instead of comedic, a distinction I shall discuss later. I wish here to acknowledge my profound indebtedness to Barry Sanders, my colleague and friend, who lived this "Stück" with me.

[2] "'Cock-A-Doodle-Doo!' and Transcendental Hocus-Pocus," *New England Quarterly*, XXI, 204-216 (June, 1948). "This story of course is symbolical," Oliver wrote, "but the intent of the symbols and the satirical depth of the fable are only apparent as it is read in the light of a passage in Thoreau. . . ."

tion are questionable, as I shall indicate. At this point I only raise the obvious questions—namely, *why* a well-known author like Melville would wish to satirize an obscure passage in an obscure book by an unknown writer (*A Week*, of course, was Thoreau's first book and its total distribution was less than three hundred copies), and *who* was to understand the point of his satire, for what value has satire if the object of its ridicule is unknown? The fact that Oliver has also found that Thoreau, or at least Thoreau's ideas, are satirized in "Bartleby" and *The Confidence-Man* is even more disturbing.[3] For the ground of his argument becomes clear: Melville was fixated on Thoreau, despite the fact that there is no evidence that he ever met the man. If the point has any validity, there would surely be some direct reference to Thoreau or to Thoreau's work somewhere in Melville, if only in his letters. All we have is Duyckinck's list which shows the books he lent Melville. For the year 1850 this list indicates that Melville borrowed fifteen titles (a total of twenty volumes), among them "Thoreau's Merrimack."[4]

That "Cock-A-Doodle-Doo!", not to mention certain passages in

[3] "A Second Look at 'Bartleby,'" *College English*, VI, 431-439 (May, 1945); and "Melville's Picture of Emerson and Thoreau in *The Confidence-Man*," *ibid.*, VIII, 61-72 (Nov., 1946).

[4] Willard Thorp, *Herman Melville: Representative Selections* (New York, 1938), p. xxviii n. Inadvertently, Oliver specifies the date of Melville's borrowing of *A Week* as 1849. It may be pointed out here, for what it is worth, that Melville also borrowed *Sartor Resartus* in 1850; that earlier, in September, 1849, he asked Lemuel Shaw to secure a letter of introduction from Emerson to Carlyle (see Eleanor Melville Metcalf, *Herman Melville: Cycle and Epicycle*, Cambridge, Mass., 1953, p. 64); and that, if we use Oliver's logic, Melville might have been influenced by the "Everlasting Yea" as opposed to the "Everlasting No" in conceiving of "Cock-A-Doodle-Doo!" At all events, Oliver's conclusions regarding "Bartleby" and *The Confidence-Man* have already been questioned. Edward H. Rosenberry voices my judgment when he writes that Oliver's "formal attempt to prove 'Bartleby' a . . . satire on Thoreau . . . is badly hampered by lack of facts and lack of decisive satiric tone in the story itself" (*Melville and the Comic Spirit*, Cambridge, Mass., 1955, p. 198, n. 20). And Elizabeth S. Foster, whom Harrison Hayford calls "the most thorough critic" of *The Confidence-Man*, tell us that she does not find "Mr. Oliver's identification of Winsome's disciple Egbert with Thoreau . . . convincing," for reasons which she gives at length (see her edition of *The Confidence-Man*, New York, 1954, pp. 351-354). In addition, we have Melville's own comment on "Bartleby," which in no way indicates satirical intent: "My first emotions [toward Bartleby] had been those of pure melancholy and sincerest pity; but just in proportion as the forlornness of Bartleby grew and grew to my imagination, did that same melancholy merge into fear, that pity into repulsion. . . . [That repulsion] proceeds from a hopelessness of remedying excessive and organic ill" (Jay Leyda, *The Melville Log*, New York, 1951, I, 481-482. The narrator-protagonist of "Cock-A-Doodle-Doo!," as we shall see, has no organic ill; only those who cannot hear the cock have organic ill.

other Melville works, is to be read as a kind of *Fable for Critics* has another proponent in William Bysshe Stein.[5] Stein also alleges that "Cock-A-Doodle-Doo!" satirizes Thoreau, but the source he adduces is not a passage in *A Week* but Thoreau's "essay, 'Walking'." Here, too, the argument proceeds by a comparison of parallel passages, but Stein errs in a significant fact; for though Thoreau delivered lectures on "Walking" in 1851 and 1852, and again in 1856 and 1857, the *essay* "Walking" was published only posthumously (in June, 1862, in the *Atlantic Monthly*), some nine years after Melville published "Cock-A-Doodle-Doo!" (in December, 1853, in *Harper's New Monthly Magazine*).[6]

Legends by their nature are accretive, and no less so with this legend. Citing Oliver's articles, Frederic Ives Carpenter, by substituting Emerson's name for Thoreau's, asserted that Melville in "Cock-A-Doodle-Doo!" and "Bartleby" "satirized Emerson's self-reliance by the process of *reductio ad absurdum*, the one story describing the absurdly tragic results of an active absolute idealism (like *Pierre*), and the other the tragic results of a passively 'self-reliant' withdrawal from society."[7] Edward H. Rosenberry also accepts the legend concerning "Cock-A-Doodle-Doo!" Accretively, too, he asserts that the tale contains "parodic echoes" of Emerson and Wordsworth as well. While he offers no evidence for the Thoreau and Emerson "echoes," he claims to find documentation for the Wordsworth parody in Leon Howard's biography of Melville.[8] But the fact is that Howard thinks "Cock-A-Doodle-Doo!" is

[5] "Melville Roasts Thoreau's Cock," *Modern Language Notes*, LXXIV, 218-219 (March, 1959). Stein writes: "Readers of *Pierre* and *The Confidence-Man* are familiar with Melville's scorn for the philosophy of Thoreau and other Transcendentalists."

[6] See Walter Harding, *A Thoreau Handbook* (New York, 1961), p. 70; and Henry Seidel Canby, ed., *The Works of Thoreau* (Boston, 1937), p. 640. In a subsequent article, Stein shifted his ground somewhat to argue the point that the "real target of Melville's ridicule" in "Cock-A-Doodle-Doo!" is the apostle Paul; but he repeats that the narrator-protagonist of the tale is a "burlesque Thoreau. . . ." ("Melville's Cock and the Bell of Saint Peter," *Emerson Society Quarterly*, No. 27, pp. 5-10, 2d Quart., 1962).

[7] *Emerson Handbook* (New York, 1953), p. 232. Carpenter added: "These stories were all so exaggerated as to destroy much of their effect."

[8] According to Rosenberry, Howard "asserted that the story is a parody on Wordsworth's 'Resolution and Independence'," and on this basis Rosenberry avers that the "woodcutter Merrymusk," not the narrator-protagonist, as Oliver and Stein urge, "is the victim" of Transcendental principles. Rosenberry concedes, however, that the "story moves with a remarkable comic lightness and rewards even the reader who is not attuned to parodic echoes of Emerson, Thoreau, or Wordsworth" (*Melville and the Comic Spirit*, pp. 163, 198, n. 20).

"serious at the core," though admittedly he does say that Melville parodied "Resolution and Independence." In context, however, Howard clearly intended to say that Melville *adapted* two lines from Wordsworth for his purposes:

The Agatha theme of nonaggressive but unshakable patience continued to haunt his mind. . . . "Bartleby". . . gave some indication of the sort of secret power which he conceived as existing in quiet stubbornness. . . . In the power of his quiet resolution and independence lay one of the mysteries of humanity. . . . In his next story . . . he found a symbol which suggested his analysis of it. For in . . . "Cock-A-Doodle-Doo!" a character like Bartleby reappeared in the person of Merrymusk. . . . Melville interpreted the humble patience which fascinated him as an expression of pride, and, as such, it struck a strong responsive chord in his own being.[9]

Given the assumption that "Cock-A-Doodle-Doo!" *must* be a satire of Thoreau or of whomever, pertinent passages are not hard to come by, though the process vulgarizes a small masterpiece. There are, for instance, passages in *Walden* that with equal validity could be cited as the object of Melville's mockery. In his epigraph to that work, Thoreau wrote: "I do not propose to write an ode to dejection, but to brag as lustily as chanticleer in the morning, standing on his roost, if only to wake my neighbors up." Or the chapter on "Sounds," in which Thoreau confesses that he thought of keeping a cockerel whose note:

certainly the most remarkable of any bird's, . . . would soon become the most famous sound in our woods, surpassing the clangor of the goose and the hooting of the owl . . . [with its] clarions. To . . . hear [it] crow clear and shrill for miles over the resounding earth . . .—think

[9] Leon Howard, *Herman Melville: A Biography* (Berkeley, 1951), pp. 208-209. See also p. 210 for Howard's remarks on Melville's "parody" of Wordsworth's poem. For further discussion of the "Agatha theme," see Patricia Lacy, "The Agatha Theme in Melville's Stories," *University of Texas Studies in English*, XXXV, 96-105 (1956). So far as I can determine, Jay Leyda in the *Complete Stories of Herman Melville* (New York, 1949), p. xxiv, and Richard Chase in *Herman Melville: A Critical Study* (New York, 1949), p. 163, were the first to point out Melville's use of Wordsworth in "Cock-A-Doodle-Doo!"—something about which I shall say more later. I might add here that, to my knowledge, Howard and Chase are the only scholars whose regard for this tale begins to approximate my own. Though Howard's remarks are to the point, they are necessarily brief; and though Chase is too narrow in his reading of the tale (this "remarkable story," he tells us, deals with "the artist's need for the sense of power and the guilt-feelings which accompany it"), he fully appreciates its magnificence.

of it! It would put nations on the alert. Who would not be early to rise, and rise earlier and earlier every successive day of his life, till he became unspeakably healthy, wealthy, and wise?

It could be argued, of course, that Melville might have taken such passages in the positive rather than in the negative sense; that is, he might have been "inspired" to dramatize Thoreau's love of life— Melville, after all, was a life-lover—rather than mock it. But then there is the problem of fact. "Cock-A-Doodle-Doo!" was published in 1853 and *Walden* in 1854.[10]

II

If neither Thoreau nor Wordsworth is the object of satire in "Cock-A-Doodle-Doo!," surely, many would argue, the tale, like passages in *Pierre* and *The Confidence-Man*, satirizes such Transcendental principles as self-reliance and optimism. My reply to this contention can only be discursive. For Melville's attitude toward Transcendentalism is at once the simplest and knottiest problem, knotty and distorted if we adopt an either-or position, simple, and undistorted if we do not. Anyone who has examined the evidence must conclude, as F. O. Matthiessen reluctantly did, that Melville "felt a strong attraction in the transcendental beliefs. . . ."[11] For Melville's attitude toward Transcendentalism, and it was not especially concerned with "modern" versions of it[12] (in fact, it

[10] A likelier object of satire than has yet been adduced by anyone is Cornelius Mathews's *Chanticleer: A Thanksgiving Story of the Peabody Family* (1850), a narrative advertised in the *Literary World*, popular in its time (it ran through two editions in 1850), and written by a man whom few people besides Evert Duyckinck could abide, and whom Melville knew. In Mathews's story the prescient red rooster crows three times at certain crucial points and "knows more than anybody about this farm, except old grandfather." But again, except for both tales using a cock in certain unusual ways, there is no relation whatever between the two tales.

[11] F. O. Matthiessen, *American Renaissance* (New York, 1941), p. 184. Perry Miller, fighting fire with fire, has asserted, much too sweepingly in my judgment, that *Moby-Dick* and *Pierre* "are, to the end, implacably, defiantly, unrepentantly, Transcendental" in the sense that they "reject tragedy" ("Melville and Transcendentalism," *Virginia Quarterly Review*, XXIX, 556-575, Autumn, 1953, reprinted in an enlarged version in *Moby-Dick Centennial Essays*, Dallas, 1953, pp. 123-152).

[12] See Merton M. Sealts, Jr., "Melville's 'Neoplatonical Originals,'" *Modern Language Notes*, LXVII, 80-86 (Feb., 1952). In this essay Sealts tells us that, in part at least, the object of Melville's satire in *Mardi* was *The Six Books of Proclus on the Theology of Plato*, and that his "satirical treatment of this abstruse source-material and his later reference to Proclus in *The Confidence-Man*, both so different in tone from Emerson's attitude, are an indication of Melville's hostility to certain characteristics of Transcendentalism, ancient and modern." See also Melville's ambivalent reactions to Goethe's "Live

would have made little difference to Melville's temperamental problem if French, German, British, and American Transcendentalism had not been in the air), was not so complex as ambivalent. Struggling to reconcile the dissonant elements of life, he was impelled to search for the "Talismanic Secret," as he called it in *Pierre*, but could not find it, or at least could not accept it, and in despair or rage he labeled those who claimed they had a "guild of self-imposters"—namely, "Plato, and Spinoza, and Goethe . . . with a preposterous rabble of Muggletonian Scots and Yankees, whose vile brogue still the more bestreaks the stripedness of their Greek or German Neoplatonical originals."[13]

In short, Melville, as Hawthorne noted, could "neither believe nor be comfortable in his unbelief"; and he was "too honest and courageous not to try to do one or the other."[14] Hawthorne understood Melville's problem, for caught in the same dilemma, he had himself flirted with Transcendentalism—had, in fact, joined Brook Farm and married a Transcendentalist—before he "settled" the problem once and for all by locking himself uncomfortably into negativism: his hostility to idealistic enthusiasms, his skepticism about social reform, and his noncommittal attitude; turning, in short, anti-intellectual and assuring himself all the while that he was happy—a locking-in that spelled, in my judgment, his artistic death. Melville was too honest and courageous, as Hawthorne saw, to accept such defeatism, and he kept struggling for a way out. And as D. H. Lawrence noted in his foreword to *Women in Love*, "Every man who is acutely alive is acutely wrestling with his own soul. The people that can bring forth the new passion, the new idea,

---

in the all" (*The Letters of Herman Melville*, ed. Merrell R. Davis and William H. Gilman, New Haven, 1960, pp. 130-131). Henry A. Murray in his edition of *Pierre* (New York, 1949), p. lxxvii, points out that among the "numerous roots of 'Chronometricals and Horologicals'" are passages in "Plutarch, St. Paul, Plato, Bacon, Pascal, Jeremy Taylor, Shaftesbury, Mandeville, and others. . . ."

[13] *The Works of Herman Melville* (Constable ed.; New York, 1963), IX, 290.

[14] *The English Notebooks by Nathaniel Hawthorne*, ed. Randall Stewart (New York, 1962), p. 433. For this reason I think Matthiessen was in serious error when he wrote: "How an age in which Emerson's was the most articulate voice could also have given birth to *Moby-Dick* can be accounted for only through reaction" (*American Renaissance*, p. 184). Melville, given his temperament, would have been of two minds at any point in history. Brom Weber's statement about *Moby-Dick*, that the universe is "tragic for Ahab but, in a religious and physical sense, comic and hopeful for Ishmael" (*Anthology of American Humor*, p. 301), seems much closer to the truth than Matthiessen's in that it catches Melville's fundamental dualism.

these people will endure. Those others, that fix themselves in the old idea, will perish with the new life strangled unborn within them." No more than the Transcendentalists of his time could Melville be unaware that modern man is divided—divided from God, from nature, from society, and from himself.[15] As he wrote to Hawthorne in 1851, this sense of dividedness is the "knot with which we choke ourselves. As soon as you say *Me*, a *God*, a *Nature*, so soon you jump off from your stool and hang from the beam."[16] The Transcendentalists were proposing a means of reintegration, and their work was no "hocus pocus." Rather, they were addressing themselves to the same problem as Karl Marx was at the same time, if by another method. The central idea of these thinkers, and Emerson of course was among them, was that modern man assumes dividedness to be a metaphysical fact when it is largely a psychological symptom of the divisiveness intensified by modern capitalist society, especially in its overpowering demands for economically useful activities and its indifference to, if not hostility toward, activities that are privately and psychologically useful and integrative.[17]

Those scholars who have recognized Melville's ambivalence to

[15] I am not saying, of course, that modern man alone suffers this dividedness. Such examples as the Book of Job, *Oedipus Rex*, and *Hamlet* would flatly deny this. I am only saying that the problem becomes more afflictive in modern times. For suggestive evidence that Hawthorne was locking himself into negativism, I point out the following: In the original version of "The Hall of Fantasy," Hawthorne said of Emerson, "No more earnest seeker after truth than he, and few more successful finders of it" (*Pioneer*, I, 52-53, Feb., 1843). By 1846, however, in the "Old Manse" sketch, Hawthorne began to deny the possibility of finding truth or even the worthwhileness of the pursuit: "For myself, there had been epochs of my life when I too might have asked of this prophet [Emerson] the master word that should solve me the riddle of the universe; but now, being happy, I felt as if there were no question to be put, and therefore admired Emerson . . . but sought nothing from him as a philosopher." It was a strange kind of happiness that, in an age when sleep was the dominant metaphor of death-in-life, Hawthorne could, in the same sketch, argue that "the great want which mankind labors under at this present period is sleep. The world should . . . take an age-long nap." Or that he should "pray," again in the same sketch, "that the world may be petrified and rendered immovable in precisely the worst moral and physical state that it ever yet arrived at, rather than be benefited by such schemes of such philosophers." (See *The Complete Writings of Nathaniel Hawthorne*, Riverside ed., Boston, 1900, IV, xx and 39-43 *passim*.) By 1856 Hawthorne considered such intellectual and emotional struggles as Melville was undergoing "deserts." Melville "will never rest," he noted, "until he gets hold of a definite belief. It is strange how he persists . . . in wandering to-and-fro over these deserts" (Stewart, *Hawthorne's English Notebooks*, pp. 432-433).

[16] *Melville's Letters*, p. 125.

[17] One of the most discerning introductions to the Transcendentalists is that by George Hochfield, *Selected Writings of the American Transcendentalists* (New York, 1966), esp. pp. xxiv-xxvii.

Transcendental thought have had good reason to re-examine his alleged thrusts at Emerson. Henry A. Murray, for instance, is convinced that Plotinus Plinlimmon in *Pierre*, far from being a caricature of Emerson, is a "striking and psychological likeness of Hawthorne. ..." "Chronometricals and Horologicals" "echoes views expressed by Hawthorne. ... Strip Plinlimmon of the disguising title of Grand Master ... and you have ... Hawthorne. ...." Murray adds that Plinlimmon's pamphlet "is scarcely Emersonian in temper. Certainly Emerson did not start a 'surprising sorcery' upon Melville in the writing of *Moby-Dick*. He was not a Paul Pry of the guilty heart, nor a compound of Apollo and Saturn, nor characteristically inscrutable. His philosophic attitude was not depressing. *There was no Death in him*" [italics added].[18] Rosenberry agrees with Murray, at least to the extent of saying that "it is probably misreading Melville to identify ... [Plinlimmon] with any single personality as an intentional portrait."[19] And William Braswell, on the basis of his study of the Melville-Emerson relationship, has said that "*The Confidence-Man* as ... a satire on the Transcendentalists seems to me unfounded."[20]

If these statements regarding Melville's attitude toward Transcendentalism and especially Emerson's version of it seem too conjectural, let us look at the known facts. By his own admission, Melville's initial exposure to Emerson occurred when he heard him lecture in Boston on February 5, 1849.[21] As he wrote to Evert

[18] Introduction to *Pierre*, pp. lxxvii-lxxix and 475-477 *passim*.
[19] *Melville and the Comic Spirit*, p. 166.
[20] "Melville as a Critic of Emerson," *American Literature*, IX, 319, n. 9 (Nov., 1937). The criticism of *The Confidence-Man* is so snarled that nothing can be gained, least of all clarity, by adding one more argument. We have gone all the way from Carl Van Vechten's assertion that "Emerson is the confidence man," to Richard Chase's statement that the confidence-man is a composite figure, to Leslie Fiedler's observation that he is Christ come "to *bamboozle* us into belief," to John W. Shroeder's contention that the confidence-man is the Devil or one of his legion, to Rosenberry's judgment that "Mark Winsome and his disciple are only two of the masks that the Confidence-Man assumes. Their relatively minor role and late placement in the story might even persuade the reader that Melville did not, after all, attach much thematic importance to them." It may be, as Fiedler has suggested, that the "clue to the primary ambiguity of the book" is that Melville himself "was just not sure." See Van Vechten, *Excavations* (New York, 1926), p. 87; Chase, *Melville*, p. 188, *et passim*; Fiedler, *Nation*, CLXIX, 494-496 (Nov. 19, 1949); Shroeder, "Sources and Symbols for Melville's *The Confidence-Man*," *PMLA*, LXVI, 363-380 (June, 1951); Rosenberry, *Melville and the Comic Spirit*, p. 170.
[21] The editors of *Melville's Letters*, p. 77, n. 2, supply this date, as they do the two Melville letters I quote subsequently (pp. 76-80).

Duyckinck on March 3 of that year, "I had only glanced at a book of his once in Putnam's store—that was all I knew of him, till I heard him lecture." His reaction to that lecture, still exuberant some two weeks later (in a letter dated February 24), was: "Say what they will, he's a great man."

Melville had reason to say only this much about Emerson, for he knew what "they" would say, "they" being Evert Duyckinck; for Duyckinck, fixed in his Episcopalian orthodoxies, was decidedly hostile to Emerson's heresies. In reviewing *Mardi* for the *Literary World* (Duyckinck's magazine), "they" would say, hesitantly at first, that Melville's "ingenious moral writing" was such that "Emerson would not disclaim."[22] Of *Moby-Dick*, however, "they" would say it was rashly "daring in speculation, reckless at times of taste and propriety. . . . This piratical running down of creeds and opinions, the conceited indifferentism of Emerson, or the run-a-muck style of Carlyle . . . is out of place and uncomfortable. We do not like to see what, under any view, must be to the world the most sacred associations of life violated and defaced."[23] And of *Pierre* "they" would say:

The combined power of New England transcendentalism and Spanish Jesuitical casuistry could not have completely befogged nature and truth, than this confounded Pierre has done. . . . The most immoral *moral* of the story, if it has any moral at all, seems to be the impracticability of virtue; a leering demoniacal spectre of an idea seems to be peering at us through the dim obscure of this dark book, and mocking us with this dismal falsehood. Mr. Melville's chapter on "Chronometricals and Horologicals," if it has any meaning at all, simply means that virtue and religion are only for gods and not to be attempted by man. But ordinary novel readers will never unkennel this loathsome suggestion. The stagnant pool at the bottom of which it lies, is not too deep for their penetration, but too muddy, foul, and corrupt. If truth is hid in a well, falsehood lies in a quagmire.

Duyckinck concluded by saying that if *Pierre* represented a development in Melville, we are not "sufficiently advanced in trans-

[22] *Literary World*, IV, 333-335 (April 14, 1849).

[23] *Literary World*, IX, 403-404 (Nov. 22, 1851). Evert Duyckinck also noted in this review what I have pointed out earlier, that there was in Ishmael "the self-torturing agency of a mind driven hither and thither as a flame in a whirlwind. . . ." If one believes, as I do, that Melville in his maturer fiction was finding metaphors for his temperamental problems, the conclusion is obvious.

cendentalism to lift ourselves skywards and see clearly the coming light with our heads above the clouds."[24]

Evidently, tasked by Duyckinck for simply averring that Emerson is "a great man" (we do not have Duyckinck's letter), Melville was forced to defend himself in another letter (dated March 3, 1849). He said that he did not "oscillate in Emerson's rainbow," but preferred, given his inability to accept Emerson's optimism:

to hang myself in mine own halter. . . . Swear he is a humbug [had Duyckinck alleged as much?]—then is he no common humbug. Lay it down that had not Sir Thomas Browne lived, Emerson would not have mystified [had Duyckinck charged that Emerson was derivative and unintelligible?]—I will answer, that had not Old Zack's father begot him, Old Zack would never have been the hero of Palo Alto. . . . No one is his own sire.— I was very agreeably disappointed in M[r] Emerson. I had heard of him as full of transcendentalisms, myths & oracular gibberish. . . . To my surprise, I found him quite intelligible. . . . And, frankly, *for the sake of the argument* [italics added], let us call him a fool;—then had I rather be a fool than a wise man.

Not that Melville could not see a "gaping flaw" in Emerson—his intellectual arrogance, "the insinuation, that had he lived in those days when the world was made, he might have offered some valuable suggestions." Yet this statement, though Melville had occasion to make similar ones in later years, might well have been at this time a concession to Duyckinck's sensibilities. For Melville also found himself apologizing in the same letter for remarks he had made about Shakespeare in his earlier one—namely, that "he's full of sermons-on-the-mount, and gentle—aye, almost as Jesus. . . . And if another Messiah ever comes twill be in Shakesper's person." His apology was: "I . . . only *seemed* irreverent." He would, he added, no more burn "tuns of rancid fat" at Shakespeare's shrine than, presumably, he would at Emerson's or any man's.

Whatever the reasons for the four-year hiatus in their friendship, and the reasons are not altogether clear, Melville must have been stung at being flogged with the Transcendental stick; and on February 14, 1852, sometime between the *Moby-Dick* and *Pierre* re-

[24] *Literary World*, XI, 118-120 (Aug. 21, 1852). See also Paul Smith, "*The Confidence-Man* and the Literary World of New York," *Nineteenth-Century Fiction*, XVI, 329-337 (March, 1962).

views, he curtly addressed a letter to the "Editors of Literary World" canceling his subscription and obviously his friendship with Duyckinck.[25]

Melville's second known exposure to Emerson occurred the following year when he visited the Hawthornes. Careful "not to interrupt Mr. Hawthorne's mornings," as Sophia Hawthorne wrote, Melville "generally walked off somewhere—& one morning he shut himself into the boudoir & read Mr. Emerson's Essays,"[26] an act that reveals at once his interest in and superficial knowledge of Emerson. His only other known exposure to Emerson occurred after he had published *Pierre* (1852), "Bartleby" (1853), "Cock-A-Doodle-Doo!" (1853), and *The Confidence-Man* (1857). Hardly affluent, he was nevertheless curious enough about the sage of Concord to buy three of his books, if only in secondhand copies. These were *Essays: First Series, Essays: Second Series* (both purchased in the early sixties), and *The Conduct of Life* (purchased in 1870). The annotations Melville made in these books indicate a sense of discovery and are, on the whole, in approbation of Emerson. Such expressions as the following regularly appear as marginalia: "Bully for Emerson!— Good"; "A noble expression, with a clear strong meaning"; "All this is nobly written, and proceeds from noble thinking, and a natural sympathy with greatness"; "True"; "True & admirable! Bravo." When he took exception to Emerson, it was to his rejection of evil, his occasional intellectual smugness, and to what Braswell calls his "imperfect appreciation of the suffering of mankind. . . ."[27]

This is the known evidence, and it does not suggest that Emerson was Melville's bête noire or that he had satirized him in book after book. Duyckinck did not recognize Emerson in Plinlimmon, nor did he see Thoreau in "Bartleby," nor anti-Transcendentalism

[25] See *Melville's Letters*, p. 149; Leyda, *Melville Log, passim*; and Howard, *Melville*, p. 236, who correctly notes that on October 1, 1856, Melville "sloughed off his four years of sensitive estrangement from Evert Duyckinck and spent the evening . . . with him."

[26] Metcalf, *Melville*, p. 91. Though the letter is undated, it is clear from the context that it was written in the fall of 1850.

[27] "Melville as a Critic of Emerson," p. 331. I have not called attention to the fact that Melville owned a copy of Emerson's *Poems* (7th ed.; Boston, 1858), a gift he received from Samuel Shaw in 1859, because there is nothing in his mere scoring of two passages of "Merlin" and the quotation from Anacreon that he wrote beside a stanza from "The Humble-Bee" that is at all revealing about his attitude toward Emerson. See Leyda, *Melville Log*, II, 607.

in "Cock-A-Doodle-Doo!"[28] Common sense would tell us that if Emerson or Thoreau were satirized by Melville, someone would have observed that fact somewhere, if only in a review or letter. To repeat, then, Melville was ambivalent to Transcendental thought, both ancient and modern; and to demonstrate that he was not implacably opposed to it and that once, in a joyous moment, he surrendered to its "comedic" vision, we shall have to turn to "Cock-A-Doodle-Doo!"[29] Before we do, however, a word needs to be said about the "comedic vision" inasmuch as it is so badly confused with the "comic vision."

The comic vision (and I can only be suggestive here) has a large gamut, running the range from seeing the amusing incongruities of life to observing the yawning disparities between the ideal and the real and being roused to the harsh satire and black humor of, say, Swift in the Fourth Book of *Gulliver's Travels*. The comedic vision is entirely different; in fact, it is the obverse of the tragic vision. If the tragic vision sees man as passing from innocence and freedom to corruption, necessity, and finally death, the comedic vision sees the possibility, even the actuality, of a glorious reversal, as Whitman does in "Song of Myself." Not that the comedic vision refuses to recognize the brute facts of man's subjection to necessity, his proneness to evil, and the imminence of his death. It simply refuses to settle for this limited view. Instead, it encompasses these

[28] Duyckinck, in the *Literary World*, XIII, 295 (Dec. 3, 1853), noted that "Bartleby" was a "Poeish tale, with an infusion of more natural sentiment. . . ." Earlier, on Nov. 26, 1853, p. 278, he had observed that "Cock-A-Doodle-Doo!" "is an imaginative, descriptive, sentimental paper, dramatically moralizing in a northern New England landscape, the sound of the farmyard trumpeter—in a strain for humor and poetry which would make merry the heart of old Dan Chaucer. . . . It is not at all difficult to recognise, in this paper, the best qualities of one of the foremost of American writers. Herman Melville never was in better trim than in this resonant 'article.'" Some two years later Duyckinck called "Cock-A-Doodle-Doo!" "one of the most lively and animated productions of his pen" (Evert A. and George L. Duyckinck, eds., *Cyclopaedia of American Literature*, II, New York, 1855, 674).
[29] When Melville read Emerson's "Heroism" in *Essays: First Series*, he came upon the following passage that would serve, with minor revisions, to define the theme of "Cock-A-Doodle-Doo!": "Self-trust is the essence of heroism. It is the state of the soul at war, and its ultimate objects are the last defiance of falsehood and wrong, and the power to bear all that can be inflicted by evil agents. . . . It is generous, hospitable, temperate, scornful of petty calculations and scornful of being scorned. It persists; it is of an undaunted boldness and of a fortitude not to be wearied out. Its jest is the littleness of common life. That false prudence which dotes on health and wealth is the foil, the butt and merriment of heroism." Melville "drew a marginal line beside these sentences and observed: 'This is noble again'" (Braswell, "Melville as a Critic of Emerson," p. 325).

facts at the same time that it transcends them. The comedic vision
has its own integrity and is an answer to the easy and even posturing
despair of modern times, a despair seldom so hard-bought as Melville's; and if it is foolishness, then, in Melville's words, it is better
to be a fool than a wise man.

The comedic vision has reaches beyond the power of the tragic
vision to explore, for, as has been remarked, the tragic vision is self-
limiting. It is Dante's *Paradise* rather than his *Inferno,* Shakespeare's *The Tempest* rather than *Macbeth,* Eliot's *Four Quartets*
rather than *The Waste Land*. It is the biblical statement, "the peace
of God, which passeth all understanding," as against the despair
expressed by Septimius Severus, *"Omnia fui et nihil expedit"* ("I
have seen all things and it availed nothing"). It is Emily Dickinson's
awareness that "Much Madness is divinest sense" and Robert Frost's:

> Ah, when to the heart of man
>   Was it ever less than a treason
> To go with the drift of things,
>   To yield with a grace to reason,
> And bow and accept the end
>   Of a love or a season?

If, in short, the comedic vision has any one characteristic, it is its
defiance of life-denying forces.

III

On the basis of Melville's adaptation of two lines in "Resolution
and Independence," Richard Chase has made the telling point that
Wordsworth's poem may have "quite possibly suggested" "Cock-A-
Doodle-Doo!," for its "whole meaning is similar to that of the
poem." And not only its meaning, I might add, but its structure,
development, and characterization as well. As Wordsworth despairs
at the beginning of his poem, so does the narrator at the outset of
the tale. As Wordsworth projects his despair upon the universe, so
does the protagonist of "Cock-A-Doodle-Doo!" Where Wordsworth
writes:

> We Poets in our youth begin in gladness;
> But thereof come in the end despondency and madness.

Melville wrote, adapting the verses to the exigencies of his narrative:

> . . . Of fine mornings,
> We fine lusty cocks begin our crows in gladness;
> But when eve does come we don't crow quite so much,
> For then cometh despondency and madness.

And as Wordsworth rejects despair after his encounter with the leech-gatherer, so the narrator of the tale achieves his full comedic vision after his final meeting with the Merrymusks.

But though Melville owed much to Wordsworth's poem in theme, design, and in many details, he owed nothing to him in execution and tone. For where Wordsworth narrates and is didactic, Melville dramatizes and writes a small but exultant masterpiece. Since the story has been misread so often, and since my major intention in this essay is to rescue the narrative from the near-oblivion into which it has fallen, I may be pardoned for making a detailed analysis of the tale.

The narrator tells us that despotism and casuality rule the times. Despotism has put down "high-spirited revolts"; casuality has injured or destroyed "high-spirited travelers"; and his own "private affairs are also full of despotisms [and] casualities. . . ." He who was once high-spirited is now "full of hypoes": he sleeps poorly or not at all, finds the "air damp, disagreeable," the "country . . . underdone." In short, to use Melville's figure, it is as if he were butting his head against the world.

But it is a time of death and rebirth in the world and in himself, a struggle for life against life-denying forces. The earth about him shows "tokens of a divided empire": the "old grass and the new grass" are striving together, and the woods are "strewn with dry dead boughs, . . . while the young trees" are beginning to bud. But he is still in his "old grass," "dead bough" frame of mind. He broods about the fate of his "good friend and thirty other good fellows" who "were sloped into eternity at the bidding of a thick-headed [steamboat] engineer, who knew not a valve from a flue," and of a "crash on the railroad" when "near a score of noble hearts, a bride and her groom, and an innocent little infant," all on the verge of a new life, were "disembarked into the grim hulk of Charon. . . ." In despair, he tells himself that casuality is the inexor-

able fact of life, so "what's the use of complaining," especially as
the ultimate despotism may be "the heavens themselves" that
"ordain these things. . . ." Yet he cannot "go gentle into that good
night," to use Dylan Thomas's expression; rather, he rages "against
the dying of the light." With consummate futility, he rants against
the "thousand villains and asses who have the management . . . [of]
vital things in the world" and against the alleged "great improve-
ments of the age" like the railroad, which he calls a Moloch, a
chartered murderer, and a death monopolizer.

The thought of death makes him think at once of his creditor
"who frightens the *life* out of me more than any locomotive"
[italics added], a "smaller dunning fiend . . . who seems to run on
a railroad track, too," a demon who "duns me even on Sunday . . .
and . . . shoves himself between me and salvation"—a "lean," "lantern-jawed rascal" who personifies everything mechanistic, ma-
terialistic, and destructive in his private life.

Happening to feel in his pocket, he finds a powder he "was
going to send to the sick baby in yonder hovel," and he thinks of
all the sick children on the verge of life carried off by disease, of
his powerlessness against such universal evil, and even the punishment he now endures for having tried to help. For he got "rheumatics" in his shoulder, the good one of course, when "in a crowded
boat, I gave up my berth to a sick lady, and stayed on deck till
morning in drizzling weather. There's the thanks one gets for
charity! Twinge! Shoot away, ye rheumatics! Ye couldn't lay on
worse if I were some villain who had murdered the lady instead of
befriending her."

At this moment of helpless despair, he hears the "triumphant
thanksgiving of a cock-crow! *'Glory be to God in the highest!'* "[30]

[30] It seems necessary to point out that there is a "cock tradition" in religious thought,
which critics of this story seem unaware of. On gravestones, in sermons, and in religious
writing in general, cocks appear with fair regularity for obvious symbolic reasons. If
death is like sleep, the cock's crow is like a call to resurrection. Failing to understand
the religious symbolism of the cock, some commentators insist upon interpreting the cock
in sexual terms, though for this tale such an interpretation has no relevance whatever.
Among these commentators is one English critic (Martin Green) who faults American
critics for misreading and even inventing texts. See his *Re-Appraisals: Some Common-
sense Readings in American Literature* (New York, 1967), pp. 11 and 108-112. The cock
as symbol of death-defiance also appears in *Moby-Dick*, as Lynn in *The Comic Tradition in
America*, pp. 232-233, has also noted. In "The Doubloon" (chap. 99) Ahab considers
the cock on the coin as "the courageous, the undaunted, and victorious fowl. . . ." And

Immediately, both he and the world change; more precisely, his view toward himself and the world changes. He begins to "feel a little in sorts again"; the mist seems to lessen; the sun starts to show itself. Again he hears the cock whose crow plainly says to him, *"Never say die!,"* for there is no death and defeat except as we yield to them. The cock's crow is so "blessed" that he finds himself addressing the calves in the field, and he realizes that he has been a calf to fall into despondency and madness. For what has he to despair of when a cock can cry "like a very laureate," though, like all mortals, it has "death hanging over him at any moment"? At the next crow of the cock, which is so "clamorously-victorious," he finds himself flapping his elbows and crowing too.

But despite his sense of exultation, he is not yet fully reborn. Doubt obtrudes: Has he overestimated the cock's pluck? Will it crow so well at noon or at nightfall? After all, "even cocks have to succumb to the universal spell of tribulation. . . ." Nevertheless, he is marvelously invigorated. He will now eat "something hearty," not his parsimonious tea and toast. Moreover, his whole perception of life is changed. The train now flashes "through the trees like a vein of silver" instead of coming "like the Asiatic cholera cantering on a camel"; its "steam pipe chirps" instead of going "snort! puff! scream!"; and its passengers are gay, hardly sacrifices to Moloch. Everything, in short, has fallen into exquisite harmony— train, passengers, earth, river, sky. "The old grass," he thinks now, playing on the word *knock*, "has to knock under to the new," as his dun—his life-denying force—must knock under to him, by a club if need be, for there have been enough "knockings on the heads" of high-spirited people.

When the dun plies him again, he turns him out, for nothing frightens him now: "Duns!—I could have fought an army of them!"

in "Queequeg in His Coffin" (chap. 110) Pip calls "for a game cock now to sit upon his head and crow!" For "Queequeg dies game! I say, game, game, game!" For cocks on gravestones, see Allan I. Ludwig, *Graven Images: New England Stonecarving and Its Symbols, 1650-1815* (Middletown, Conn., 1966), pp. 133 ff. For cock metaphors in religious writing, see, for example, *Images or Shadows of Divine Things*, ed. Perry Miller (New Haven, 1949), p. 92, in which Jonathan Edwards writes: "The crowing of the cock to wake men out of sleep and to introduce the day seems to signifie the introducing the glorious day of the church by ministers preaching the Gospel. Many shall be awakened and roused to preach the Gospel with extraordinary fervency, to cry aloud and lift up their voice like [a] trumpet." Trumpet, of course, is the name Melville gave to his cock.

He also learns that the cock's crow is mightiest "at the darkest," that it is clearly "a cock who had fought the world and got the better of it, and was now resolved to crow, though the earth should heave and the heavens should fall." Reassured, he returns home "dauntless"; and now, when he considers the life-crushing forces that put down the "risings of the poor oppressed" and destroy people in "railroad and steamboat accidents," including his own friend, it is to his astonishment "with a calm, good-natured rapture of defiance," which would enable him to "meet Death, and invite him to dinner, and toast the Catacombs with him, in pure overflow of self-reliance and a sense of universal security."

The next morning, his spirit and body miraculously refreshed, he decides to buy the cock, the "bird rightly offered up by the invincible Socrates, in testimony of his final victory over life,"[31] for while the cock's crow reinforces him, the cock's spirit is not yet his. In searching for it, he can only determine that the crow of this "Brother of the Sun," "this bird of cheerful Socrates—the game-fowl Greek who died unappalled," comes from the East (life), not from the West (death). No one he asks can help him, for none of them can hear the cock, for they are "uncheerful and uncheerable. . . ." But though he is not yet aware of the fact, he hardly needs the cock, for his own "soul . . . would turn chanticleer, and clap her wings, and throw back her throat, and breathe forth a cheerful challenge to all the world of woes."

To interiorize the cock's spirit and become fully reborn and independent, he has yet to go through one more stage, a stage through which Merrymusk guides him. Merrymusk, a man who sawed and split his wood and who endures such torments of despotism and casuality as trivialize his own, appears for his pay. He gives Merrymusk what he can, and in a day or two proceeds to his shanty, where the sawyer lives with his four ailing children and invalid wife, to pay him the rest of his wages. The closer he comes to the shanty, the more clearly he hears the cock, until finally he sees the creature whose appearance is in every way as martial and victorious as its voice. It is "like a golden eagle," "a Field-Marshal," "Lord Nelson, with all his glittering arms on, standing on the *Vanguard's*

---

[31] Socrates's last words to Crito in the *Phaedo*, it will be recalled, were: "I owe a cock to Asclepius; will you remember to pay the debt?"

quarter-deck going into battle"; the "Emperor Charlemagne in his robes at Aix-la-Chapelle. . . ." Its crest is "like unto Hector's helmet"; its "embroidered trappings" like those of "some Oriental king. . . ."

Merrymusk, despite his miserable poverty, refuses to sell him the cock, for it is the pearl beyond price. Its presence is so celestial that it irradiates the shanty; its voice gives such stuff against despair that it transfigures the children and makes them seem the offspring of "emperors and kings"; and, in Merrymusk's words, the cock glorifies "this otherwise inglorious, lean, lantern-jawed land," adjectives that the narrator had applied to the dun. To prove his point, Merrymusk bids the cock crow its best, at which the cock delivers a blast comparable only to that of "some overpowering angel in the Apocalypse." It seems to herald the defeat of evil in the world and the rise of righteousness, for the cock "seemed crowing over the fall of wicked Babylon, or crowing over the triumph of righteous Joshua in the vale of Ashkelon."

Recovering from his fright at hearing this preternatural blast, the narrator asks Merrymusk if there is any hope for the recovery of his wife and children. "Not the least," Merrymusk replies, adding, nevertheless, that he is "a very rich man, and a very happy one."

On the way home, the narrator has his last doubt, for he is "not wholly at rest concerning the soundness of Merrymusk's views of things, though full of admiration for him"; but it is a doubt that the cock's crow dispels once and for all. Thus, when some of his relatives die, he wears no mourning but drinks "stout in preference to porter," for he no longer acknowledges death, only life.

Some weeks later, returning to Merrymusk's shanty, he finds the "whole house . . . a hospital. . . ." Yet when he would make Merrymusk aware that he and his family are dying, Merrymusk also refuses to acknowledge death and insists, instead, that all is well. Merrymusk dies protesting this fact; and, as if the family were a single organism, each of them dies quickly in turn, with the cock crowing as if it meant the blast to thrust their souls "sheer up to the seventh heavens" and to rejoin them "in the upper air." Then, sounding one last "supernatural note," the cock too drops dead.

The narrator buries the family and erects a gravestone over them. But the stone bears no image of skull and crossbones, the tokens of man's mortality and death's victory. Instead, the stone bears the image of "a lusty cock in act of crowing" in sign of man's immortality, the call to resurrection, and of death's defeat, in token of which he had these words chiseled into the stone:

> *O death, where is thy sting?*
> *O grave, where is thy victory?*

But that is not the end. Though the cock is dead, its spirit, phoenix-like, has risen in the narrator's own person. So that now he too can crow amid universal tribulation, "Cock-a-doodle-doo!—oo!—oo!—oo!—oo!"

"Cock-A-Doodle-Doo!" is clearly a companion piece to "Bartleby." Apart from the fact that they appeared concurrently in 1853, they represent opposite positions. Where Bartleby is defeated by life and withdraws even into death, the narrator of "Cock-A-Doodle-Doo!" comes to defy and even deny death while exulting in life. Perhaps the final comment should be left to Yeats who in "Sailing to Byzantium" shared in his own way Melville's comedic vision:

> An aged man is but a paltry thing,
> A tattered coat upon a stick, unless
> Soul clap its hands and sing, and louder sing
> For every tatter in its mortal dress. . . .

Melville and the Negro:
From *Typee* to "Benito Cereno"

Eleanor E. Simpson

I NASMUCH AS MELVILLE PUBLISHED most of his best work in the years
between the Mexican and Civil Wars—the years during which the
interconnected problems of westward expansion and slavery reached
crisis stage—it might seem, as Sidney Kaplan thinks, "not surprising that from *Typee* in 1846 to the *Battle-Pieces* of 1866 there is
scarcely an important item in the Melville canon that does not contain Negro characters or touch in some way the question of bondage
and revolt."[1] Yet the frequency and importance of the Negro's role
in Melville's work is, in fact, surprising in view of the absence of
black men from the work of his contemporaries.

Though Negroes figure prominently in such abolitionist efforts
as *Uncle Tom's Cabin,* they seldom appear in the nonpropagandistic
writings of Melville's literary peers. Emerson, Thoreau, and Whittier, for example, may have spoken and editorialized against the
evils of slavery and the wickedness of Daniel Webster and Judge
Shaw, but Negroes as individuals have no place in their poetry.
Negroes do, of course, figure in Whitman's work, but *Leaves of
Grass* was published four years after *Moby-Dick,* and Whitman
was not widely known until still later. Mention of Negroes and
slavery is also conspicuously absent from the stories and novels of
Melville's close friend and correspondent Nathaniel Hawthorne
(though he discusses the slavery issue in his campaign biography of
Franklin Pierce, whose administration was pro-slavery). Furthermore, Melville's correspondence makes no reference to the slavery
issue. Even the letters to his father-in-law and confidant, Judge
Lemuel Shaw, contain no mention of either Negroes or slavery,
though Shaw was at the time embroiled in the fugitive slave cases

[1] Sidney Kaplan, "Herman Melville and the American National Sin," originally published in the *Journal of Negro History,* XLI, 311-338 (Oct., 1956) and XLII, 11-37 (Jan.,
1957). My references are to the article as reprinted in *Images of the Negro in American
Literature,* ed. Seymour L. Gross and John Edward Hardy (Chicago, 1966), p. 135.

and the Boston school segregation case which made him famous (or infamous, if one took the abolitionists' view). Considering this lack of literary precedent, then, we should not expect to find Melville in his fiction creating black characters and dealing with slavery as he does.

In discussing Melville's attitudes toward Negroes and slavery I have tried to avoid treating the stories and novels solely as historical documents—that is, as statements apart from the literary traditions and conventions in which they were written, because these often help to account for the way in which he portrays Negroes. When, for example, we find Melville relying on a literary convention or stereotype (the Rousseauistic "noble savage" or the "jolly African"), we may conclude one of four things: (1) he accepts the convention or stereotype as true, (2) he is not sufficiently interested in that particular character to go beyond the convention, (3) he desires to individualize the character but has been unable to break out of the convention, (4) he is consciously and deliberately using the convention, or stereotype, for thematic or artistic purposes. It would seem that Kaplan in his study, "Herman Melville and the American National Sin," has erred badly on occasion (as will be discussed below) by ignoring the possible relevance of such literary factors and by crediting only the first of these alternatives—that the stereotypes he uses actually represent Melville's own convictions.

I

The influence of literary tradition is most noticeable, as might be expected, in Melville's first two novels, the fledgling efforts of a young writer. Thus the liberal, equalitarian treatment of the island natives in *Typee* (1846) and *Omoo* (1847) is probably to be accounted for largely in terms of the literary convention of the "noble savage," rather than taken as a conscious exposition of racial attitudes.

In these early novels Melville was, after all, writing a couple of potboilers and although they contain many passages of serious, thoughtful prose, they should be seen in the light of the expectations of the reading public of the day. The account of travel to exotic lands—especially the still (for most Americans) idyllic South Sea Islands—was popular among nineteenth-century readers, and such accounts often included sentimentalized portraits of the natives. Since Melville had decided on a career as a professional writer and desired financial as well as artistic success, he was probably only giving the public what it had come to expect when he pictured the islanders as innocent, robust, charming people to whom the corruptions of civilization were unknown. Melville, of course, also had before him the example of Cooper, with his largely conventional and sentimental treatment of "nature's nobleman."

Since, then, Melville at this point would seem to be following established romantic conventions in his portraits of dark-skinned peoples, his praise of the natives and condemnation of exploitive white traders and missionaries is not to be wondered at, and probably not too much significance should be attached to what Kaplan calls "the clean atmosphere of physical democracy" present in *Typee* and *Omoo*.[2] Similarly, the stereotyped figures of "the jolly little Negro," Billy Loon, and the old cook, Baltimore, probably have little relevance to Melville's actual attitudes toward Negroes, except as perhaps demonstrating that at this early period he evidently had no deep convictions on the subject and accepted ready-made stereotypes without really examining them. That this acceptance was unconscious and uncritical would seem the more probable inasmuch as the stereotypes he uses in *Typee* and *Omoo* are the partially conflicting ones of the Negro as happy-go-lucky, mindless buffoon (Billy Loon) and as "noble savage" (the Typee warrior), with its implications of dignity and strength. It should be noted also that these early portraits of the islanders are not unequivocally laudatory. Their romantic coloring is somewhat qualified, for example, by the fact that Tommo's injury continues to trouble him despite his idyllic surroundings. Also, there is no gainsaying the repulsion aroused in the narrator by his hosts' cannibalism and by their violent attempt to prevent his escape from the island.

In *Mardi*, Melville's next novel (1849), most of the dark-skinned islanders encountered merely serve the allegorical purpose of the author and are on the whole treated in the same manner as those in the earlier books. Exceptions to this generally causal treatment are Samoa and Annatoo, an islander and his termagant wife encountered aboard an abandoned brigantine. Annatoo is primarily a

[2] Kaplan, p. 136.

comic character who, having fulfilled her duty to amuse the reader, conveniently falls overboard. Though at first depicted comically as her henpecked husband, Samoa soon acquires an individualized personality of considerable dignity and, with it, the narrator's increasing respect. The narrator imputes to him the capacity for both good and evil action, thus breaking from stereotypes of uncivilized persons as either "jolly" or vicious. Samoa is "a man who, without precisely meditating mischief, could upon occasion act an ugly part." Although the narrator's description still retains a hint of condescension ("of his courage and savage honor, such as it was, I had little doubt"), Samoa is on the whole characterized primarily in terms of the noble savage, but with some attempt at individualization. Like the later Queequeg, of whom he is partially a prototype, Samoa is something of a "George Washington cannibalistically developed"; though he wears a knife sheathed in an earlobe and a polished nail through his nose, he is a "hero" reminiscent of Lord Nelson and Napoleon, and he has "a soul in his eye looking out upon you there, like somebody in him."[3]

Mardi contains Melville's most explicit attack on slavery. In the course of their allegorical journey, the narrator Taji and his companions enter the Republic of Vivenza (the United States). Its motto, "In this republican land all men are born free and equal," is followed by an Orwellian postscript in very small letters: "except the tribe of Hamo." In the Temple of Freedom (the United States Senate) caricatures of Webster and Calhoun debate the Fugitive Slave Act. Among these "dogmatically democratic" Vivenzians, "there's not so much freedom . . . as these freemen think," as the philosopher Babbalanja observes. The Temple of Freedom is, after all, "the handiwork of slaves" (p. 431).

In the extreme south of the republic the travelers see slaves at work in the fields; it is a static, decaying and cheerless land over which "men with thongs" rule. Portraying Calhoun (called "Nulli" for his nullification doctrine) as a harsh overseer, Melville mocks the argument that Negroes have no souls and are thus not fully human. "Their ancestors may have had," Nulli asserts, "but their souls have been bred out of their descendants, as the instinct of scent is

---

[3] *Mardi, and a Voyage Thither* (New York, 1964), pp. 91-93. Hereafter, page numbers of Melville's works will be cited in parentheses in the text for convenience; all citations refer to editions given in the notes.

killed in pointers." Yoomy, the poet, remains unconvinced. After carefully examining one of the slaves, he muses, "I swear he is a man." "Under the lash," replies the Negro, "I believe my masters and account myself a brute, but in my dreams bethink myself an angel. But I am bond, and my little ones—their mother's milk is gall." Nulli finds it advantageous to evade this dangerous debate about the Negro's soul and counters with the well-known assertion that his slaves are at least well fed and cared for. They are content in their ignorance and are better off than the "serfs" who work in Northern factories and mills. To Nulli these skeptical visitors are "incendiaries" and "fanatics" come to instigate revolt, always the most sensitive issue for Southerners, as Melville knew (pp. 439-442).

Despite the travelers' unmistakable sympathy for the slaves, in *Mardi* their future is left in doubt. Though slavery is a sin, "a blot foul as the crater poor of hell," though the narrator knows that lamenting the slaves' lot does not help to alleviate it ("tears are not swords"), he is nevertheless unwilling to precipitate civil war in order to free the slaves (pp. 441-442). Kaplan objects to what he considers Melville's defeatist attitude: "Whereas the abolitionists are optimistic actionists of one kind or another, for Melville the slaves' plight is completely hopeless."[4] Such a judgment, I suggest, errs in confusing literature with history; its implied demand that Melville be an "optimistic actionist" ignores the fact that the writer's first duty is to his art as art, not as propaganda. Further, to chide Melville for this position is to assume that his characters' opinions are his own, certainly a doubtful assumption.

II

Melville's characterization of Negroes in *Redburn* (1849) and *White-Jacket* (1850) is more equalitarian and less indebted to literary convention and stereotype than in any of his previous works. On the whole, Negroes in these two books are neither patronized as jolly minstrels nor sentimentalized as noble savages. This is especially appropriate in that these novels of the seaman's life are based closely on Melville's own experience, and it is probable that most of his first-hand contact with Negroes came during those years

[4] Kaplan, p. 139.

when he shared the forecastle and seamen's mess with them aboard whalers and frigates.

The two Negroes on board Redburn's ship are both types, it is true, but the interesting thing is that they are not particularly Negro types; most of the narrator's description of them would apply just as well were they white. The steward, "a handsome, dandy mulatto" (p. 80), is, like innumerable fictional stewards, fastidious of his dress and "a sad profligate and gay deceiver ashore, addicted to every youthful indiscretion" (p. 51).[5] The second Negro is the cook, Mr. Thompson. Secreted away in his shack, from which emerge the proverbially rank odors and bad coffee, he reads his greasy Bible in the manner of several fictional old cooks and spends his spare time trying to reform the steward.

Like *Mardi, Redburn* was written during the course of the Congressional debates over the Fugitive Slave Act and the Compromise of 1850. As in the earlier book, Melville has something to say in *Redburn* about slavery and also about the condition of the free Negro. The young protagonist, wandering around Liverpool on leave, comes upon the statue of Lord Nelson. The manacled figures ornamenting the base of the statue, though meant to represent Nelson's victories, remind the American of "four African slaves in the market place." Musing on the historical position of Liverpool as a center of the slave trade, Redburn involuntarily associates the city with Virginia and Carolina. His are abolitionist sympathies; he sees those who defend slavery as defenders of a "sordid interest" against the claims of humanity (pp. 148-149).

The narrator also finds himself comparing the status of Negroes in Liverpool with that of free Negroes in the northern cities of the United States. He notices, for example, that the Liverpool slums are inhabited by whites, in contrast to those of the "free states," where black people "almost always form a considerable portion of the destitute" (p. 194). Redburn also remarks that American Negro sailors are much freer in Liverpool than in their own country: "In Liverpool indeed the negro steps with a prouder pace, and lifts his head like a man; for here, no such exaggerated feeling exists in respect to him, as in America." Redburn has several times encountered the mulatto steward out with white women, something which

[5] *Redburn, His First Voyage* (Garden City, N. Y., 1957).

he realizes would provoke mob violence in New York, but which in the English city is not at all remarkable. He acknowledges that, "unconsciously swayed in some degree by those local and social prejudices that are the marring of most men," he was "surprised that a colored man should be treated as he is in this town; but a little reflection showed that, after all, it was but recognizing his claims to humanity and normal equality. . . ." And he adds wryly that "in some things, we Americans leave to other countries the carrying out of the principle that stands at the head of our Declaration of Independence" (p. 195).

In *White-Jacket* Melville attacks all forms of arbitrary government and legalized brutality. Though his immediate target is the military machine as codified in the Articles of War, his whole stance is one of democratic rebellion against any law or act of government which undermines or simply ignores the dignity and rights of men. There is an unusually large number of Negroes among the *Neversink's* crew. Four of them—the cook, Old Coffee, and his three assistants, May-day, Rosewater, and Sunshine—are essentially portrayed in the same vein as Billy Loon; that is, though treated sympathetically, they are not really taken seriously as human beings. The same does not apply, however, to the two Negro seamen. One, captain of White Jacket's gun crew, is a "fine negro" who, prefiguring Daggoo and Queequeg of *Moby-Dick,* commands the narrator's outspoken admiration. The other, Tawney, is described as intelligent and dignified and is highly regarded by his fellow seamen. It is especially significant that these two Negroes are delineated as individuals, with little of the stereotype about them, as this would indicate that Melville is coming to rely less on conventional images and more on personal evaluation.

III

Probably for most Americans of the period the best-known literary statement on slavery and the Northerner's obligation to the fugitive slave was *Uncle Tom's Cabin* (1852). There is evidence, however, that Melville's alertness to the problem and dissatisfaction with the Fugitive Slave Act had found expression in *Moby-Dick* a year earlier. Two men close to Melville were involved in the case of Thomas Simms, a fugitive slave from Georgia, who was tried

before the Massachusetts Supreme Court in April, 1851. Melville's
father-in-law, Lemuel Shaw, was Chief Justice of that court, and
his friend Richard Henry Dana was one of the attorneys retained to
defend Simms.

Shaw had made himself widely unpopular in Massachusetts when
in a similar case in 1842 he had ordered the return of the slave
George Latimer to Virginia. At that time 50,000 citizens of the
state had signed a petition protesting his decision, a petition which
former President John Quincy Adams had tried—unsuccessfully—
to present to Congress. Whittier had written his poem "Massachusetts to Virginia" in protest, and Garrison and Phillips had
joined in the attack on Shaw.

The Simms case served to revive the abolitionists' animosity. The
runaway, arrested in Boston, was ordered by Shaw returned to
Savannah, where he received a public whipping. During his trial
an iron chain had encircled the court building, together with an
armed guard of police. This chain furnished the Judge's critics
with a ready-made propaganda weapon. Wendell Phillips, for example, castigated him for having "betrayed the bench and the
courts of the Commonwealth, and the honor of a noble profession
when . . . he crept under a chain into his own courtroom." The
chain, Phillips continued, was a mark of "wanton servility to the
slave power . . . and wanton flattery to Daniel Webster."[6]

Lemuel Shaw had been a close friend of the Melville family
even before Herman's marriage to his daughter, after which the
bond of affection between the two men had grown stronger. It is
certainly possible, therefore, that Melville discussed with his father-
in-law the Latimer and Simms cases and others (such as the Roberts
school segregation case of 1849, in which Shaw, upholding Boston's
segregated school system, had established the "separate but equal"
doctrine). Despite his knowledge of Shaw's position and his own
affection for the Judge, however, Melville had not hesitated to speak
out against slavery in *Mardi* and in favor of free Negroes' rights in
Redburn and to delineate many Negroes sympathetically in his
novels. Though not an abolitionist and consistently skeptical of

[6] Wendell Phillips, "Surrender of Sims," in *Speeches, Lectures, and Letters*, First Series
(Boston, 1891), p. 62. For a summary of these incidents, see Charles H. Foster, "Something in Emblems," *New England Quarterly*, XXXIV, 3-35 (March, 1961).

reform movements, Melville probably was in conflict with his family's patriarchal head on this matter.

Though I do not think the evidence supports Professor Foster's thesis that in *Moby-Dick* Melville produced "a democratic, antislavery fable, . . . a revolt against Judge Shaw," it would appear that, as he suggests, particular passages do allude to slavery and perhaps specifically to the Simms case.[7] There are many indications that Melville, who reported to Dana in May, 1850, that he was half-way through the novel, later began rewriting it, perhaps radically changing its course. Although he originally assured his publisher that the book would be ready by fall, 1850, it was not sent off until September of the next year. Leon Howard suggests that Melville's radical rewriting began in September, 1850, the month in which the Fugitive Slave Act took effect.[8] George R. Stewart, working from internal evidence, also concludes that major revisions were made in the course of composition.[9] Some of them may well have come during the spring of 1851, possibly at the time of the Simms trial. Thus, two events pertinent to the fugitive slave issue took place during the course of the composition of *Moby-Dick* and may have figured in its repeated revision.

Building on Stewart's analysis, Foster suggests that Father Mapple's sermon (Chapter 9) and the role of the Negro Pip were among Melville's later insertions, and that the sermon covertly expresses Melville's dissatisfaction with Judge Shaw's handling of the Simms case. This would seem plausible in view of the preacher's exhortation that we must destroy all sin, though "[we] pluck it out from under the robes of Senators and Judges" (p. 57).[10] Foster is surely right in thinking that for many New Englanders of the day, the most sinful senator was Daniel Webster, and that, for Melville especially, Judge might well mean Lemuel Shaw.[11]

Even if Melville's characterization of the Negroes aboard the *Pequod* was not consciously intended as a reaction to Shaw's conservatism, it is difficult to conceive how he could have more effectively refuted the assumptions which underlay that conservatism—

[7] Foster, p. 21.

[8] Leon Howard, *Melville: A Biography* (Berkeley, 1951), pp. 162-172.

[9] George R. Stewart, "The Two *Moby-Dicks*," *American Literature*, XXV, 417-448 (Jan., 1954).

[10] *Moby-Dick: or, The Whale*, ed. Alfred Kazin (Boston, 1956).

[11] Foster, pp. 16-20.

the assumption that the slave was property rather than person, that legalism rather than conscience or humanitarianism was adequate to decide the Negro's status. Certainly Ishmael's statements about Queequeg conflict radically with then-current notions concerning the Negro's supposed inferiority, his limited intelligence, his lack of morals, and brutishness. Though perhaps not technically a Negro—he is from one of the South Pacific islands—Queequeg is described as though he were. He worships a Negro idol (a "black manikin," a "Congo doll"), and Ishmael's reflection that a white man is really "a white-washed negro" implies that he was thinking of Queequeg in these terms.

The most fervent abolitionist could hardly have asked for anything more liberal than Ishmael's attitude toward Queequeg; in fact, Ishmael is frequently more radical in his equalitarian views than the abolitionists themselves who, though unwavering in their opposition to slavery, were considerably less certain about the desirability of social equality and integration. Though they realized that to be consistent they also had to work for equal rights for free Negroes, most abolitionists were nonetheless reluctant to flout custom and mix socially with black men. The contention aroused over the question of admitting Negroes to the antislavery societies demonstrates how strong this inhibition was.[12] The Garrisons, Phillipses, Whittiers, and their like had, it is certain, never experienced the close contact with Negroes which Melville had known as a seaman. Therefore, the picture of Ishmael, descended (like Redburn and Melville himself) from a genteel Yankee family, sharing a bed and becoming "chums" (the seaman's word) with Queequeg, was probably a bit extreme even for the most advanced antislavery man.

Ishmael, faced with the prospect of close contact with Queequeg, is, in fact, less concerned about the latter's race than about his "heathenish" appearance and his cannibalism. Ishmael's decision that "the man's a human being just as I am, . . . better sleep with a sober cannibal than a drunken Christian," recalls the attitude of the narrator of *Typee* (*Moby-Dick*, p. 40). Queequeg, he discovers, has "a simple honest heart; his countenance yet had a something in it which was by no means disagreeable. You cannot hide the soul"

[12] See Leon F. Litwack, "The Abolitionist Dilemma: The Anti-Slavery Movement and the Northern Negro," *New England Quarterly*, XXXIV, 50-73 (March, 1961).

(p. 58). There is "a certain lofty bearing about the pagan. . . . He looked like a man who had never cringed and never had had a creditor." Queequeg is nothing less than "George Washington cannibalistically developed," self-sufficient, serene, with a "Socratic wisdom" (p. 58).

Queequeg, of course, plays a crucial role in one of the novel's major thematic developments—the redemption of Ishmael from his initial despair and, in the epilogue, his symbolic redemption from the destruction which has befallen the rest of the crew. Queequeg's forthright and unsentimental offer of friendship dissolves the mood of despair in which Ishmael had set out: "No more my splintered heart and maddened hand were turned against the wolfish world. This soothing savage had redeemed it. There he sat, his very indifference speaking a nature in which there lurked no civilized hypocrisies and bland deceits. . . . I'll try a pagan friend, thought I, since Christian kindness has proved but hollow courtesy" (p. 59). The references to "soothing savage" and "civilized hypocrisies" may reveal some lingering influence of the noble savage convention, but the relationship between Ishmael and his friend is developed for the most part in terms not marred by resort to such models.

The genuineness of Ishmael's attitude is affirmed by an incident which might well have had its parallel whenever a white and a Negro were seen together: on the crossing to Nantucket, Ishmael and Queequeg draw "jeering glances" from their fellow passengers, "who marvelled that two fellow beings should be so companionable; as though a white man were any thing more dignified than a white-washed Negro" (p. 65). This last statement is startling in that it goes far beyond the position of most abolitionists. Later white liberals, in fact, seldom achieve this detachment, for the assumptions implicit in Ishmael's phrase are the opposite of those which underlie, for example, Kenneth Stampp's faintly condescending comment that Negroes are "white men with brown skins."

Daggoo, a "gigantic, coal-black negro-savage," is, like Queequeg and the Indian Tashtego, one of the *Pequod's* harpooners. Again in Melville's description of the African there is something of the noble savage convention ("Daggoo retained all his barbaric virtues"), but at the same time Melville takes the opportunity to introduce explicit Negro-white comparisons, in which the latter comes off second best: "a white man standing before him [Daggoo] seemed a white flag come to beg truce of a fortress" (p. 108). Furthermore, Melville's African in no sense fits the complacent American stereotype of the Negro as docile and self-effacing. Daggoo, proud of his race ("Who's afraid of black's afraid of me! I'm quarried out of it!"), is challenged by another sailor who taunts him: "Thy race is the undeniable dark side of mankind—develish dark at that." The African calls the other's bluff, and in the ensuing fight Melville makes clear that this is not just another skirmish between sailors. It is a contest between black man and white man: "White skin, white liver!" Daggoo cries, leaping on his opponent (p. 148). Though Melville will in "Benito Cereno" develop thematically the white seaman's identification of the Negro with diabolism, he is here clearly on the Negro's side.

The cabin boy Pip is another Negro who plays a significant role aboard the *Pequod*. Introduced as the happy-go-lucky, tambourine-playing black boy of the stereotype, he is soon given another, more serious and more individualized dimension. It is Pip who perceives the full significance for himself and the rest of the crew of Ahab's determination to hunt down the white whale: "Oh, thou big white God aloft there somewhere in yon darkness, have mercy on this small black boy down here; preserve him from all men that have no bowels to feel fear!" (p. 149). His prayer, with its race-conscious overtones and following as it does immediately upon Daggoo's fight with the white sailor, would seem to be part of that racial theme first noted in relation to Queequeg, a theme which reappears in Pip's later scenes.

As Foster has observed, the cabin boy becomes a really significant figure only toward the end of the book, and then rather suddenly and inexplicably. Approximately one-third of the novel's bulk separates Pip's prayer to the "big white God" and the very important scene as castaway which grooms him for his role as Fool to Ahab's Lear. If, however, as Foster believes, Melville created Pip toward the end to humanize the mad Ahab and then went back and inserted the earlier mention of him, Pip's prayer is to be seen as congruent with the later episode, in which the fact of his race is also emphasized.[18] Too, if Melville had been interested only in the Lear's-Fool quality

[18] Foster, pp. 24-25.

of Pip, a white cabin boy would have served as well; yet he makes Pip a Negro and calls attention to this fact both in the prayer and in the opening lines of "The Castaway."

The possibility that Pip is meant to function as—among other things—a vehicle for comment on slavery may account for the otherwise somewhat superfluous incident of his first leap overboard and Stubb's subsequent lecture on the relative value of whales and black men. Pip first leaps out of the whaleboat when, put in as a substitute oarsman, he becomes frightened during the chase. With the bowline wrapped around his chest and neck, he is being drawn through the water beside the boat while Stubb, the mate, must decide whether to cut the line, thus saving Pip but losing the whale. The rope is cut and Pip saved, but only to take a tongue-lashing from the boat's crew for costing them their catch. The terms of profit and loss in which Stubb and the narrator comment on Pip's action gives this episode more than passing significance. After Stubb has "in a plain, business-like, but still half humorous manner, cursed Pip officially," he advises him never again to jump from a boat. But, as the narrator comments, though "stick to the boat" is usually the best motto in whaling, there are occasions when "leap from the boat" is even better. Stubb is aware of this, yet

as if perceiving at last that if he should give undiluted conscientious advice to Pip, he would be leaving him too wide a margin to jump in for the future; Stubb suddenly dropped all advice, and concluded with a peremptory command, "Stick to the boat, Pip, or, by the Lord, I won't pick you up if you jump; mind that. We can't afford to lose whales by the likes of you; a whale would sell for thirty times what you would, Pip, in Alabama."

And the narrator adds, "perhaps Stubb indirectly hinted, that though man loved his fellow, yet man is a money-making animal, which propensity too often interferes with his benevolence" (pp. 320-321).

This passage, whose length and detail is unnecessary to the major castaway scene which follows, constitutes, I think, another of those oblique comments on Negro-white relations which are to be found scattered throughout the novel. It is certainly pertinent to the problem which fugitive slaves posed for Northern commercial interests, circa 1851. From an ideological and humanitarian standpoint, the North would be expected at least to admit—if not actually encourage—fugitives. But, as Melville's narrator observes, "man is a money-making animal," and Northern businessmen were overwhelmingly opposed to the abolitionists' efforts to encourage runaway slaves. Abolitionist agitation, in the eyes of such men, posed a dangerous threat to profits, and they were loath to exchange a whale—or anything else—for a black man like Pip. I conclude, then, that two aspects of Pip's role are important for this study: (1) the fact that he is delineated as a rather complex individual with a crucial part to play in the drama, rather than as a stereotyped Sambo, and (2) the fact that the prayer and castaway scene reveal Melville's continued concern with slavery, especially the plight of the fugitive slave.

The last Negro to appear in *Moby-Dick* is the old cook Fleece, whose sermon to the sharks mixes humor with a serious bit of philosophizing pertinent to the novel's theme. Beyond this moment of seriousness, however, Fleece is definitely a comic character. Stubb has some fun ordering the "old black" around, and though the ordering is harmless enough and not of a malicious sort, it places the cook in the convention of the stage "darky" who shuffles through his part, speaking in thick dialect and obeying the white man's orders, however sulkily (pp. 235-238). Kaplan, incidentally, disagrees; in his view, Fleece is saved from the stereotype by his sardonic remark about church membership ("unlike his predecessors, he is no devout Uncle Tom") and his sermon to the sharks.[14] The scene between Fleece and Stubb, however, continues for two pages beyond this sermon, and in those pages Fleece plays his comic role on cue. It might be interesting to speculate why Melville has stereotyped this one Negro when he has taken care to avoid such treatment of the others in *Moby-Dick*. Since we can only speculate, it seems reasonable to accept the simplest explanation—that he needed comic relief at this point and furnished it through the cook and Stubb.

IV

Melville's work between *Moby-Dick* and "Benito Cereno" contains little that is relevant to this study. The playing off of the blonde Lucy against the dark Isabel in *Pierre* (1852), for example, seems an entirely conventional use of dark-light symbolism similar to the

---

[14] Kaplan, p. 150.

opposition of the blonde Yillah and the dark Hautia in *Mardi*. "Benito Cereno," then, of the many short stories Melville wrote in these years, is the one most clearly concerned with Negroes.

This novella, originally published in the October, November, and December, 1855, issues of *Putnam's Monthly Magazine*, was included the next year in the *Piazza Tales*. In view of his sustained interest in racial themes, it is not surprising that Melville would have written a story of slave revolt, especially at the height of the Southern panic on the subject. It is interesting, however, that not one of the eight periodicals which reviewed the *Piazza Tales* suggested that the story might be of topical interest. Even George W. Curtis, editorial consultant to the publisher of the *Piazza Tales*, who thought the story "very good," evidently failed to see in it any significance for contemporary events.[15]

Yet these were, after all, years not only of mounting fear of slave revolts in the South, but years also of fighting over the extension of slavery in Kansas, in which a large contingent of New Englanders took part, and of increasing traffic on the underground railroad. The thesis that Melville is in fact talking about slave insurrection here is substantiated by H. Bruce Franklin's observation that one of the changes Melville made in his source (*Narrative of the Voyages and Travels of Amasa Delano*) was to move the date from 1805 back to 1799, thus making Babo's revolt correspond to the rule of Toussaint L'Ouverture on Santo Domingo.[16]

Despite the wishful thinking of some well-intentioned liberals, it is clear that Melville did not intend Babo and his mutinous Negroes to come off as heroic fighters against oppression and injustice, thus allowing us to read the story as an antislavery tract. Melville wastes no time making clear what it is about the Negroes aboard the *San Dominick* that Captain Delano fails to see: it is their malice, their evil. On the story's opening page we are told that Captain Amasa Delano is "a person of a singularly undistrustful good nature, not liable, except on extraordinary and repeated incentives, and hardly then, to indulge in personal alarms, any way involving the

[15] These reviews are listed in Jay Leyda, *The Melville Log* (New York, 1951), II, 500-501.

[16] H. Bruce Franklin, "Apparent Symbol of Despotic Command: Melville's *Benito Cereno*," *New England Quarterly*, XXXIV, 470 (Dec., 1961).

imputation of malign evil in man" (p. 3).[17] Moreover, the whole technique of the story rests upon Delano's inability to distinguish between appearance and reality, thereby insuring the reality of anything he persists in believing unreal—such as the possibility of foul play on the part of the blacks. Neither should Cereno's last words leave any room for doubt concerning their real character. Throughout the story Don Benito is consistently portrayed as the man whose eyes have been opened—the good man who trusted only to have that trust betrayed, the Old World European whose sense of the reality of evil has not been dulled by the bland optimism of nineteenth-century America. Therefore, when he answers "The Negro" to Delano's query, "You are saved; what has cast such a shadow over you?" it is clear that to the Spaniard—the perceiver of truth— "Negro" is synonymous with "evil" (p. 90).

Don Benito's perception of the Negro is true; Delano's false— that much is clear. What, then, had Delano's perception been before his horrifying discovery? The American had complacently seen Negroes in terms of the prevailing stereotype—as docile, good-natured, and incapable of malice or any action that demanded intelligence or calculated planning. "The whites," he thought, "were by nature the shrewder race . . . the blacks too stupid" to connive (p. 39). The Negroes have a "peculiar love . . . of uniting industry with pasttime," he remarks with unconscious irony on seeing four old men busily polishing hatchets on deck. Fit by nature for menial tasks, they perform them zealously and thus make "the most pleasing body servant[s] in the world"; they are "natural valets and hairdressers" particularly suited to domestic employments by their "great gift of good humor . . . a certain easy cheerfulness, harmonious in every glance and gesture; as though God had set the whole negro to some pleasant tune." Delano's complacent and benevolent nature is especially impressed with the Negro's "docility, arising from the unaspiring contentment of a limited mind, and that susceptibility of blind attachment sometimes inhering in indisputable inferiors. . . ." Delano applauds that something about the Negro which—as he thinks—"exempts him from [that] inflicted sourness of the morbid or cynical mind" which in Don Benito so depresses him (p. 49).

[17] "Benito Cereno," in *Selected Tales and Poems by Herman Melville*, ed. Richard Chase (New York, 1950).

Captain Delano is by nature "not only benign, but familiarly and humorously so" and is patronizingly benevolent toward Negroes in a way that passed for tolerance in that day (as in this). He enjoys watching them at work or play and likes to be "on chatty and half-gamesome terms" with those among his crew. "In fact, like most men of a good, blithe heart, Captain Delano took to negroes, not philanthropically, but genially, just as other men to Newfoundland dogs" (p. 50).

If it is this complacent, stereotyped image of the Negro that Melville's story declares false—as it surely is—what are we to put in its place? For purposes of this particular story at least, the transformation of images is clear: the idyllic picture of the sleeping Negro woman, "like a doe in the shade of a woodland rock" (p. 36), gives way abruptly to the vision of that same woman, more sadistic even than the male, urging the slaves on to bloodthirsty revolt. Has Melville, then, gone to an opposite extreme from that which delineated Queequeg, Daggoo and Pip? Has he, as Kaplan asserts, repudiated "his superficial, old notions (which were Delano's too) about the innately jolly, minstrel, religious nature of Negroes" only to transmute them into "hatred of the 'ferocious pirates' of the *San Dominick. . .*"?[18]

Kaplan sees "Benito Cereno" as "an artistic sublimation of . . . notions of black primitivism dear to the hearts of slavery's apologists, a sublimation in fact of all that was sleazy, patronizing, backward and fearful in the works that preceded it." As such, he says, the story is a failure: "looked at objectively, the tale seems a plummet-like drop from the unconditionally democratic peaks of *White-Jacket* and *Moby-Dick. . . .*" Melville, Kaplan thinks, is well rid of his shallow primitivistic notions, but has overreacted and failed to "perceive the free spirit of the Tawneys and the Daggoos as the reality behind the masks."[19]

A number of comments might be made on this evaluation. For one thing, Kaplan has erred rather badly in confusing the criteria appropriate to a work of fiction with those appropriate to a tract on race relations. When he judges "Benito Cereno" a failure, he is really saying that Melville has failed to take what Kaplan thinks is the proper attitude toward Negroes. But literary works are not to

[18] Kaplan, p. 155.
[19] *Ibid.*, pp. 154-155.

be judged in these terms. Kaplan, moreover, is hardly being more "objective" than Melville; he is merely biased in another direction, as his glorification of "the free spirit of the Tawneys and the Daggoos" reveals. Furthermore, he makes the gratuitous assumption that Delano's attitudes are Melville's, a confusion which adherence to the most elementary principles of literary criticism would have helped him avoid. It is particularly strange that Kaplan would impute "superficial old notions" to Melville, inasmuch as he spends the bulk of his essay insisting that Melville was seldom dominated by such prejudices.

Finally, we must ask whether Melville is in fact seeking to destroy the image of "black primitivism dear to the hearts of slavery's apologists" in order (presumably) to warn Southerners of the real dangers lurking among carelessly guarded slaves. I don't think so. In the first place, Southern slaveholders evidently did not believe those platitudes about black primitivism and docility that they published for Northern consumption—and perhaps as reassurance for Southern ladies. The existence of the slave codes and the care taken to prevent slaves from acquiring anything which might be used as a weapon indicates this much.

It was, rather, the Northerner, whether abolitionist or not, who was most likely to accept the image of the Negro as primitive. It was an abolitionist, James Freeman Clarke, who in an article addressed to free Negroes inadvertently associated them with animals (and apes at that); admonishing them to acquire wealth as the surest way to social acceptance, he assured them that "no race in this country will be despised which makes money. If we had in Boston or New York ten orang-outangs worth a million dollars each, they would visit in the best society. . . ."[20] Another antislavery man, Charles Stuart, asserted, Delano-like, that Negroes were guilty of fewer "atrocious crimes" because they were "less ferocious, less proud, and passionate and revengeful, than others."[21] William Ellery Channing, in an essay on "The African Character," with which Melville may have been acquainted, claimed that Negroes were by nature docile, friendly, and cheerful and that if they possessed less

[20] James Freeman Clarke, "Condition of the Free Colored People of the United States," *Christian Examiner*, LXVI, 264 (March, 1859).

[21] Charles Stuart, "On the Colored People of the United States," *Quarterly Anti-Slavery Magazine*, II, 16 (Oct., 1836).

energy and courage than whites and were inferior intellectually, they compensated for this in their "amiableness, tranquillity, gentleness, and content."[22]

The abolitionists thus helped perpetuate both the docile primitive and Sambo stereotypes; instead of questioning these images, they claimed that such qualities—since they rendered Negroes both harmless and likable—formed no obstacle to political and social rights for free Negroes or to freeing the slaves. White spokesmen for Negro rights probably relied on such stereotypes to evoke sympathy, inasmuch as they permitted the public to retain undisturbed its assumptions of the Negro's inferiority and at the same time to be "tolerant" and "Christian" at no risk. It is well known that any demonstration of intellectual or moral superiority by Negroes was apt to cause the abolitionists considerable embarrassment; Frederick Douglass's refusal to act the role of Uncle Tom for them is a case in point.

Northern whites thus accepted and perpetuated images of the Negro which were not only false and derogatory, but which masked the depth of that hatred and violence which slavery could breed in its victims. In "Benito Cereno" Melville has indeed struck through the mask. He has said, not that Negroes in general are bestial and malevolent, but that Negroes—like other men—are capable of extreme violence and sadistic cruelty, especially when subjected to the dehumanizing conditions of slavery. Given this capability, bland stereotypes are not only irrelevant but dangerous. It is not Delano's faith in human goodness that saves him, but Don Benito's appreciation of the possibilities of human malevolence. It would seem, then, that in Amasa Delano, Melville has portrayed—indeed, parodied—certain of his fellow Northerners. Delano, significantly, is a Massachusetts man; in fact that is the first thing we are told about him.

It is interesting to speculate as to how much Melville knew or suspected about Negro role-playing and accommodation techniques. Inasmuch as he was capable of seeing the inconsistencies and dangers of Delano-like complacency, it is not unlikely that he also suspected that Sambo was essentially a role which the Negro played, often consciously and shrewdly, but which could be shed when circumstances permitted. For this is exactly what the Negroes aboard

[22] William Ellery Channing, "The African Character," in *The Anti-Slavery Picknick: A Collection of Speeches, Poems, Dialogues and Songs; Intended for Use in Schools and Anti-Slavery Meetings*, ed. John A. Collins (Boston, 1842), pp. 56-58.

the *San Dominick* are doing—Babo especially. He is role-playing to the hilt, making use of techniques learned as a slave. Ironically, that is also what Don Benito is doing, and it is his role-playing which ultimately saves both his own life and the more candid, utterly guileless Delano's. As he reminds Delano at the end, the latter had been walking on treacherous ground all along, but lulled by his trust in the "docile" Negro—which the slaves had done everything possible to confirm—he had been unaware of his danger.

In objecting to Melville's imputation of malice to Negroes, Kaplan reveals that, like many white liberals, he wishes to exchange one stereotype (Negro as primitive) for another (Negro as hero— as "free spirit"). But if one must go to extremes, it is surely more complimentary to the Negro to credit him with Babo's intelligence and boldness than to perpetuate the prevailing image of guileless— because mindless—docility. Moreover, evil is always more real for Melville than good, and life for him is never one-sided. It was the ambiguity and mystery of man's nature—black and white—that fascinated him, and it is the artistically successful creation of these elements that makes "Benito Cereno" a work of art—not a propaganda tract.

In reviewing Melville's treatment of Negroes and slavery from his first novel to the story in which these themes are most fully explored, we have perceived several changes in attitude. By the time of "Benito Cereno," Melville had come so far from the relatively facile, conventional portrayals of *Typee* and *Omoo* that the Negro Babo is not only individualized, but individualized in a manner radically opposite to all prevailing stereotypes. This would indicate that in the ten years between *Typee* and "Benito Cereno," Melville grew more thoughtful about and more deeply concerned with the Negro and slavery, as reflected in the increasing originality of his portrayals and his decreasing reliance on literary convention and popular stereotypes. Finally, he was able, unlike most people of his day—in North or South—to see Negroes as multifaceted, complex individuals, capable of both good and evil and neither simply docile not simply vicious. He had portrayed with equal accuracy— and artistic success—both Daggoo and Babo.

Melville's Bachelors and Maids:
Interpretation Through Symbol and Metaphor
Beryl Rowland

CRITICAL EXEGESIS of "The Paradise of Bachelors and the Tartarus of Maids" has focused on the longer of the two sketches. The first seems to acquire its significance largely through illumination thrown back on it by the tale of the maids, a work which could easily stand alone. There is little argument about the levels of meaning in the latter: in the general view, E. H. Eby's comment that the tale presents both the biological and social burdens of women is still valid. Related to the first part of the diptych, the two levels of meaning are appropriately extended or modified. For Eby, the maids' drudgery and female subjugation to biological processes contrast with the bachelors' happy life and male freedom.[1] For C. G. Hoffmann, W. R. Thompson, and R. H. Fogle, further dimensions are apparent: a distinction between "Old World leisure and New World industrialism";[2] an indictment of the moral weaknesses of both civilizations;[3] an attack on "mass production, the publishing business, and some theories of American democracy,"[4] with the first tale serving to point up comparison and contrast.

Most critics feel that the diptych is technically unsuccessful. The second tale is "bristling . . . with sexual symbols,"[5] but when the allegory is correlated with the first tale it seems to illustrate some tritely obvious fact of life. Melville's serious critical purpose in linking the civilizations of Europe and America does not come through because of a "structural flaw."[6] His oblique approach ob-

---

[1] E. H. Eby, "Herman Melville's 'Tartarus of Maids,'" *Modern Language Quarterly*, I, 100 (March, 1940).

[2] C. G. Hoffmann, "The Shorter Fiction of Herman Melville," *South Atlantic Quarterly*, LII, 424 (July, 1953).

[3] W. R. Thompson, " 'The Paradise of Bachelors and the Tartarus of Maids': A Reinterpretation," *American Quarterly*, IX, 44-45 (Spring, 1957).

[4] R. H. Fogle, *Melville's Shorter Tales* (Norman, Okla., 1960), pp. 53-54.

[5] Thompson, p. 35.

[6] Thompson, p. 34; Hoffmann, p. 424.

scures his honest, if pessimistic, analysis of the contemporary condition.

We know that Melville's vision was complex: his world was vast, strange, and of multiple meaning. He recognized that if he was to achieve his purpose and present timeless and unrestricted truth, he needed to find the right relation between subjective and objective modes of experience. His short fiction, written in the four-year period following the completion of *Pierre* in 1852, seems to have provided experimental answers to the problem raised in his now well-known letter to Hawthorne, June, 1851,[7] and to the difficulties of structural and artistic control which troubled him in longer works. In most instances he took some aspect of experience that defied expression and projected it into a single block of material which could be given pattern and structure.

Essential to his purpose was the employment of two interdependent strategies: the first-person narrator who, while posing as a rational, humane man, addressing readers similarly inclined, could become sufficiently disturbed by the action he related to reveal thoughts and behavior inconsistent with his chosen self-image; metaphors and symbols which served as vehicles for parabolic truth and had an organic, unifying function. The tropological approach was the natural outcome of Melville's "transcendentalism," which saw an infinity of correspondences between the visible and invisible world; symbol and metaphor were his principal means for revealing the "fruyt" beneath the "chaf."

In this diptych, the levels of meaning so far postulated, valid as they are, are subordinate. They fail to realize that a metaphor lies at the heart of the work. They reach only the cortex and miss the organic experience. Central to the diptych is a traditional metaphor which Melville uses in a highly original way, structuring his tales upon it with meticulous craftsmanship. I believe that he derived it from the argot of the streets and that he intended that it should control meaning, action, form, and imagery in the two parts of the diptych.

The mill may have originated in a documentary account of a visit to a New England paper factory, but it is also an almost bla-

[7] *The Letters of Herman Melville*, ed. Merrell R. Davis and William H. Gilman (New Haven, 1960), p. 128: "What I feel most moved to write, that is banned,—it will not pay. Yet, altogether, write the *other* way I cannot."

tant, basic symbol with very long traditions. When we perceive the figurative meaning, we find that the hell with which the diptych is concerned is not only that of woman in her service to the machine and to biology but that of man in his relationship or, rather, his *service* to woman. The concealment of the tenor is not due to artistic perversity or ineptness; it was the only way whereby Melville could communicate the incommunicable.

On one level the first part of the diptych is an ironic dissection of the "bachelors"—Melville's half-jocular term for those who think that they know how to live the good life, how to close their eyes to evil and pain, and who are, in reality, smug, unperceptive, and inadequate.[8] But the dominant protagonist here, as in the second part, is a man who, like Actaeon, is finally compelled to accept a role which he had not recognized as his, that of the impotent *voyeur*. For all the whimsy and nostalgia accompanying the description of the bachelors in their "snug cells,"[9] the irony indicates that, just as the girls are "mere cogs to the wheels" of the machine,[10] so these men live routine lives of quiet negation. The paradox is that while the narrator conveys their atrophied condition with such sensuous perceptiveness, experience topples him from a sophisticated and confident knowingness to the disturbed recognition that he is one of their company. The dinner, the journey, the exploration of the mill all become vehicles for conveying an aspect of human suffering epitomized in the "I" of the diptych.

The slang metaphor of the mill is of ancient origin, the grinding of the corn into life-giving flour being regarded as analogous to the creative act. Man was the miller, woman the mill, and the *Talmud*, commenting on Samson grinding in the prison-house, states: "It teaches that everyone brought his wife to him to prison that she might bear a child by him."[11] Job and Isaiah use the same imagery and St. John symbolizes the destruction of the Whore of Babylon as a stone "like a great millstone" cast into the sea.[12]

[8] On Melville's "bachelors" see Fogle, pp. 14 and n., 46 f., 50-51, 105, 132 f.
[9] "The Paradise of Bachelors and the Tartarus of Maids," in *The Complete Stories of Herman Melville*, ed. Jay Leyda (New York, 1949), p. 189, l. 5. All quotations are from this edition.
[10] P. 202, ll. 16-17.
[11] *The Babylonian Talmud*, ed. I. Epstein (London, 1936), Sotah, 10a.
[12] Job 31:9-10; Isa. 47:1-2; Rev. 18:21-24.

In England the idea was proverbial in Chaucer's day,[13] as it was in France,[14] and I have found numerous examples of its use in ballads and scurrilous verse from the fifteenth to the nineteenth century.[15] John Florio defines the associated verb in *A Worlde of Wordes*, 1598, when he translates *mancinio* as "the grinding or greest, also taken for carnall copulation,"[16] but by Burns's day the metaphor had been dropped from polite society.[17] It survives in "Bawdyhouse Blues," reputed to be a very old jazz song,[18] and is current today with all its associated imagery in a lively song of a reluctant but "cuddlesome lass" and an enterprising young man who "leapt with a will / And found her mill."[19] While "to do a grind" may simply refer to a rotation of the pelvis, it still most commonly denotes *futuere* and, indeed, might be a straight translation of *molere* as anciently used by Petronius and others.[20]

The early use of mill to express a fundamental concept, its persistence in proverb and in literature, point to continuous colloquial usage. It could apply to an individual woman or to women collectively as prostitutes,[21] and there is no reason to suppose that the metaphor ever lost its vitality.

Melville is known to have made extraordinary use of the resources of the language, particularly those of the vernacular. He had an intense interest in cant languages, and in *Moby-Dick* alone

---

[13] *The Works of Geoffrey Chaucer*, ed. F. N. Robinson (Boston, 1957), p. 80, l. 389; W. W. Skeat, *Early English Proverbs* (Oxford, 1910), p. 112.

[14] *Le Roman de la Rose*, ed. Ernest Langlois (Paris, 1920-1924), IV, 13145–13149; *Le Parnasse satyrique du quinzième siècle*, ed. M. Marcel Schwob (Paris, 1905), pp. 89, 220.

[15] BM. AD MS 22311, fol. 119; BM. AD MS 22312, fol. 188; the ballad of "my ladyes water-myll," *The Early English Carols*, ed. R. L. Greene (Oxford, 1935), p. 311; Henry Neville, *The Ladies' Parliament* (London, 1647), ll. 69-70, 139-140 ("Digbie's lady takes it ill, / that her lord grinds at her mill"; "Simons may rejoice still / that the Priest doth ply her mill"); Thomas d'Urfey, *Wit and Mirth or Pills to Purge Melancholy* (London, 1719-1720), I, 120, II, 61, V, 139; *The Tea-Table Miscellany*, ed. Allan Ramsay (Edinburgh, 1724), p. 153.

[16] London, 1598, p. 210.

[17] *The Letters of Robert Burns*, ed. J. De Lancey Ferguson (Oxford, 1931), II, 167: "The original song 'The Mill mill O' though excellent is, on account of decency, inadmissible." Burns to George Thompson, April 7, 1793.

[18] S. Longstreet, *The Real Jazz Old and New*, 52, cited in *Dictionary of American Slang*, ed. Harold Wentworth and Stuart Berg Flexner (New York, 1960), p. 230.

[19] Contributed to the writer by Earle Birney.

[20] *Satiric.*, xxiii, 4, Varro, *Menippearum Reliquiae*, 331.

[21] See "Colin Blowbol's Testament," *Nugae Poeticae*, ed. J. O. Halliwell (London, 1844), p. 5; "The Bel-man," *The Non-Dramatic Works of Thomas Dekker*, ed. Alexander B. Grosart (London, 1885), III, 52.

he employed some thirty terms for which the *New English Dictionary* and the *Dictionary of American English* quote him as being the first or sole user.[22] These are not words which he coined: they belong to argot which seldom finds it way into print. As C. M. Babcock has remarked:

His firsthand acquaintance with usages developed among the American people and his employment of these hitherto unrecorded words of the "national blood" makes of his published works an invaluable source book for American lexicographers. . . . Herman Melville derived his unique vocabulary from the "plain facts" of experience, observed in "the vulgar cauldron of an everlasting uncrystallising Present."[23]

Life was Melville's dictionary in the true Emersonian sense. His reading was astonishingly eclectic, as Sealts has shown, but it was probably from the streets that he acquired the metaphor of the mill and other comparable figurative expressions which he employs in other tales.[24] When we reexamine the diptych and interpret the mill in its popular sense, we find that the metaphor integrates the two experiences and milieux which, superficially, may seem so disparate.

At the time when Melville wrote the diptych the question whether the Templars were innocent of the charges for which they were condemned early in the fourteenth century was warmly debated. Chief among the charges was that of sodomy which had been "documented" as early as 1654 by Pierre du Puy, librarian to the Bibliothèque Royale, in order to exculpate the French monarchy.[25] In the nineteenth century the discussion received fresh impetus with the spirited defense of F. J. M. Raynouard in his *Monumens historiques, relatifs à la condamnation des chevaliers*

[22] C. Merton Babcock, "The Language of Melville's Isolatoes," *Western Folklore*, X, 286, n. 3 (October, 1951).

[23] C. Merton Babcock, "Melville's 'Moby Dictionary,'" *Word Study*, XXIX, 7-8 (December, 1953).

[24] In *Pierre* the guitar on which Isabel focuses her affections is clearly intended to be a symbol of the womb. Such symbolism is very ancient and can be traced back to the Egyptian sistrum. In "I and My Chimney" the chimney is, among other things, a symbol of virility. See E. Hale Chatfield, "Levels of Meaning in Melville's 'I and my Chimney,'" *American Imago*, XIX, 163-169 (Summer, 1962); Darwin T. Turner "Smoke from Melville's Chimney," *College Language Association Journal*, VII, 107-113 (September, 1963).

[25] *Traittéz concernant l'histoire de France: sçavoir La Condamnation des Templiers, avec quelques actes: L'Histoire du Schisme, les Papes tenans le siège en Avignon: et quelques procez criminels* (Paris, 1654).

du Temple, Paris, 1813, and with the reply by the famous oriental-
ist, Friedrich von Hammer-Purgstall, five years later, who, con-
tending that the Templars were Gnostic Ophites, produced repre-
sentations of obscene ceremonies and mystic signs alleged to have
been found in the Templars' buildings.[26] A succession of German
and French scholars upheld the innocence of the order, and their
views were popularized in England by C. G. Addison in the 1840's.[27]
On the other hand, the famous historian Jules Michelet, who had
supported the Templars in his history of France, then accepted the
original charges, republishing them in detail in his *Procès des
Templiers*, the first volume of which appeared in 1841. The accu-
sation that the Templars practiced unnatural vice was reaffirmed.
Whether they had any relations with women was debated on scanty
evidence. Women were officially banned from their society, but du
Puy's charge that any child born from intercourse between a Templar and a virgin was roasted and made into an unguent[28] certainly
implied heterosexual relations. Through Michelet the alleged prac-
tices of the Templars gained wide currency. They were accepted
without qualification by Thomas Wright, the well-known anti-
quarian, who subsequently expanded them to support his thesis in
The Worship of the Generative Powers, and with reservation by
Charles Knight, whom Melville met in London.[29]

In the United States the Templars also aroused wide interest.
In 1821 a freemason called Jeremy Cross asserted in *The Templars'
Chart or Hieroglyphic Monitor* that the modern order of the
Knights Templars stemmed directly from the ancient one, and he
later listed fifty-one grand masters from Hugh de Payens to Sir

[26] *Mysterium Baphometis revelatum* in *Fundgruben des Orients*, VI (Vienna, 1818).
On Melville's familiarity with the Ophite heresy see Lawrance Thompson, *Melville's Quarrel
with God* (Princeton, 1952), pp. 430-431.
[27] *The History of the Knights Templars, the Temple Church, and the Temple* (1st and
2nd ed., London, 1842; 3rd ed., London, 1852).
[28] *Histoire de la condannation des Templiers* (Brussells, 1713), I, 27-28: "Praeterea,
si ex Templarii coitu, infans ex puella virgine nascebatur, hunc igni torrebant; exque
eliquata inde pinguedine, suum simulachrum, decoris gratia ungebant."
[29] *Journal of a Visit to London and the Continent by Herman Melville*, ed. Eleanor
Melville Metcalf (Cambridge, Mass., 1948), p. 80; for Wright, see *A Contemporary Narrative of the Proceedings against Dame Alice Kyteler* (London, 1843); *The Worship of
the Generative Powers* (London, 1866). See also *London*, ed. Charles Knight (London,
1841-1844), III, 316: "There seems little doubt but that the body grew in many respects
more and more lax in their observance of many of the virtues for which they had at
one time been so distinguished." Melville purchased a copy of *London*, December 15,
1849.

Sidney Smith (1838). In his manual, which ran into sixteen editions by 1851, he stressed that the Templars took the oath of chastity, and he maintained that they were much maligned by their oppressors:

What were their crimes? It was said that they burnt their own infants! and yet an instance was never yet produced, in which the child of a Templar had disappeared. . . . They were said to have committed upon one another the most unnatural of all crimes! and yet no individual produced a specific instance which he could corroborate by indubitable proof.[30]

Melville may have known of the modern movement: the "general encampments" (organizational meetings) of the American Templars were held in Boston, and lodges were located in Massachusetts. The nine Brethren may even have originated in the nine Knights Templars who were required before a new lodge or "encampment" could be officially recognized. But his motive for choosing the subject, affected as it may have been by the contemporary interest and by his own visit to the Temple, was governed by his artistic purpose: the equivocal nature of the Knights' mode of life made the subject uniquely suited to the experience which he wished to convey.

From the beginning Melville's "Paradise" is shot through with relevant ironic undertones: "Templar? That's a romantic name. Let me see. Brian de Bois-Guilbert was a Templar, I believe."[31] In *Ivanhoe* Brian de Bois-Guilbert tries to rape a Jewish girl and when she repulses him he trumps up a charge of witchcraft against her. The language describing the Templars' downfall is oblique: "Though no sworded foe might outskill them in the fence, yet the worm of luxury crawled beneath their guard, gnawing the core of knightly troth, nibbling the monastic vow, till at last the monk's austerity relaxed to wassailing, and the sworn knights-bachelors grew to be but hypocrites and rakes." In the popular medieval sense "the worm of luxury" was the Tempter himself, the Old Serpent urging man to the deadly sin of *Luxuria*. Here it is an ingenious reminder of the more famous prelapsarian Paradise and

[30] *The Templars' Chart or Hieroglyphic Monitor* (New York, 1852), p. 53.
[31] P. 186, ll. 1-2.

seems to imply that the Templars' guilt, like that commonly attributed to Adam and Eve, was sexual knowledge.

The passage immediately following the reference to Brian de Bois-Guilbert suggests that the modern bachelors are even further debased. They are "so entirely secularized as to be reduced from carving out immortal fame in glorious battling for the Holy Land, to the carving of roast-mutton at a dinner-board. Like Anacreon, do these degenerate Templars now think it sweeter far to fall in banquet than in war?"

But we must note the increase in humor. The values are made deliberately ambivalent. The ironic undertone which pervades the whole tale makes it impossible to know how seriously we are to regard the degeneracy with which he charges the present-day representatives of the Templars; whether Anacreon is introduced because he was a great exponent of love or because he choked to death on a grape.

Impotency, sodomy, unnatural vice—any of these modes of behavior may be implicit in the charges which Melville admits against the original Templars. But if the Templars were "hypocrites and rakes," their descendants are "Brethren of the Order of Celibacy," and the nine diners "represent the general celibacy of the Temple." Their fraternal love for one another appears to be beyond reproach. It evinces itself in a conviviality which is never indecorous nor forgetful of the comfort of others. If the name Socrates has a special significance it may simply be to remind us of an inquiring mode of discourse often accompanied by a special kind of irony rather than of the leisurely intellectual life of the male clique which he dominated.

What emerges is the hint that the bachelors' mode of living is enjoyable because it is second-hand, that the tragedy of the Tartarus arises because the narrator leaves the "dreamy Paradise of Bachelors," as he calls it, to seek direct experience. The bachelors dine in a fashion that can be described in terms of military maneuvers, but they no longer fight. One diner tells spicy anecdotes not about himself but of former companions; another has a strange characteristic tale about the Duke of Wellington. Almost all of them "were travelers, too," but those who describe their travels are concerned with the splendors of antiquity, not with present human relations. Women are excluded from this society; yet some of the bachelors go back to their chambers to read a fourteenth-century collection of tales of heterosexual love.[32]

The climax of the evening is the appearance of the "immense convolved horn," brought in by Socrates. This horn was the symbol of Israel's military triumph of which it was both instrument and inspiration. It came from the ram, and Melville appears to emphasize its phallacism by giving it two protuberant horned heads, those of the goat, the symbol of male lust. This horn now conquers no cities. Its function, so Melville implies, is both more innocuous and more enjoyable. Jericho means "sweet-smelling," and appropriately the horn is filled with snuff. It is not called a snuffbox. Because of its size, silver mounting, and ornamentation, it is properly termed a *mull*, as he observes himself: "... my nostrils were greeted with the smell of some choice Rappee. It was a mull of snuff." The use of the word derives from the fact that snuff is a powdered preparation, ground from tobacco. In Scotland it referred both to the early machines which made the snuff and to the containers themselves; in England it usually applies to the table model as distinct from the small portable box for the pocket. It is from the Scandinavian. The form from the Old English is *mill*. As would be obvious, not only to an etymologist but to anyone who considered their application, *mull* and *mill* are the same word.

It is this snuff-taking, freely enjoyed yet in such a manner that none "so far violated the proprieties, or so far molested the invalid bachelor in the adjoining room as to indulge himself in a sneeze," which concludes the evening, with the narrator admiringly exclaiming to his smiling host that "this is the very Paradise of Bachelors!"

This mull appears to be a further token of the bachelors' vicarious mode of living: the horn of Jericho has become an ornamental container, a symbol of pleasure instead of a summons to war and destruction. Whether it has some sexual significance we cannot determine. We may see parallels between the convoluted nature of the horn and the vaginal imagery in the second part of the diptych, and we may regard the use of the word *mull*

[32] P. 195, l. 3.

as suggestive that the horn represents at least a quasi-sexual experience for the bachelors and the narrator. But such features are not "clues." On the contrary, they contribute to the intentional ambiguity which controls the effect: Melville sees to it that the intimate lives of the bachelors remain private and gives the reader the choice of either suspending moral judgment or making one colored by individual prejudice. All we know is that the rite of the mull is important in the social intercourse of the bachelors and appears to afford complete satisfaction to the narrator. The second part of the diptych pivots around a different kind of mill. Whereas the bachelors' mull appears only toward the conclusion of the evening, Melville, with a firm sense of meaningful structure, makes the mill central to the tale of the maids because the experience it involves, culminating in the personal failure of the narrator, is central to the meaning of the diptych as a whole.

There are three consecutive descriptions of the route to the paper-mill, each given by the narrator. The first is a general pseudogeographical account, telling of "the Mad Maid's Bellows-pipe" (a dusky pass), "the Black Notch" (a sudden contraction of the gorge, with steep black walls), and a huge purple hopper-shaped hollow called "the Devil's Dungeon," with an abandoned saw-mill on a bluff on one side, and itself the locale of both the turbulent waters of the Blood River and the paper-mill.

The second description, subjectively and intensely felt, consists of the narrator's journey in his pung drawn by his horse Black. While the landscape on the first occasion was sinister, the effect being enhanced by adjectives associated with death or violence and proper names of evil connotation, in the second it is sensuously brittle. The frosty trees groan with the petrifying cold as the cutting blast sweeps through them. Only the horse impels the rider on. It starts at a fallen hemlock but still goes forward through the Black Notch, speeding "madly past the ruined saw-mill." The terrified rider almost collides "with the bleak nozzle of a rock, couchant like a lion in the way," and has difficulty in discovering the mill in the bleak snowy landscape.

The third description begins in retrospect and then continues with the narrator's discoveries from the point at which they were broken off previously. In reviewing his approach to the sinister Black Notch, he compares it with the first sight of the Temple

Bar. This comparison is extended when he arrives at the mill and exclaims: "This is the very counterpart of the Paradise of Bachelors, but snowed upon, and frost-painted to a sepulchre."

More than one writer has pointed out the equations of the landscape. The description of the mountain scenery is, as Richard Chase observes, "expressed in kinaesthetic and visual imagery appropriate to the mythical identification of the body with the landscape."[33] Valid and illuminating comments have been made on the function of such imagery both as a description of the sexual act and as an anticipation of the gestation allegory. But we may further discover that the meaning of the descriptions relates specifically to the introspections of the narrator as part of the total experience of the diptych, and that the imagery conveys sensations which are intended to account, in part, for the final trauma, for an experience which is truly Tartarean compared with the Paradise left behind.

We realize, as soon as he introduces himself, that the seedsman has a symbolic function, and this function has been fully explicated by critics in terms of the allegory of procreation and parturition. The nightmare ride is also obviously symbolic. Traditionally, from Plato onward, the horse and rider have been used to denote body and soul. The rider who is unable to control his horse or chariot is a man who has succumbed to physical desire.[34] Psychologists have noted the recurrence of the same image in the *angstvolle Traumfahrt* of the nightmare in which the terrified victim of unresolved sexual fears is depicted as either riding or being ridden upon to some kind of hell where mutilation and death await him.[35] It has its counterpart, too, in the folklore of the Furious Host, the ghostly huntsmen and their baying hounds who are psychopomps seeking to carry off guilty souls to the world below.[36] In the seedsman's journey the horse seizes control. The

[33] *Herman Melville: A Critical Study* (New York, 1949), p. 160.

[34] Plato, *Phaedrus*, ed. W. H. Thompson (London, 1868), pp. 247, 253-256; James 3:2-3; Plutarch, *Opera*, ed. J. G. Hutten (Tübingen, 1796), X, 219; St. Augustine, "De moribus ecclesiae," *Patrologia Latina*, ed. J. P. Migne, XXXII (Paris, 1841), col. 1313; Philo Judaeus, "De Agricul., *Opera Omnia*, ed. C. E. Richter (Leipzig, 1828), II, 15-19.

[35] For the anatomy of the nightmare ride, see Ernest Jones, *On the Nightmare* (New York, 1959), Part III.

[36] See Guillaume d'Auvergne, "De universo," *Opera* (London, 1674), I, 1066; Gervase of Tilbury, *Otia imperialia, Scriptores rerum Brunsvicensium*, ed. G. Leibnitz (Hanover, 1707), I, iii, 62, 92; Reginald Scot, *The Discoverie of Witchcraft* (London, 1886), p. 37.

rider likens his horse to a runaway London bus dashing through an ancient arch. Significantly, he projects himself into both experiences and finds the similitude tinged "not less with the vividness than the disorder of a dream."

Related to the protagonist, as Melville obviously intended that it should be, the trip into the funnel is a representation of a sexual encounter attended by deeply rooted anxieties. Dominant among these is the fear of the *vagina dentata*, conveyed in symbols which appear also in folklore.[37] The rider is terrified by the Black Notch, by the saw-mill which, if it is in ruins, still retains its sawn-up logs, the symbols of castration, by the fallen hemlock compared to an anaconda—the gigantic snake which crushes its prey to death and then swallows it. Still consumed with fear, acutely conscious of the physical harms from which he has so narrowly escaped, the narrator moves from one fantasy of female exploration to another, to a whole factory of women, at the sight of which not even his instinctual drive will carry him on. The image clusters—the "redly and demoniacally boiled Blood River," the "long woodpile . . . all glittering in mail of crusted ice" ready to be cut up, the horse-posts "their north sides plastered with adhesive snow,"[38] show that he associates the impending experience with female heat and male frigidity. Not surprisingly, his good horse cannot manage the last dangerous declivity, and the rider is unmounted when the icy wind finally shoots him into the square beside the main edifice.

Horse-posts betoken riders, and the narrator immediately thinks of the Temple and asks: "But where are the gay bachelors?" His question is prefixed with an "inverted similitude." Using images which ironically recall Spenser's great "spousall" poem, he remarks: "The sweet, tranquil Temple garden, with the Thames bordering its green beds." The garden, the traditional symbol of woman herself, is paradoxically used here for an all-male Paradise. Its counterpart is "frost-painted to a sepulchre."[39] The de-

---

[37] See G. Legman, *The Horn Book* (New York, 1964), pp. 191-193.

[38] The color of the landscape may owe something to the Templars. Their uniform was white with a red cross, their banner striped black and white and charged with a red cross.

[39] Two further metaphors, both apposite, may be concealed here: *whited sepulchres*, originally referring to the scribes and Pharisees but later proverbially denoting the prostitute, as a deceptive repository of corruption; *painted Jezebels*, also denoting women of "loose morals"—see E. C. Brewer, *Dictionary of Phrase and Fable* (London, 1900), p. 681.

scription is followed by an action in which the woman is rejected. He wants to know where to put his horse, which is now shivering in the wind. He finds a girl, only to be repelled instantly at the sight of her: "'Nay,' faltered I, 'I mistook you. Go on; I want nothing.'"

He knocks on a dormitory door. Another girl appears and the expletive with which he dismisses her suggests that his repulsion is intensified: "'Nay, I mistake again. In God's name shut the door. But hold, is there no man about?'" Finally he gets directions from Old Bach, the overseer. Making every effort to cover up his horse in the woodshed, he then runs on foot, "lamely, . . . stiff with frost," and hampered by his driver's dreadnaught, into the factory. Here the slavelike submission of the operatives to the machine appals him. A moment later he is dragged outside by Old Bach because his face is frostbitten.

The symbolism of the factory operation is not consistent. Some of the processes are not fully correlated with the dominant symbols of the paper as the infant, the machine as the womb, and the contents of the two vats as sperm. Melville characteristically allows the symbols to accumulate meanings so that their complexity enhances the ambiguity behind which he can efface himself, leaving the reader to make his own evaluations. This pervasive ambiguity is intensified by the dreamlike role of the narrator, an isolato, sympathetically portrayed, seeking to identify himself with a social group. The introspective seedsman "finds" himself in strange places, is "amazed," "fastened" with a "spell," filled with "curious emotion" or with "awe." Like the typical protagonist of a dream, he is baffled, terrified or impressed by mysterious operations, and he can communicate only intermittently with other people. He is in the upside-down world of the nightmare in which the symbolic appear to have an exclusively immediate, nonsymbolic function, and the concrete "I" is confused and conscious of appearing stupid to others.

Cupid gives the visitor a guided tour of the machinery, during which, as various critics have pointed out, the process of insemination is presented allegorically. The narrator is particularly disturbed by the inevitability of the processes which he witnesses. He has the painful illusion that he sees the pallid faces of the girls imprinted on the moving pulp: "Slowly, mournfully, beseechingly,

yet unresistingly, they gleamed along, their agony dimly outlined
on the imperfect paper, like the print of the tormented face on
the handkerchief of Saint Veronica." The room is intensely hot
but he feels cold. He has to be taken outside again, and this time
he does not return.

In his transactions at the mill the visitor is inhibited by the
fears so graphically symbolized in his previous journey. He
watches. He cannot participate. His reaction is clarified by the
episode of the frozen cheeks.

. . . the dark-complexioned man, standing close by, raised a sudden cry,
and seizing my arm, dragged me out into the open air, and without
pausing for a word instantly caught up some congealed snow and began
rubbing both my cheeks.

"Two white spots like the whites of your eyes," he said; "man, your
cheeks are frozen."

"That may well be," muttered I; " 'tis some wonder the frost of the
Devil's Dungeon strikes in no deeper. Rub away."

Soon a horrible, tearing pain caught at my reviving cheeks. Two
gaunt blood-hounds, one on each side, seemed mumbling them. I seemed
Actaeon.

Concealed here is the typical folk figure, occurring in several
ballads of a huntsman, accompanied by two dogs, exemplifying
coitus.[40] The dogs wait outside while the huntsman enters a pond
or looks into it. In this situation, Actaeon, confronted with the
primordial femaleness of Diana bathing naked, was destroyed by
his own dogs—rendered impotent by a woman. When this image
is applied to the seedsman, we are no longer in doubt as to his
intentions and the reason for his involuntary recoil. Significantly,
it is not Cupid but the celibate, Old Bach himself, the man to
whom he turned in his initial repulse of the mill girls, who saves
him now.

Impotency continues to make him an observer rather than a
participant even in the experiment undertaken to prove that the
paper-making process takes only nine minutes. He starts with
the *end* product and even that he hands over to Cupid to drop
into the mass of pulp. In his service to the machine, it is as far as
he can go: "My travels were at an end, for here was the end of the
machine."

[40] Legman, p. 193.

The fantasy which finally drives him away further illuminates his reactions. In his illusion, the faces of the girls bear the tormented impression on the handkerchief of St. Veronica—the print of Christ on his way to Calvary. He conflates the agony of the girls with the far greater agony of celibate male suffering.

Various images in the subsequent scene support the significance of the basic metaphor and convey the nature of the activity. The women are called mares, animals which, as early as Aelian,[41] were popularly believed to be so lascivious that they might be impregnated by the wind, and to be so acquiescent that, unlike other animals, they would receive the male at any time. In an extension of mill imagery to be found in the popular songs, they are also likened to the cogs of wheels.[42] The maleness of the iron animals which they serve is never in doubt. Common phallic symbols show that in this female world Man is present as an inexorable generative organ. He is the rider whose horse can be accommodated along with the mounts of other riders at the horse-posts. He is the long, glittering scythe, an instrument which, by its position, indicates its antagonism to the female principle. He possesses no further identity. He services the machine impersonally. The transaction is as meaningless as discarding an old shirt. The bachelors, the narrator suggests, may furnish old shirts for rags but not the buttons with them; nor are there any bachelor's buttons to be found there except on the chest of Old Bach. Proverbially, to lose one's bachelor's buttons is to marry.[43] Here the male participant evidently never stays, never sets up a human relationship.

The intense cold so frequently remarked upon is probably not an image of female frigidity as has been suggested. It appears to be a shifting symbol, standing both for male impotence and for the nature of man's association with woman, as the narrator sees it. This association, if it brings suffering to the woman, is agonizing for the man: "That moment two of the girls, dropping their rags, plied each a whetstone up and down the sword-blade. My unaccustomed blood curdled at the sharp shriek of the tormented steel."

[41] *De natura animalium*, ed. F. Jacobs (Jena, 1832), I, iv. 6, 11.

[42] Cf. *The Tea-Table Miscellany*, p. 153.

[43] Brewer, p. 82; J. O. Halliwell, *A Dictionary of Archaic and Provincial Words* (London, 1847), I, 130.

To Old Bach the women are simply classified as unmarried, but to the seedsman, for good reason, they are all virgins at the end, and "some pained homage to their pale virginity" makes him "involuntarily bow." They are virgins because he cannot touch them: the only relationship possible for him is that which he found at the Temple among the bachelors.

His cheeks, which evoked the comparison to Actaeon, are whitish yet and will not mend, as he himself observes, until he gets out of the Devil's Dungeon. His horse is equally affected—"all cringing and doubled up with the cold." What has resulted from this experience when contrasted with that previously recounted is a bitter kind of self-awareness and a recognition of how disparate the two worlds are for him: "At the Black Notch I paused, and once more bethought me of Temple Bar. Then, shooting through the pass, all alone with inscrutable nature, I exclaimed—Oh! Paradise of Bachelors! and oh! Tartarus of Maids!"

The final exclamation serves to convey his pleasure in the bachelors' world and his recoil from the world of women, which have been the subjects of the diptych. The extent of the deviation which the first world represents we never know. The "Paradise" reveals an exclusively male society, urbane, leisured, mannerly, comfortable, intellectual, with the rite of the mull representing the climax of satisfaction. The "Tartarus" describes the experience of a man who enjoys this society of bachelors but is compelled by his instinctual drive to explore the sexual nature of woman. For him, woman has no identity, no meaning, beyond her physical function, and his deep-rooted fears based on a castration fantasy, his association of the sexual act with commercial exploitation, his repugnance for the inexorable nature of sex which turns the whole world of women into a brothel and lying-in hospital simultaneously, result in his impotence. His revulsion is imaginatively conveyed through concrete description, incident, and dialogue in which irony and metaphor remain just below the surface, with the mill, simultaneously representing the *pudenda* and women collectively engaged in the hold-door trade—an assembly line of parts servicing and being serviced by man—as the controlling symbol.

The "I" of the diptych, while he leaves no doubt as to the world he wants, never understands his motivation. That he

should think of Temple Bar on the two occasions when he approaches Black Notch seems meaningful:[44] we perceive that there
is an association between his preference and the site of his deepest
apprehensions. The narrator is confused and disturbed by the
juxtaposition the first time, but the second time he simply pauses
and makes good his escape. He sees himself "all alone with inscrutable nature." The statement epitomizes his plight. Caught
in a limbo between hell and heaven, this solitary deviate can
only acknowledge that the complexities governing man's strongest impulses are unfathomable. The trite and deliberately inadequate phrase is the culminating irony; it is also Melville's
perception of truth.

[44] Melville's predilection for puns, particularly those which were "both intricate and
problematical," makes one suspect that Temple Bar means *mental barrier*. Melville clearly
appreciated that sexual inhibitions stemmed from psychological causes.

Melville and the Theme of Timonism:
From *Pierre* to *The Confidence-Man*
Charles N. Watson, Jr.

N OT MANY MELVILLE readers would dispute the idea that between 1851 and 1856 Melville's vision of life darkened. By late 1856, with the manuscript of *The Confidence-Man* deposited at the publisher's, Melville was sufficiently exhausted and depressed for his family to send him off to Europe and the Middle East for a traveling rest-cure. His family, to be sure, was *always* fussing about the state of his nerves; but there can be little doubt that when he arrived in England his friend Hawthorne was accurate in judging him "much overshadowed" since their last meeting four years earlier. This state of depression has been variously explained. For one thing, it was the result of a religious disillusionment, an increasing skepticism about the benevolence and even the existence of God. Though such doubts had begun well before 1851, after *Moby-Dick* they became, if anything, more pronounced. Another dimension, as Edgar A. Dryden has persuasively shown, was artistic.[1] Increasingly Melville came to doubt the ability of literary art to perform the lofty truth-telling function he had conceived for it in 1850, at the time of his absorption in the writings of Shakespeare and Hawthorne. Instead, he began to suspect—with an ultimate kind of epistemological nihilism—that truth either cannot be known or does not even exist.

What I should like to suggest here, however, is that Melville's disillusionment during these years had still a third dimension: an increasing belief that his career had been betrayed and destroyed by his family, friends, and readers. His final disillusionment thus concerns not only the capacity of his art to *tell* the truth but also the capacity of his audience to *receive* the truth when it is told. In one sense, certainly, there is nothing new in the notion that Melville had troubles with his readers. While deep in the throes of *Moby-*

[1] *Melville's Thematics of Form: The Great Art of Telling the Truth* (Baltimore, 1968).

Dick, he had written to Hawthorne the widely-quoted and prophetic statement of his dilemma: "Dollars damn me. . . . My dear Sir, a presentiment is on me,—I shall at last be worn out and perish, like an old nutmeg-grater, grated to pieces by the constant attrition of the wood. . . . What I feel most moved to write, that is banned,—it will not pay. Yet, altogether, write the *other* way I cannot."[2] If he was wrong in concluding that all his books were "botches," he was prescient in his recognition of the toll that this conception of his audience would take on his inner resources. And like the other forms of his disillusionment, this one was bound to find embodiment in his fiction.

The extent of this fictional embodiment, though it has often been touched on, has not yet been fully explored; nor have its biographical implications been satisfactorily explained. More and more, in the works after *Moby-Dick*, Melville found a metaphor for his disillusionment in the theme of Timonism—a theme which took its name from his reading of Shakespeare's *Timon of Athens* and which implies a betrayal and desertion by one's friends.[3] During these years, with his health and finances precarious and his early literary admirers falling away, he seems to have had an increasing sense of Timon's plight as an analogue to his own. Following such a betrayal, he saw two alternatives: to withdraw, like Timon, into misanthropic solitude; or to engage the public on its own terms, taking on the protective coloring of an artistic confidence-man, playing with a grim humor on the egotism and gullibility of his audience. In the works prior to *The Confidence-Man*, the first of these reactions is embodied in such characters as Hunilla, Bartleby, Israel Pot-

[2] *The Letters of Herman Melville*, ed. Merrell R. Davis and William H. Gilman (New Haven, Conn., 1960), p. 128.

[3] *Timon of Athens* was one of the plays that Melville read and annotated in the edition of Shakespeare he acquired in early 1849. Although it is one of Shakespeare's weaker plays, Melville was sufficiently impressed with its central character to include him in the company of Hamlet, Lear, and Iago when, in his review of Hawthorne's *Mosses* (1850), he wanted to suggest that the essence of Shakespeare's genius lay in his ability to say, or insinuate, "the things which we feel to be so terrifically true that it were all but madness for any good man, in his own proper character, to utter, or even hint of them." As others have observed, the statement is highly pertinent to Melville's own artistic method. The suggestion that after *Moby-Dick* Melville went through a period of Timonism first appeared in Lewis Mumford's *Herman Melville* (New York, 1929) and was invoked occasionally thereafter by other early critics and biographers. After the "normalizing" biographical work of the early 1950's, however, the term was relegated to the status of an unscholarly myth and has languished there ever since.

ter, and Benito Cereno. The second appears most fully in Oberlus
and Babo, while a combination of the two responses appears in
Pierre and Jimmy Rose. The occasional pairing of these characters
(Hunilla-Oberlus, Babo-Cereno) suggests that in contemplating
the appropriate response to betrayal and desertion Melville was
engaged in a kind of inner debate—a debate finally resolved in
The Confidence-Man, where the same patterns of response can
be traced through a series of characters with a progression that
implies Melville's increasing disillusionment with the role of professional author.[4]

The composition of *Pierre*, during the winter of 1851–52, was
clearly influenced by Melville's increasing disappointment over the
reviews of *Moby-Dick*. From the "rural bowl of milk" he had promised Mrs. Hawthorne during the early stages, the novel followed a
downward path into an agonized despair unequaled in all his fiction. After the rescue of Isabel, the action is dominated by a series
of Timon-like betrayals: banished and disinherited by his mother,
spurned by Falsgrave and Glen Stanly, Pierre at last feels deserted
by "even the paternal gods."[5] Despite the companionship of Isabel
and eventually Lucy, his withdrawal to the Church of the Apostles
is a Timon-like retreat into spiritual isolation: though he is "one
in a city of hundreds of thousands of human beings," he is "solitary
as at the Pole" (p. 398).

With this bitter isolation comes a progressive absorption in the
solitary labor of his writing. But, like Melville himself, having been
flattered by obsequious editors and witless readers for his trivial early
writings, Pierre soon learns that "though the world worship Medi-

[4] Though the pattern of betrayal and desertion by one's friends is most clearly ex-
emplified by these characters, there are many others who are peripherally related to it:
Redburn, Jackson, and Harry Bolton (*Redburn*); Ishmael, Ahab, Perth the blacksmith, and
Pip (*Moby-Dick*); the narrator and Merrymusk ("Cock-a-Doodle-Doo!"); the Coulters
("Poor Man's Pudding"); Hautboy and the narrator ("The Fiddler"); the uncle ("The
Happy Failure"); and Bannadonna ("The Bell-Tower"). These bankrupts, outcasts, failed
artists, and wounded Titans have one thing in common: the world has not treated them
kindly.

[5] *Pierre; Or, The Ambiguities*, ed. Henry A. Murray (New York, 1949), p. 349. References to other works by Melville are to the following editions: *Moby-Dick*, ed. Harrison
Hayford and Hershel Parker (New York, 1967); *The Complete Stories of Herman Melville*, ed. Jay Leyda (New York, 1949); *Israel Potter* (Garden City, N.Y., 1965); *The
Confidence-Man*, ed. H. Bruce Franklin (Indianapolis, 1967). References to *Timon of
Athens* are from the Yale Shakespeare, ed. Stanley T. Williams (New Haven, 1919). Citations appear hereafter in the text.

ocrity and Common-Place, yet hath it fire and sword for all contemporary Grandeur" (p. 310). In short, he is "Timonized" (p. 300).
As the world's flattery turns to hostility, he counters by becoming a
literary con-man, giving back "jeer for jeer, and taunt[ing] the apes
that jibed him. . . . For the pangs in his heart, he put down hoots on
the paper. And every thing else he disguised under the so conveniently adjustable drapery of all-stretchable Philosophy" (p. 398–399).
At last, hounded by his cousin as a lying seducer and cast off by
his editors as a blaspheming swindler, he can summon one more
effort at revenge and can then take refuge only in death. Pierre thus
encompasses, to a violent extreme, both of the reactions to Timon's
plight—a misanthropic withdrawal into spiritual isolation and a
cunning game of literary imposture.[6]

Both Hunilla and Oberlus, whose stories form companion pieces
in "The Encantadas" (1854), have suffered Timon's misfortune of
betrayal and desertion; but their reactions are strikingly different.
Hunilla, along with her husband and brother, has been left on an
island by a French sea captain, who has promised to return for her.
But the two men are accidentally drowned, and it soon becomes clear
that the French captain has abandoned her. Later, after a long
period of increasing despair, she signals a passing whaler in the
hope of rescue, but is instead raped by the ship's crew. Her last hope
apparently betrayed, she retreats into a spiritual isolation which is
scarcely relieved even when she is at last rescued.

At the opposite extreme from Hunilla's blank despair is the
Timon-like misanthropy of the hermit Oberlus. At first glance, it
would seem absurd to imply even the slightest resemblance between
Oberlus and Melville. But so excessive is the narrator's condemnation of him that by the time he is described as "a creature whom
it is religion to detest, since it is philanthropy to hate a misanthrope"
(p. 112), we may begin to suspect the possibility of irony. He is
bestial, true; but his bestiality is of a rather regal sort: he is com-

[6] Raymond J. Nelson has recently argued against biographical and psychological interpretations by dissociating Melville from Pierre on the interesting supposition that the
narrator is not Melville but Pierre himself ("The Art of Herman Melville: The Author
of Pierre," Yale Review, LIX, Winter, 1970, 197–214). The evidence for this supposition,
however, seems fully insufficient. Much as one may share the desire to acquit Melville
of the novel's weaknesses, it still appears far more likely that the weaknesses stem from
Melville's increasing inability to keep a saving distance between himself and his author-
protagonist.

pared to a bear and a tiger; and, like Ahab, he is a "Lord Anaconda."
Though he is as treacherous as the most Satanic of Melville's characters, he has a kind of perverse pride and resilience that at times
makes him look almost heroic. When, after an act of especially
diabolical malice, he is outwitted and captured, his punishment is
harsh enough to draw our reluctant sympathy: he is severely
whipped, and all his possessions—his hut, food supply, garden,
and money—are either seized or destroyed. Thereafter, Ahab-like
(and Timon-like), "brooding among the ruins of his hut, and the
desolate clinkers and extinct volcanoes of this outcast isle, the insulted misanthrope . . . meditates a signal revenge upon humanity,
but conceals his purposes" (p. 107). If this sounds a bit like Pierre's
literary revenge, we soon learn that Oberlus, too, was an "accom-
plished writer, and no mere boor; and what is more, was capable
of the most tristful eloquence" (p. 110). In the wily role-playing of
his letter to his antagonists (pp. 110–111), he embodies the second
response to the Timon-like plight of betrayal and desertion, the
artistry of a Satanic con-man.

In "Bartleby" (1853), the pattern continues. The heart of the
story lies in the way the lawyer-narrator, despite his initially well-
intentioned efforts to deal with Bartleby's perverse "preferences,"
finally betrays and abandons the scrivener to a Timon-like isolation and death. As the narrator correctly perceives, Bartleby is
"alone, absolutely alone in the universe." He is a "bit of wreck in
the mid-Atlantic" (p. 29), who seeks only shelter from the storm of
life that has wrecked him. But at the end, the eminently sane, practical, reasonable Wall Street lawyer—for all his good will—denies
his responsibility for Bartleby's plight and takes refuge in Pilate-like
rationalizations: "I distinctly perceived that I had now done all that
I possibly could . . . to benefit Bartleby, and shield him from rude
persecution. I now strove to be entirely care-free and quiescent; and
my conscience justified me in the attempt; though, indeed, it was
not so successful as I could have wished" (p. 42). With Bartleby
near death inside the walls of the Tombs, the narrator makes a
fatuous (and again implicitly self-justifying) attempt to persuade
him that the prison "is not so sad a place as one might think"
(p. 43), and urges him to find consolation in the sky and the grass.
But Bartleby knows where he is. Confronted with a universe of

blank walls and dead letters, he has found in the lawyer's office an island of comparative safety, only to be driven finally to the silence of the Tombs.[7]

When in his search for new materials Melville turned in 1854 to the little volume of Israel R. Potter's *Life and Remarkable Adventures*, which he had acquired a few years earlier, he might have taken a sardonic satisfaction in noting that Israel, like himself, was born on the first of August. But the parallels between their lives did not stop with that one coincidence. Like an earlier quasi-autobiographical character, Ishmael, Potter was driven to sea by his disappointments on land and eventually shipped on a whaling vessel. Melville's description of his motives (which does not appear in the source) echoes Ishmael's wry assertion that the sea is his "substitute for pistol and ball." "With a philosophical flourish," says Ishmael, "Cato throws himself upon his sword; I quietly take to the ship" (p. 12). In the parallel passage in *Israel Potter*, the allusion to Timon is clear: "A hermitage in the forest is the refuge of the narrow-minded misanthrope; a hammock on the ocean is the asylum for the generous distressed" (p. 20).

But what may have been still more appealing to the Melville of the mid-1850's was Potter's reason for telling his story, his bitterness over the government's failure to recognize his heroic service in the Revolution. In the novel, Melville transforms this motive into the heavy pathos of the ending, where Israel languishes in a crushing poverty and obscurity, ignored by the government he has served. The abandonment of the deserving Israel is reminiscent of Melville's own failure to secure a consular appointment and, more broadly, of the public's indifference or hostility toward his most ambitious literary efforts. Once again, therefore, a quasi-autobiographical character responds to betrayal by a stoical withdrawal that conceals an underlying bitterness. At the end, Israel's distress is no longer "generous."

The lugubrious pathos of the ending of *Israel Potter* is repeated

[7] The general resemblance between Melville's situation and Bartleby's has been pointed out often before and need not be reviewed here. One of the best of the biographical readings, however—Leo Marx's "Melville's Parable of the Walls," *Sewanee Review*, LXI (Oct., 1953), 602–627—seems to me to err in concluding that the story offers "a compassionate rebuke to the self-absorption of the artist" and "a plea that he devote himself to keeping strong his bonds with the rest of mankind" (p. 627). The autobiographical motive is not, I think, self-castigation, but rather self-justification mixed with a touch of self-pity.

with more restraint in the ending of "Benito Cereno" (1855), when Cereno, overwhelmed by Babo's treachery, withdraws to a monastery to await an imminent death. Having trusted the slaves to roam the deck unfettered, he now sees "the negro" as a symbol of all the treacherous forces of the universe, much as the blank walls and dead letters become symbols to Bartleby. And just as Bartleby has his Job's-comforter in the genially superficial lawyer, Cereno has the blithely commonsensical Captain Delano to try ineffectually to persuade him of the benignity of nature: "But the past is passed; why moralize upon it? Forget it. See, yon bright sun has forgotten it all, and the blue sea, and the blue sky; these have turned over new leaves" (pp. 351–352). But Cereno cannot forget, and his disullusionment is a spiritual death shortly to become physical.

Between the passive withdrawal of the disillusioned master, however, and the savage heroism of the rebellious slave, there is very nearly a thematic balance—just as there is an implied balance between Hunilla and Oberlus. Like Oberlus, Babo is the perpetrator of evil, but he is also its victim. Betrayed into slavery, he devotes all his considerable cunning to turning the tables on his captors. Once he has achieved the upper hand, the skill with which his masquerade dupes Captain Delano casts him as another artistic con-man, whose ingratiating art can be used for purposes of revenge on his betrayers. For Babo, such revenge—however terrifyingly bloodthirsty—is the only possible route to physical survival and a measure of human dignity. In his "voiceless end," with his impaled head meeting, "Unabashed, the gaze of the whites" (p. 353), there is an incipient "revenger's tragedy" with something of the power of Ahab's. If Babo also reminds us of Iago, we may recall that Iago was one of those "dark characters," including Timon, in whose words Melville detected a terrifying truth.[8]

One other story of 1855, "Jimmy Rose," brings us still closer to *The Confidence-Man* in its detailed repetition of the theme and action of Shakespeare's *Timon*. At the height of his wealth, Jimmy, like Timon, wines and dines his friends in a spontaneous outpouring of generosity, only to find that after his financial collapse his friends have deserted him. He thereupon retires to his house, locking him-

[8] The most persuasive case for viewing Babo as something more than a mere personification of evil has been made by Allen Guttmann, "The Enduring Innocence of Captain Amasa Delano," *Boston University Studies in English*, V (Spring, 1961), 35–45.

self away in misanthropic solitude, just as Timon retires to his hermitage in the forest. At this point Melville seems almost to have been working with a copy of *Timon* in front of him when the narrator, calling on Jimmy at his retreat, hears a "hollow, husky voice" addressing him through the keyhole:

"Who are you?" it said.
"A friend."
"Then shall you not come in," replied the voice, more hollowly than before.

.   .   .   .

"Let me in, Rose; let me in, man. I am your friend."
"I will not. I can trust no man now."
"Let me in, Rose; trust at least one, in me."
"Quit the spot, or—" (p. 248)

This dialogue appears to have been shaped by two related sequences in *Timon*. In the first, Alcibiades visits Timon's cave and protests, "I am thy friend and pity thee, dear Timon," to which Timon growls, "How dost thou pity him whom thou dost trouble? I had rather be alone" (IV.iii.97–98). Later, Timon's steward, Flavius, approaches and hails Timon as "My dearest master":

Timon. Away! What art thou?
Flavius. Have you forgot me, sir?
Timon. Why dost ask that? I have forgot all men;
   Then, if thou grant'st thou'rt a man, I have forgot thee.
Flavius. An honest poor servant of yours.
Timon. Then I know thee not. . . . (IV.iii.481–485)

Thereafter, allowing his protagonist to mask his bitter misanthropy, Melville concludes the story by having Jimmy take the advice that Apemantus vainly offered to Timon: "Be thou a flatterer now, and seek to thrive / By that which has undone thee" (IV.iii.211–212). Jimmy thus begins a kind of desperate confidence-game, resuming his round of buoyant social activity by ingratiating himself with his former friends and keeping up the pretense of his earlier mastery until he dies pathetically in his "lone attic," accompanied by the narrator's reiterated lament, "Poor, poor Jimmy—God guard us all—poor Jimmy Rose!" (pp. 252, 253).

The residue of self-pity that weakens such stories as "Jimmy Rose" is finally dissolved in the bitter comedy of the last work of Melville's career as a public author, *The Confidence-Man*. Like any of the greatest of Melville's works, this novel defies a restrictively biographical interpretation. Ultimately it transcends even the brilliance of its satire to become a parable of the human situation. As the punning title suggests, we are all either confidence-men, victimizing our fellows, or men of confidence, extending our trust at the risk of becoming victims. From the horns of this dilemma no one in the novel escapes.

This movement between the extremes of charity and misanthropy is also the movement of Timon, and it is no accident that Shakespeare's embittered protagonist is invoked a number of times in Melville's novel. Here for a final time Melville is facing the problem of Timonism, brooding on the disappointments of his own life, and transforming them into a work that moves beyond self-justification or self-pity. But however superbly transformed, the roots of the novel in Melville's experience can still be traced and some conclusions can be drawn about his state of mind at the close of his public career. Throughout the novel we find characters who embody the problem of Timonism and who are also symbolic authors— that is, ones whose activities bear an implied resemblance to authorship. The theme of confidence increasingly becomes the theme of friendship, and, more specifically, the theme of the relationship between an author and his public.[9]

The theme emerges in the first three chapters, where three characters—the lamb-like man, Black Guinea, and the wooden-legged cynic—embody the entire range of responses to Timon's plight, from passive withdrawal to cagy role-playing to snarling misanthropy. Furthermore, each of these characters is a symbolic author who is reviled by the crowd for his efforts at symbolic authorship. The first of them, the lamb-like man, writes on his slate the litany of charity from Paul's epistle to the Corinthians and for his pains is buffeted and jeered by the passengers, who clearly do not know what

---

[9] One of the notable accomplishments of recent criticism of *The Confidence-Man* is its discovery of the extent to which the novel deals with the problem of fiction-writing and truth-telling. Far from being confined to the apparent digressions (chapters 14, 33, and 44), this theme pervades the entire novel, constantly raising the question of whether a work of fiction can convey any truth at all—and indeed whether there is any to be conveyed.

to make of him, labeling him (among other things) an "odd fish," a "humbug," and a "moon-calf." Thereafter, he mutely steals into Timon-like retirement, where, "going to sleep and continuing so, he seemed to have courted oblivion, a boon not often withheld from so humble an applicant as he" (p. 12).

The second figure, a Satanic counterpart of his Christlike predecessor, is Black Guinea, a Negro cripple who earns a few meager coins through a grotesque travesty of the game of authorship, in which to be an author-like public entertainer is the ultimate in degrading servility, with the audience paying for the privilege of heaping abuse on the performer:

Still shuffling among the crowd, now and then he would pause, throwing back his head and opening his mouth like an elephant for tossed apples at a menagerie; when, making a space before him, people would have a bout at a strange sort of pitch-penny game, the cripple's mouth being at once target and purse, and he hailing each expertly-caught copper with a cracked bravura from his tambourine. To be the subject of alms-giving is trying, and to feel duty bound to appear cheerfully grateful under the trial, must be still more so; but whatever his secret emotions, he swallowed them, while retaining each copper this side the esophagus. And nearly always he grinned, and only once or twice did he wince, which was when certain coins, tossed by more playful almoners, came inconveniently nigh to his teeth, an accident whose unwelcomeness was not unedged by the circumstance that the pennies thus thown proved buttons. (p. 17)

Soon, however, the crowd begins to turn from degrading patronage to overt hostility. Like the lamb-like man, Black Guinea seems none too surprised at the crowd's inconstancy, "as if instinct told [him] that the right or the wrong might not have overmuch to do with whatever wayward mood superior intelligences might yield to" (p. 18). The crowd's reversal of attitude then provokes the narrator to compare Black Guinea to a Timon-like man "proved guilty, by law, of murder, but whose condemnation was deemed unjust by the people, so that they rescued him to try him themselves; whereupon they . . . found him even guiltier than the court had done, and forthwith proceeded to execution; so that the gallows presented the truly warning spectacle of a man hanged by his friends" (p. 19). This contagion of distrust has been spread to the crowd by the third of the trio of characters, the wooden-legged cynic, the only one of the three who is explicitly compared to Timon. He is also the one who most fully sees the game of authorship for what it is, an act of crowd-pleasing imposture. Such knowledge may even have come from his own experience as an author, for there may be an allusion to Hawthorne in the comparison of the cynic to "some discharged custom-house officer, who, suddenly stripped of convenient means of support, had concluded to be avenged on government and humanity by making himself miserable for life, either by hating or suspecting everything and everybody" (p. 17). If the allusion is indeed to Hawthorne, it hardly matters here that Melville is exaggerating his friend's misanthropy; what is important is the way he has transformed it into the experience of the cynic, which has led him to distrust the authorial role as public entertainer and benefactor and to see it instead as a cynical confidence-game. The cynic thus foreshadows the final stage of Timonism in the novel as a whole—total disillusionment with the role of public author.

These early indications that an author is necessarily a con-man and impostor are borne out by two later Timon-like episodes, the stories of the "unfortunate man" and the "soldier of fortune." Each of these characters has been betrayed by his friends, each narrates his own history, and each is involved with the question of authorial imposture. The unfortunate man's story concerns his effort to rescue his daughter from his shrewish wife, Goneril, with the result that his wife and friends conspire against him, reduce him to poverty, destroy his reputation, nearly succeed in getting him committed, and finally drive him into a lonely exile. Significantly, however, the very telling and retelling of this Timon-like tale raises the question of its truth—or at least the question of whether its audience will receive it as such—for in the next chapter one of its hearers tries to persuade another hearer that the unfortunate man is in reality a person of "great good fortune. . . . Lucky dog, he dared say, after all" (p. 92). One liability of the teller of unhappy truths like the Timon story, therefore, is that he is forever afflicted with an audience that persists in turning his message of darkness into a blithe reassurance that God's in his heaven and all's right with the world.

The crippled "soldier of fortune," who is linked to the "unfortunate man" by the similarity of their epithets, is linked also to an earlier crippled author-figure, Black Guinea (his is "much such a case as the negro's" [p. 138]). Taken to jail as the witness to a murder, the soldier has no money for bail and no friends to provide any. He is therefore left to rot in prison until the trial, at which the murderer—who, unlike the soldier, has friends—is acquitted. The soldier, now hopelessly crippled by the prison dampness, is forced to conclude that not having friends is a "worse crime than murder" (p. 133). Reduced to beggary, he knows (like Black Guinea) that the only way to retain the favor of the mob is to dress up his misfortune in a more appealing form. "Hardly anybody believes my story," he says, "so to most I tell a different one" (p. 135). Posing as a wounded veteran, he goes about soliciting "a shilling for Happy Tom, who fought at Buena Vista . . . , something for General Scott's soldier, crippled in both pins at glorious Contreras" (p. 135). After witnessing this act of author-like imposture, the herb-doctor neatly sums up the kind of compromise that the act of public authorship entails: "For all that, I repeat he lies not out of wantonness. A ripe philosopher, turned out of the great Sorbonne of hard times, he thinks that woes, when told to strangers for money, are best sugared" (p. 136).

But a crucial turning point in this procession of Timon-like symbolic authors is marked by the appearance of the gruff Missouri backwoodsman named Pitch, who is explicitly compared to Timon and who embodies a Timon-like combination of magnanimity and misanthropy. Though the P.I.O. agent temporarily persuades him to take on another boy, there is little chance of his surrendering his conviction that "boyhood is a natural state of rascality" (p. 162)— a conviction drawn from the seemingly invincible evidence of thirty-five successive boys who have betrayed his confidence in them. But unlike the earlier symbolic authors, Pitch is a misanthropic truth-teller who is unwilling to sugarcoat the pill. Truth, he says, is "like a thrashing-machine; tender sensibilities must keep out of the way" (p. 166). His last opponent, the Cosmopolitan, urges the familiar kind of authorial role-playing: "Life is a pic-nic *en costume*; one must take a part, assume a character, stand ready in a sensible way to play the fool" (pp. 187–188). But by declining to "play the fool"—by declining to compromise his gloomy vision by transforming it into narrative art—Pitch marks the first of three steps toward Melville's valediction as a professional author.

The second step is taken by Colonel Moredock, the Indian-hater. Like Pitch, Moredock is a backwoodsman who combines fierce misanthropy with benevolent humanity, for he is a "species of diluted Indian-hater, one whose heart proves not so steely as his brain" (p. 213). In contrast, the theoretical "Indian-hater *par excellence*" is more fully Timon-like, one who, "with the solemnity of a Spaniard turned monk . . . takes leave of his kin" and "commits himself to the forest primeval; there . . . to act upon a calm, cloistered scheme of strategical, implacable, and lonesome vengeance" (p. 212). Since the Indians in question seem symbolic of the savage propensities in all men (Moredock "hated Indians like snakes" [p. 198]), Indian-hating implies a broader kind of Timon-like misanthropy. When Melville has the Cosmopolitan facetiously call the colonel "a Moredock of Misanthrope Hall—the Woods," he manages, in a single brilliant pun, both an allusion to Timon and a sly hint that Moredock is not so much a real person as a fiction contrived by a misanthropic author, Judge Hall.[10] As recreated by a misanthropic Hall and revised by a misanthropic Melville, Moredock is another truculent realist, whose awakening to the facts of Indian (hence human) nature came when his entire family was wiped out in a massacre. And finally, Moredock, too, must decide (author-like) whether to compromise his grim vision by playing a public role:

If the governorship offered large honors, from Moredock it demanded larger sacrifices. These were incompatibles. In short, he was not unaware that to be a consistent Indian-hater involves the renunciation of ambition, with its objects—the pomps and glories of the world; and since religion, pronouncing such things vanities, accounts it merit to renounce them, therefore, so far as this goes, Indian-hating, whatever may be thought of it in other respects, may be regarded as not wholly without the efficacy of a devout sentiment. (pp. 219–220)

By declining the governorship, Moredock, like Pitch, renounces the

[10] The fact that Melville thus implies a kinship between himself and Hall would seem one piece of evidence against Edwin Fussell's contention that Melville was covertly attacking Hall's supposed racism (*Frontier: American Literature and the American West*, Princeton, 1965, pp. 318–325). A convincing argument for viewing the Indians as symbols and Moredock as a hero is presented by Merlin Bowen, "Tactics of Indirection in Melville's *The Confidence-Man*," *Studies in the Novel*, I (Winter, 1969), 401–420.

kind of author-like imposture that the world applauds, and thereby
retains his integrity.

The final stage in this procession of symbolic authors is contained in the story of China Aster. As the culmination of the theme
of friendship betrayed, it is carefully prepared for by the episodes
that precede it: the conversation between the "boon companions,"
Frank Goodman and Charlie Noble, at the end of which Charlie
changes abruptly from friend to enemy when Frank solicits him
for a loan; the story of Charlemont, the gentleman-madman, who
withdraws, Timon-like, from the scene of his earlier bankruptcy,
returning years later with an outward good cheer but a deep inward
disillusionment; and the role-playing conversation between the "hy-
pothetical friends," in which Egbert (as "Charlie") expounds his
coldly self-serving notion of friendship. At this point Egbert tells
the story of the Timon-like China Aster, which turns out to be a
veiled allegorical account of the literary and financial humilations
that beset Melville's entire career as an author.[11] By disclaiming the
spirit of the style and distorting the meaning, Egbert provides a final
instance of Melville's unsanguine view of the fate of unpleasant
truths in a complacent world.

First, China Aster is a candle-maker, "one whose trade would
seem a kind of subordinate branch of that parent craft and mystery
of the hosts of heaven, to be the means, effectively or otherwise, of
shedding some light through the darkness of a planet benighted"
(p. 291). If this sounds strongly like Melville's earlier conception of
the artist's role as cosmic truth-teller, the note of self-mockery ("effectively or otherwise") reflects his current disillusionment with so
lofty an aim. But there are more specific parallels to Melville's career in the account of China Aster's financial dealings. Lured on by
the seemingly beneficent loan from his friend Orchis, and by the

[11] Edwin Fussell has briefly suggested that the China Aster story is "a rather transparent
allegorical parody of Melville's disastrous literary career and of its relation to Hawthorne"
(*Frontier*, p. 314n.), and Walker Cowen has similarly proposed that "a Hawthorne may
be urging a Melville to continue writing great books which will not sell" ("Melville's
Marginalia," in *The Recognition of Herman Melville*, ed. Hershel Parker, Ann Arbor, Mich.,
1967, p. 388). Finally, after the present article was completed, Hershel Parker's " 'The Story
of China Aster': A Tentative Explication" was published for the first time in the Norton
Critical Edition of *The Confidence-Man* (New York, 1971), pp. 353–356. Parker's suggestive but rather inconclusive observations surely need some sort of clarifying context,
and perhaps the most appropriate is the autobiographical theme of Timonism explored
here.

appearance in a dream of an angel called "Bright Future," who showers gold upon him, China Aster follows Orchis's advice to "drop this vile tallow and hold up pure spermaceti to the world" (p. 292), which Orchis promises to buy from him. Similarly, Melville was lured on toward a seemingly bright future by the enthusiasm for his first two books on the part of his family, publishers, and literary friends. But the rapid growth of his mind in the late 1840's led him to reject such "vile tallow" and to venture instead into "spermaceti," which suggests not only *Moby-Dick* but also, more broadly, *Mardi* and *Pierre*—in short, the kind of light-giving, truth-telling book that (as he told Hawthorne) he felt "most moved to write." The disappointing reception of these three books, ending with the near-total public failure of *Pierre*, exactly parallels the fate of China Aster's three ventures into spermaceti: the first "rather disappointed [his] sanguine expectations"; the second turned out "still less prosperously"; and the third ended in "almost a total loss" (p. 298). Thereafter, when China Aster made a new beginning, "he did not try his hand at the spermaceti again, but, admonished by experience, returned to tallow" (p. 301), just as Melville began an attempt to recoup his reputation and finances by writing for the magazines.

Orchis, the fair-weather friend who betrays China Aster and drives him to destruction, may be a reflection of Melville's disillusionment with Hawthorne, as Edwin Fussell and Walker Cowen have suggested. Or he may be simply a catch-all representation of the forces that Melville felt had blighted his career: the reading public that had stopped buying his books; the editors and critics whose praise of his early books had turned to sharp attacks on the later ones; and the members of his family who were less sympathetic toward his work than he could have wished. Possibly it was this conception of an impenetrable audience that prompted the seemingly innocent whimsy of the pun on Orchis's occupation as a shoemaker, whose task was to "defend the understandings of men from naked contact with the substance of things" (p. 292). In the biographical context, the pun blossoms into a deft thrust at Orchis as a kind of guardian of the public complacency.

The final details of China Aster's death are then drawn from the death of Melville's bankrupt father. Precisely like Allan Melville, China Aster suffered a physical collapse, then "lingered a few days with a wandering mind, and kept wandering on, till at last, at dead of night, when nobody was aware, his spirit wandered away into the other world" (p. 304). To the son, the old specter of the father's failure and death must have come to seem a prefiguring metaphor of his own impending "death" as a public author, for his artistic capital at last was spent.

Though biographical conclusions drawn from an author's fiction are always hazardous, there seems a strong probability that the persistence of the Timon theme in Melville's fiction of this period tells us something about the author that a merely factual chronicle of his life tends to obscure. Both in its characters and events and in its tone of black humor and sardonic gloom, *The Confidence-Man* appears to bring to a final focus Melville's reflections on his career as a professional author—a career hampered, he seems to have felt, by the inconstancy and obtuseness of even his most ardent early admirers. The disillusioned Timon stands at last as a symbol of the disillusioned author, whose highest ambitions and greatest work now appeared headed for oblivion. Perhaps, therefore, Melville's final despair, described so memorably by Hawthorne when they met in England, stemmed not only from doubts of "Providence and futurity" but also from a deep skepticism about the possibility of combining honest artistic creativity with genuine human friendship. Certainly it is a tribute to the fundamental sanity of his genius that he could turn his disillusionment into the brilliant bitter-comedy of *The Confidence-Man*, where the benignly Satanic Cosmopolitan survives, plying his artistic trade, leading another unsuspecting reader into the dark. But as a public author, Melville may well have known that he was taking his last long dive. Though he continued to write poetry until the end of his life and returned to prose fiction in *Billy Budd*, he never again thought seriously of public success. Possibly, after all, it was the artist, as much as the religious quester, who told Hawthorne that he had "pretty much made up his mind to be annihilated."

Vere's Use of the "Forms":
Means and Ends in *Billy Budd*

Christopher W. Sten

SINCE THE 1962 appearance of the Hayford-Sealts edition of *Billy Budd, Sailor,* there has been no break in the critical inquest, initiated by Joseph Schiffman's ironist reading in 1950, into Melville's view of Vere's decision to execute Billy.[1] Edward H. Rosenberry and Paul Brodtkorb, Jr., each attempted to settle the dispute in the mid-1960's, but the more recent conflicting assessments by Bernard Rosenthal and B. L. Reid seem to imply that the two traditions in *Billy Budd* criticism will live as long as Melville's most controversial novel continues to be read.[2] The very difficulty of resolving the controversy may, however, indicate that Melville intended neither to endorse nor to condemn Vere's judgment. Indeed, Hayford and Sealts have concluded that the effect of Melville's "noncommittal 'alienation,'" achieved by his late dramatizations of what earlier had stood as partisan statements, was "often—perhaps usually—deliberately sought."[3] Still, perhaps some progress in this celebrated case can be made, first by arguing for the necessity of Vere's decision and then by suggesting what might have been Melville's purpose in creating that necessity. *Billy Budd* poses a typically Romantic question which every reader

---

[1] Harrison Hayford and Merton M. Sealts, Jr., eds., *Billy Budd, Sailor (An Inside Narrative)* (Chicago, 1962). References are to this edition and appear in the text. Besides Schiffman, "Melville's Final Stage, Irony: A Re-examination of *Billy Budd* Criticism," *American Literature,* XXII (May, 1950), 128–136, see Hayford-Sealts, pp. 26–27 and 203–212, for the other pre-1962 ironist critics; and W. G. Kilbourne, Jr., "Montaigne and Captain Vere," *American Literature,* XXXIII (Jan., 1962), 514–517; Ray B. Browne, *"Billy Budd:* Gospel of Democracy," *Nineteenth-Century Fiction,* XVII (March, 1963), 321–337; Ralph W. Willett, "Nelson and Vere: Hero and Victim in *Billy Budd, Sailor,"* PMLA, LXXXII (Oct., 1967), 370–376; and Bernard Rosenthal, "Elegy for Jack Chase," *Studies in Romanticism,* X (Summer, 1971), 213–229.

[2] Rosenberry, a non-ironist, examines the novel's tone and "ethical logic," in "The Problem of *Billy Budd,"* PMLA, LXXX (Dec., 1965), 489–498, while Brodtkorb, in "The Definitive *Billy Budd:* 'But aren't it all sham?'" PMLA, LXXXII (Dec., 1967), 602–612, argues that virtually "everything is demonstrable," because the novel is "unfinished." Rosenthal; Reid, "Old Melville's Fable," *Massachusetts Review,* IX (Summer, 1968), 529–546.

[3] Hayford-Sealts, p. 38.

is left to answer for himself: Does the end—civilization—justify the inevitable sacrifice of the natural man?

The Captain's reasoning, while it seems to have had Melville's reluctant sympathy, cannot be said to have had his full support, for in his presentation of Vere's handling of the case Melville merely brought into focus the means-and-ends dilemma. Rather than an autocratically held end in itself, every one of Vere's applications of the "forms," like each of his deviations from them, was a deliberately chosen means to the end of insuring the security of England and thence the salvation of "the Old World" (pp. 128, 54). Billy, like Christ, was sacrificed not by a "martinet" but by a benevolent despot who used inhuman means to effect ends at once tragic and potentially divine: the death of a blameless man and "the peace of the world and the true welfare of mankind" (pp. 128, 63).[4]

Although the Christian parallel need not signal Melville's endorsement of Vere's decision, it may signal his larger intent. By focusing on the means-and-ends dilemma through this secularized version of the Crucifixion story, Melville makes us sensible of the price of civilization. And he reminds us that the responsibilities of the survivors, like the "agony" of authority and the passion of the victim, are features of our everyday lives, not antique curiosities (p. 115). Civilized beings bear a responsibility to the sacrificial victim who, as an "upright barbarian," symbolizes the natural in every man; thus they bear a responsibility to themselves to make their civilized lives worthy of the ideal in whose name the sacrifice is made (p. 52). First Adamic, then Christ-like, this "child-man" whose life was taken in his twenty-first year is finally a type of us all (p. 86). His fate is the human fate. It is because Melville sought to awaken us to the common fate and its attendant responsibility that he could go no further in his defense of Vere; he had to stop where he did in order to prevent this work of imaginative literature from becoming the political treatise it is often taken to be.

II

Despite the many indictments, it is remarkable that those who condemn Vere's decision seldom offer more than *ad hominem* argu-

[4] For an earlier treatment of the means-and-ends problem, see Wendell Glick, "Expediency and Absolute Morality in *Billy Budd*," *PMLA*, LXVIII (March, 1953), 103–110.

ments based upon ironic readings of the text. Vere is viewed as a
tyrant who blindly or weakly or insanely followed, rather than man-
fully defied, the "forms, measured forms" of the Mutiny Act which
demanded death as the penalty for striking an officer. Thus he is
supposed to have violated those "primitive instincts," forming the
basis of natural law, which demand mercy for one who was not only
innocent of intent but, as even Vere felt sure, had also rid the world
of an "Ananias" (pp. 109, 100). To condemn Vere on such grounds,
however, is in itself to violate the principles of natural law. It is to
look but to the "frontage," as war and the Mutiny Act do, and to
judge Vere by the consequence of his decision rather than by his
intent, as Vere said the court must judge Billy (p. 112).

   Yet Vere's decision invites condemnation, as surely as it was meant
to. Melville knew it would because he knew from the experience of
his cousin, Guert Gansevoort, that the comparable conduct of the
Somers affair had been condemned.[5] Moreover, the *Bellipotent's* surgeon, the court, and later "some officers" criticized Vere's handling
of the case (p. 103). While Melville was concerned to demonstrate
the need for compassion, for Vere no less than for Billy, he was
equally concerned to demonstrate that compassion will suffice for
neither of these tragic figures. The power of compassion cannot
exceed the power of historical circumstance to create the tragic necessity for inhuman action, and in this Melville could rely on the authority of the Father of the crucified Christ. Sympathetic understanding of Vere's rationale is warrantable, but so is indignation at the
necessity of Billy's death. One must feel both pity and fear in response
to this tragedy.

   Melville's intention to portray the grim necessity of Billy's execution is revealed by the fact that the narrative cards could hardly have
been stacked more expertly to force Vere's hand. Indeed, that "the
unhappy event" (Claggart's death at the hand of Billy) "could not
have happened at a worse juncture was but too true." If Melville's
intention, as the ironists argue, was in fact to strike out at arbitrary
authority, it seems reasonable to ask why he bothered to place the
event at a juncture which included among its critical factors not only
the recently "suppressed insurrections" at Spithead and the Nore but
a tightly interlocked and painstakingly detailed arrangement of other

---

[5] See Hayford-Sealts, pp. 26–30, 181–183.

circumstances: that there were some on board who had participated in those insurrections; that England's defense rested on her navy; that the enemy had been sighted just before Claggart's death; that the *Bellipotent* stood at the moment "almost at her furthest remove from the fleet"; and that the incident occurred "in the latter part of an afternoon watch," when the cover of night, too conducive to the kind of intrigue earlier refused by Billy, was soon approaching (pp. 102, 90). Important as it is, the argument from the author's need for dramatic tension seems inadequate; for what on one level is dramatic tension becomes on another the source of the problem and the debate.

From the outset Vere was portrayed not as one imprisoned by forms or conventions but as one independent in mind and nonconformist in manner. In conversation, for example, the narrator remarked that the "honesty" of "natures constituted like Captain Vere's . . . prescribes to them directness, sometimes far-reaching like that of a migratory fowl that in its flight never heeds when it crosses a frontier" (p. 63). This simile, coming as it does at the end, emphasizes Vere's characterization throughout Chapters 6 and 7 as a man who did not fear to transgress the world's boundaries—its customs, its forms—in pursuit of a distant goal. More pertinently, neither was the Captain portrayed as a mechanical formalist in his attitude toward the crew or toward Billy. We are told that, "though a conscientious disciplinarian, he was no lover of authority for mere authority's sake," and in his speech to the court (" 'I feel as you do for this unfortunate boy' ") and in his closeted interview with the foretopman we witness Vere's heartfelt desire to do Billy justice (pp. 104, 113). But Billy was the "man trap" Claggart claimed him to be, one which Vere knew he must avoid (p. 94). Unlike Ahab, Vere knew the cruel injustice of the fact that "whatever devotes itself to justice at the expense of reality," in the memorable words of Frank Kermode, "is finally self-destructive."[6] But Vere knew, too, as his own subsequent death showed, that there is no cause more worthy of devotion. In the fight against the *Atheist,* he died for the same cause for which he sacrificed Billy—the defense of his nation and his view of what constitutes justice to mankind.

Unconcerned about self-destruction, Vere was unswervingly concerned about the destruction of the British community for which he

---

[6] *The Sense of an Ending: Studies in the Theory of Fiction* (New York, 1967), p. 105.

spoke and acted. He was "prompted by duty and the law," he said in formulating the case against Billy, and duty to that community demanded that he prevent a mutiny on his ship (p. 113). In this time of war, a mutiny would have endangered not simply the lives of those on board; as the spread of insurrection in the Great Mutiny had shown, it would have endangered also the very life of a fleet which was "the right arm of a Power then all but the sole free conservative one of the Old World." Hence mutiny had the potential for becoming to "the British Empire . . . what a strike in the fire brigade would be to London threatened by general arson" (p. 54). Vere had to choose, therefore, either individual justice or communal justice; for in the fate of Billy Budd possibly rested the fate of an entire nation, perhaps even of "the Old World."

Given this context, only two issues could have made Vere's decision debatable: the question whether the possibility of mutiny on the *Bellipotent* was real and present; and the danger of encountering the enemy before the case could be referred to the admiral. That Vere's fear of mutiny was not paranoiac is suggested by the narrator's assertion that "Discontent foreran the Two Mutinies, and more or less it lurkingly survived them. Hence it was not unreasonable to apprehend some return of trouble sporadic or general" (p. 59). What is even more pertinent, Vere knew that the *Bellipotent* was at the time "mustering some who . . . had taken a guilty part in the late serious troubles" and "others also" who had been impressed into her duty (p. 92). The impressed men, too, were not trustworthy: "sometimes," particularly before twilight, they were "apt to fall into a saddish mood which in some partook of sullenness" at the thought of their families at home (pp. 49–50). While "very little in the manner of the men . . . would have suggested to an ordinary observer that the Great Mutiny was a recent event," some grounds arose to substantiate Vere's sense of the potential mood of his men (pp. 59–60). At least they were not docilely responsive to his every word, as seen on three occasions—the announcement of Billy's execution, the execution itself, and Billy's sea interment—when order had to be restored by a "strategic command" for an uncustomary use of the forms. On the first occasion there went up from the crew a "confused," on the second an "inarticulate," and on the third a "strange human" murmur, the last followed by an "uncertain movement . . . in which some encroachment was made" (pp. 117, 126–127). That Vere's judgment against Billy provoked these disturbances is beyond question. But it is also true that the potential for mutiny was shown to exist among the men both before and after the judgment was announced.

According to Ralph W. Willett, Vere's "fear of mutiny serves to rationalize" his "hasty" judgment that Billy must hang; for, Willett hedgingly asserts, Melville "points out" that the possibility of mutiny "is in no way suggested by the behavior of the *Bellipotent's* crew." Attributing Vere's prejudgment to the temporary impairment of his "powers of cerebration," Willett argues that "The most clearly ironic example" of his "rashness" "begins with Vere's attempt to forestall mutiny by making an example of Billy Budd; this only serves to stimulate discontent among the crew and to make Billy a martyr."[7] There is irony here, to be sure, but "the *might-have-been,*" as the narrator observes, "is but boggy ground to build on" (p. 57). There was simply no way for Vere, as there is none for us, to be sure how the crew would have acted had Budd not been executed. Though there is no certainty that Billy's hanging prevented a mutiny, Willett begs the question when he concludes that its "only" effect is the ironic one. Furthermore, that Vere's fear of mutiny was not a rationalization but a fundamental concern can be seen as early as midway in Claggart's accusations, even before Billy had been named. Vere is said to have concluded that even "if in view of recent events prompt action should be taken at the first palpable sign of recurring insubordination . . . not judicious would it be . . . to keep the idea of lingering disaffection alive by undue forwardness in crediting an informer, even if his own subordinate and charged . . . with police surveillance of the crew" (p. 93). Thus, too, by reserving judgment about his master-at-arms's report, the Captain early revealed his willingness to deviate from the forms when his crew's steadiness was at issue.

Once again, Vere's fear of mutiny was not self-contained; it related to his more comprehensive desire to maintain full strength in the event of a confrontation with the enemy, which in turn related to his larger concerns for the defense of England and "the peace of the world and the true welfare of mankind." Such a confrontation had almost occurred just before Claggart accused Billy, when an enemy frigate was sighted and the *Bellipotent* gave chase. The fact that this

[7] Willett, pp. 370–371.

was a frigate is important, because it implies the proximity of a French squadron or fleet, frigates being sent out alone primarily as scouts; as Hayford and Sealts point out, they "formed no part of the line of battle."[8] Then, too, it was while on "a somewhat distant" expedition, the *Bellipotent* being "almost at her furthest remove from the fleet," that she unexpectedly sighted the frigate; consequently, there was time in which to encounter enemy battleships before Billy's case could be brought to Vere's superior (p. 90). Neither fanciful nor fanatical, Vere's desire to insure full strength for an enemy engagement was vindicated by the subsequent clash with the *Atheist*. Indeed, Melville seems to have been doubly willing to vindicate the Captain in this matter by contriving the French line-of-battle ship's defeat. Though Vere lost his life in this fight, like Lord Nelson he had fulfilled his duty to maintain England's security.

III

Although the possibilities of a mutiny and of a meeting with the enemy were the two critical factors in Vere's decision, his detractors have tended to focus on the first of these and on subsidiary questions relating to his conduct of the trial. Besides his failure to place the case in the admiral's hands, these include Vere's demands for secrecy in the proceedings against Billy; his determination of the irregular make-up of the court; his demand for dispatch in its reaching a verdict; his briefs to the court and virtual usurpation of its role; and, running through each of the others, the question of his mental stability at the time. It is here that examination of Vere's use of the forms most clearly reveals his deliberateness; for in each of these matters except the last—and this turns upon his thinking in the others—Vere clandestinely deviated from the forms or manipulated them to his advantage. And he did so for the same reasons he espoused in adhering to the forms of the Mutiny Act in the final verdict; he had to insure the stability of his men and thence the safety of his nation.

Vere's demands for secrecy, like his other contrivances for assuring his command, commenced immediately after Claggart accused Billy, when the Captain showed "perplexity" chiefly about "how best to act in regard to the informer." Although at first "he was naturally for

---

[8] Hayford-Sealts, p. 144.

summoning that substantiation of his allegations which Claggart said was at hand," Vere realized that "such a proceeding would result in the matter at once getting abroad, which in the present stage of it, he thought, might undesirably affect the ship's company." Thus deserting the customary course, which he felt free to do because his crew had as yet no precise expectations, Vere "would first practically test the accuser" by shifting the scene from the "broad quarter-deck" to his cabin and there scrutinizing "the mutually confronting visages" upon the reiteration of Claggart's charge. His fear of publicity even at this early stage seems appropriate, because "the interview's continuance already had attracted observation" from some of the sailors (pp. 96–98).

Vere's desire for secrecy following Claggart's death was consistent with that before it, and from then on he was even more cautious. "Here he may or may not have erred," the narrator said equivocally; but still it is suggested that this and every subsequent decision had been thoroughly considered: "Until he could decide upon his course, and in each detail; and not only so, but until the concluding measure was upon the point of being enacted, he deemed it advisable, in view of all the circumstances, to guard as much as possible against publicity" (p. 103). Thus, having earlier used Albert, in whose "discretion and fidelity" he had "much confidence," to retrieve Billy, Vere was so careful as to hide Claggart's body from the hammock-boy's view when he was summoned to send for the surgeon (p. 97). Though Vere's wariness was called into question by the surgeon, it was later seen to have been warranted by the crew's continued curiosity in the affair. For, while "less than an hour and a half had elapsed" between Claggart's disappearance and the announcement of Billy's execution, it "was an interval long enough . . . to awaken speculations among no few of the ship's company as to what it was that could be detaining in the cabin the master-at-arms and the sailor" (p. 116). Though Vere, also in the cabin during this period, did not witness their curiosity, he was a commander "long versed in everything pertaining to the complicated gun-deck life, which like every other form of life has its secret mines and dubious side, the side popularly disclaimed" (p. 93). While it can be said that there would have been no cause for rumors had Vere proceeded aboveboard throughout, as was customary in capital cases, it cannot be known whether in that event there might not have been cause for mutiny.[9]

Why Vere hastened to call a drumhead court, like the question of why he demanded dispatch in its reaching a verdict, is answered by his remark near the end of the trial: " 'while thus strangely we prolong proceedings that should be summary—the enemy may be sighted and an engagement result' " (p. 112). Thus keeping his eye on larger responsibilities, Vere deviated from usage; for the surgeon and the court agreed that it would be best to confine Billy, "and in a way dictated by usage," and wait until the matter could be referred to the admiral (p. 101). In fact, the "case indeed was such that fain would the *Bellipotent's* captain have deferred taking any [final] action whatever respecting it." But with the "self-abnegation" of a monk he chose to keep "his vows of allegiance to martial duty." This statement, suspect in isolation, is translated to mean not that Vere weakly subordinated the claims of his conscience but that he steadfastly attempted to maintain his crew's stability: "Feeling that unless quick action was taken on it, the deed of the foretopman, so soon as it should be known on the gun decks, would tend to awaken any slumbering embers of the Nore among the crew, a sense of the urgency of the case overruled in Captain Vere every other consideration" (p. 104).

There has been less dispute about Vere's determination of the court's irregular make-up, although in selecting the officer of marines to sit with the sea lieutenant and the sailing master he again "perhaps deviated from general custom." He did so because "he took that soldier to be a judicious person, thoughtful, and not altogether incapable of grappling with a difficult case unprecedented in his prior experience." Yet even as to him Vere had "some latent misgiving" about the reliability of his "extremely good-natured" character in "a moral dilemma involving aught of the tragic." Nonetheless, the marine captain seemed to be more suitable as a judge than the other two "honest natures," for "their intelligence was mostly confined to the matter of active seamanship and the fighting demands of their profession" (pp. 104–105). While they were hardly ideal jurists (Vere regarded them as "well-meaning men not intellectually mature"), in light of their demurrers during the trial—particularly those voiced by the soldier, "the most reluctant to condemn of the members"—it can-

---

[9] See C. B. Ives, *"Billy Budd* and the Articles of War," *American Literature*, XXXIV (March, 1962), 36.

not be claimed that Vere had unfairly stacked the court in this departure from custom (pp. 109, 129).

Once the court had been convened, Captain Vere interfered in its role and deliberations in at least four ways. First, though "temporarily sinking his rank" because he was the only witness in the case, he was cautious enough to maintain it "in a matter apparently trivial" by testifying from the ship's elevated side (p. 105). Second, he instructed the court to confine its attention to the blow's consequence, not its provocation or intent. Third, he assumed the role of "coadjutor," arguing against allegiance to Nature and in behalf of allegiance to the King (p. 110). And, last, he warned against mitigating the sentence. While each interference entailed a violation of due process or a departure from custom, Vere's rationale in each instance, as seen in his reply to the marine captain's inquiry about leniency, returned to his persistent fear of mutiny: " 'consider the consequences of such clemency,' " he said. " 'The people' (meaning the ship's company) 'have native sense; most of them are familiar with our naval usage and tradition. . . . [T]o the people the foretopman's deed . . . will be plain homicide committed in a flagrant act of mutiny.' " If the well-known penalty does not follow, " 'Will they not revert to the recent outbreak at the Nore?' " (p. 112).

These interferences, together with the concluding warning against clemency, make it obvious that Vere's primary interest was to bring the secret court's verdict into line with public expectations. That this verdict was demanded by "the law of the Mutiny Act" (or so Melville thought) was important to Vere because the law corresponded with and defined his crew's expectations (p. 111). If, having already decided against Billy, the Captain then railroaded his judgment through the court, why did he bother to convene it? One implicit explanation is that, because Vere could not know beforehand how the court would decide, its concurrence was an even wager. More importantly, Vere was "very far" from wishing to monopolize to himself "the perils of moral responsibility." Hence his motivation for not varying from "usage" in turning "the matter over to a summary court of his own officers" was not self-serving.[10] It stemmed from his

[10] In fact, Vere's argument from "usage" in this regard is tenuous. See Hayford-Sealts, pp. 175–176, and Ives, pp. 32–36. Apparently this was Melville's error, as he made a related mistake earlier, when it was said that Vere had been a member of "a court-martial ashore . . . when a lieutenant" (p. 94). "According to statute," the editors say, "regular naval courts-martial consisted of commanders and captains" (p. 178). See also pp. 181–182.

awareness of the limited "moral" capacity of one man to decide such an issue. Vere knew he was not God. Yet he also knew that he had sole responsibility for any of the crew's actions which might result from a lenient verdict by the court. Thus he reserved "to himself, as the one on whom the ultimate accountability would rest, the right of maintaining a supervision of it, or formally or informally interposing at need" (p. 104). Even Vere's subsequent interferences, then, had been anticipated. He was a deliberate, even a prescient, man. While his calculations, like his justifications, might still be judged "insane," it cannot be argued that he had lost self-control (p. 102). It is as true of Vere as of Nelson that "in foresight as to the larger issue of an encounter, and anxious preparations for it . . . few commanders have been so painstakingly circumspect as this same reckless declarer of his person in fight" (pp. 57–58).

Because all proceedings after the announcement of Billy's hanging were necessarily public, Vere felt an even greater need to be circumspect. Accordingly, once Billy had been transferred from the Captain's quarters "without unusual precautions—at least no visible ones," then "certain unobtrusive measures were taken absolutely to insure" that no one but the chaplain had communication with him. Contrary to the narrator's assertion, however, Vere did not observe "strict adherence to usage" in every public proceeding "growing out of the tragedy," despite the fact that in no point could usage be deviated from "without begetting undesirable speculations in the ship's company" (pp. 117–118). When Vere ordered the drummer to beat to quarters "at an hour prior to the customary one" in response to the crew's "encroachment" following Billy's burial, the narrator remarks: "That such variance from usage was authorized by an officer like Captain Vere . . . was evidence of the necessity for unusual action implied in what he deemed to be temporarily the mood of his men" (pp. 127–128). Though Vere risked the consequences of manipulating the forms in public only under the most pressing circumstances, this stratagem shows the power of the forms to have been such that their use was imperative in all dealings with the crew.

" 'With mankind,' " Vere would say, " 'forms, measured forms, are everything; and that is the import couched in the story of Orpheus with his lyre spellbinding the wild denizens of the wood.' And this he once applied to the disruption of forms going on across the Channel and the consequences thereof" (p. 128).[11] It was a mechanically inhuman, unredeemed society which Vere saw, but it was the reality he could not ignore despite his desire to do Billy justice. Vere's statement was an insight of tragic dimension and a lament for the inexorable state of things as they are, not a declaration of personal philosophy. It was not with Vere but with "mankind," and in particular these men-of-war's men who were "of all men the greatest sticklers for usage," that the forms were sacrosanct (p. 117). Almost at the moment Claggart fell, Vere, who was "in general a man of rapid decision," spoke his full comprehension of the paradoxical situation before him: " 'Struck dead by an angel of God! Yet the angel must hang!' " (pp. 103, 101). He knew, therefore, that the lyre's forms do indeed "lie." But he knew, too, that only the forms could "spell-bind" his crew. Unlike Billy and the *Bellipotent's* other prelapsarian sailors, Vere had partaken of the "questionable apple of knowledge" (p. 52). With him the forms were not "everything." There were also the otherwise "wild denizens" of the man-of-war world and the inhuman "consequences" of the "disruption of forms going on across the Channel"—the "wars which like a flight of harpies rose shrieking from the din and dust of the fallen Bastille" and the attendant chaos responsible for both the abrogation of the Rights of Man in Billy's impressment and the destruction of Starry Vere (p. 66).

Yet Vere's tragedy was not that he died in service to mankind. His tragedy was that he had to use the inhuman forms of the Mutiny Act in order to attempt to secure more human forms, and not merely in order to conserve the stability of the larger community. A "bachelor," without wife and child at home to protect, Vere "disinterestedly opposed" the theories of the revolutionary innovators "not alone because they seemed to him insusceptible of embodiment in lasting institutions, but at war with the peace of the world and the true welfare of mankind" (pp. 60, 62–63). Certainly the objective of

---

[11] A more precise parallel between Vere and Orpheus is suggested by the fact that the mythical poet is known for resolving "a quarrel among the Argonauts (on whose voyage he sailed) that enabled them to reach Colchis strand and the Golden Fleece," though, unlike Vere, Orpheus achieved control over the ship's company by the eloquence of his poetry. See Thomas H. Cain, "Spenser and the Renaissance Orpheus," *University of Toronto Quarterly*, XLI (Fall, 1971), 25. Note also that, according to one of Spenser's sources, civilization originated with Orpheus (p. 27).

"world peace" has been invoked to embolden the schemes of tyrant and madman; but, for that very reason, it is not an objective we can afford to live without. Everyone with an objective—whether Claggart, Billy, or Vere; whether Satan, Christ, or God—must use the imperfect means of the world to achieve his end. And this is, I think, the legacy of Melville's tragic, anti-Transcendentalist vision. His portrayal of Vere's dilemma presents the means-and-ends riddle with a vengeance, and our recognition of the riddle in *Billy Budd* makes it impossible to read this work as Melville's "testament of acceptance."[12] The arbitrary fate of Captain Vere makes us feel the human need for the forms, but the unjust fate of Billy Budd makes us, like Vere, feel the need to change the state of things as they are and so to make more human forms possible.

Following Billy's early morning sea burial, "the circumambient air in the clearness of its serenity was like smooth white marble in the polished block not yet removed from the marble-dealer's yard." These are the last words of Melville's narrative, save the "three brief chapters" of its "sequel," and they suggest not an end but the possibility of a new beginning. The day is pure potentiality for those who witness the common fate; the world has begun anew, as it had for the survivors of an earlier Gethsemane. But it can truly begin anew only if the sacrifice of the natural "child-man" awakens us to the recognition that our potential salvation has its price—our debt to the victim and our responsibility to create a world worthy of his sacrifice. The world as it stands, like the book which mirrors it, lacks the "symmetry of form attainable in pure fiction"; it, too, is "less finished than an architectural finial" (p. 128). Most important, it has not been, nor is it meant to be, "accepted" as it is. The marble still lies in waiting; civilized, human form has yet to be realized.

IV

In his travels, Melville had seen people in all corners cutting themselves off from Nature or ruthlessly being cut off from her by civi-

---

[12] E. L. Grant Watson coined this controversial term, in "Melville's Testament of Acceptance," *New England Quarterly*, VI (June, 1933), 319–327. See also William Braswell, "Melville's *Billy Budd* as 'An Inside Narrative,' " *American Literature*, XXIX (May, 1957), 133–146; Richard Harter Fogle, "*Billy Budd*: The Order of the Fall," *Nineteenth-Century Fiction*, XV (Dec., 1960), 189–205; Brodtkorb; and Reid.

lized man. And what he found in civilization was not sufficiently redeeming to justify the loss without perturbation. This was especially true because civilized man had blithely forgotten the loss in his pursuit of "that manufacturable thing known as respectability." The "doctrine of man's Fall," according to the narrator, was "a doctrine now popularly ignored," even though it implies the death of the Budd in every civilized man. For he observes that "where certain virtues pristine and unadulterate peculiarly characterize anybody in the external uniform of civilization, they will upon scrutiny seem not to be derived from custom or convention, but rather to be out of keeping with these, as if indeed exceptionally transmitted from a period prior to Cain's city and citified man" (pp. 52-53). Still, Melville seems not to be proposing a Rousseauist rejection of civilization. Having made the discovery more than forty years earlier when he wrote *Typee,* Melville still knew that once a mañ had bitten of "the questionable apple of knowledge" he could not return to Nature and the time before Cain. *Billy Budd* suggests that the Fall is a rite of passage as irreversible as it is perilous.

The inadequacy of the chaplain's Christian "consolation," which he extended to the still prelapsarian Billy awaiting death, seems to imply that in his last years Melville himself could not find consolation in institutionalized Christianity (p. 120). But in a work in which he more than once voiced the expectation that his readers would find the novel's "savor of Holy Writ" disagreeable, it is fitting that Melville's retelling of the Crucifixion story on the historical plane should reveal his support of the essential truth of the complexly tragic and triumphant Christian story as human drama (p. 76). Like Christ, Billy was forced to play his role by the necessities of time and by his awful responsibility to a community which failed to understand, yet unknowingly benefited from, his sacrifice. Melville's "inside narrative" strikes that uneven balance and recalls to us what we were and are, though it foretells nothing about what we shall become. Prophecy is not the function of tragedy. But, having gained the burdensome knowledge of duty, we thus are free to change ourselves and our world. Like all great literature, *Billy Budd* ends not so much with an answer and an ideological stand as with a question and a challenge to remake the world in a more benevolent image. Unless Billy's sacrifice "vitalizes into acts" the heroic potential of those in whose name the sacrifice is made, as it vitalized Vere's in his fight against the *Atheist,* then such sacrifice is indeed "vainglory," as the Benthamites claimed of the death of Nelson; then, too, "affectation and fustian is each more heroic line" of *Billy Budd,* and our investigations into its meaning are little more than antiquarianism (pp. 57–58).

The Composition of *Moby-Dick*

James Barbour

S OME TWENTY YEARS AGO George R. Stewart's "The Two *Moby-Dicks*" appeared in *American Literature*.[1] Since that time his theory of the composition of *Moby-Dick,* though often ignored, has not been seriously questioned;[2] it is, briefly, that there were two separate narratives written during two distinct periods of time and arranged back to back in the completed work. It is now time to review the theory of "two *Moby-Dicks*" in order to see whether it accurately describes either the writing of the novel or the manner in which Melville arranged the compositional parts—for undoubtedly Melville spent an unexpected length of time upon his book and probably engaged in a considerable amount of arranging and rearranging before it went through the press.

I

The "two *Moby-Dicks*" culminates a history of investigation frequently marked by shrewd and brilliant literary scholarship. From the time the book was revived in 1919 until 1939, it was assumed that *Moby-Dick* was of seriatim composition begun in February, 1850, and completed in early autumn, 1851. This assumption was first questioned by Leon Howard in a paper delivered to the MLA convention in New Orleans in 1939.[3] On the basis of the slight evidence then available he inferred that there may have been a major revision of the novel after August, 1850, when the manuscript was described as "mostly done."[4] This inference was later supported by the discovery of letters in which Melville described the stages of composition of the early narrative. In 1947 Charles Olson

---

[1] XXV (Jan., 1954), 417–448.

[2] Hershel Parker and Harrison Hayford in *Moby-Dick as Doubloon* (New York, 1970), p. 378, note that in much of the criticism that followed Stewart's article "the theory tends to be stated as fact."

[3] Printed as "Melville's Struggle with the Angel," *Modern Language Quarterly*, I (June, 1940), 195–206.

[4] Jay Leyda, *The Melville Log* (New York, 1951), I, 385.

in *Call Me Ishmael* (New York, p. 35) announced, "*Moby-Dick*
was two books written between February, 1850, and August, 1851.
The first book did not contain Ahab. It may not, except incidentally, have contained Moby-Dick." Howard P. Vincent in *The
Trying-Out of Moby-Dick* (Boston, 1949) hypothesized a revision
that began much later, in the spring of 1851, when Melville acquired
Owen Chase's *Narrative*,[5] his source for the sinking of the *Pequod*.

But the two works that were to settle matters were still to be
written. Leon Howard returned to the topic in his biography
Herman Melville (Berkeley, California, 1951, 150–179), and in his
chapter "Second Growth" he described Melville's inspirational revision of the early whaling narrative as under the tutelage of Shakespeare and Hawthorne he began philosophically and histrionically
to reshape his "whaling voyage." Finally George R. Stewart in
"The Two *Moby-Dicks*" identified the point at which the revision
began: he concluded that the early chapters (1–16) were original;
they were stitched by transitional chapters (17–22) to the revised
narrative (23–"Epilogue").

Stewart's "The Two *Moby-Dicks*" is the only study that has been
solely devoted to the problem of composition. Leon Howard was
primarily interested in Melville's intellectual growth; Howard P.
Vincent was concerned with the cetological genesis of the novel;
and Charles Olson offered an impressionistic prose poem inspired
by the book—each man touched upon the composition only in
passing. Stewart, the last to speak, seemingly untangled the compositional riddle. However, his assumptions and methodology were
too limited: he believed there was only one seam in the book, and
he ignored external evidence that would have altered his conclusions.[6]

This external evidence is available: there are letters that describe
the narrative during its various stages of writing, chapters that are
datable through external reference, and source materials that are
both identifiable and datable. This evidence indicates that there

[5] Vincent implies that the plot of *Moby-Dick* was added after September, 1850 (p. 45).
But what was included in this revision is unclear, for Vincent also states that the white
whale did not swim into the novel before March or April, 1851 (p. 47).

[6] Had Stewart employed the datable textual references and source material, he probably
would have noticed that the earliest datable chapters (78 and 90) indicate the original
narrative extends beyond chapter 22.

were not just two, but three well defined periods in the writing of
Moby-Dick:

1. The writing of an early whaling novel begun in February,
   1850, and "mostly done" by August of the same year.
2. A period from August, 1850, until early in 1851 when Melville was writing cetological chapters and perhaps interpo-
   lating adventure chapters into the narrative.
3. A final period, when, under the influence of Shakespeare and
   Hawthorne, Melville was revising the early narrative; this
   period extended from early 1851 until the publication of the
   book in the fall of the year.

II

The progress Melville made on the whaling story that he began
in February, 1850, can be followed through three letters written
between May and August.

The story is first mentioned in a letter of May 1 to Richard H.
Dana, Jr., in which Melville writes: "About the 'whaling voyage'
—I am half way in the work, & am very glad that your suggestion
so jumps with mine. It will be a strange sort of book, tho', I fear;
blubber is blubber you know; tho' you may get oil out of it, the
poetry runs as hard as sap from a frozen maple tree;—& to cook the
thing up, one must needs throw in a little fancy . . . . Yet I mean
to give the truth of the thing, spite of this."[7]

Two months later he wrote to his English publisher Richard
Bentley offering the work for publication in the fall and describing
it as "a romance of adventure, founded upon certain wild legends
in the Southern Sperm Whale Fisheries, and illustrated by the
author's own personal experience, of two years & more, as a harpooneer" [sic].[8]

A final reference comes from Evert Duyckinck, editor of the
Literary World; he evidently read Melville's manuscript, for he
wrote to his brother George on August 7, 1850: "Melville has a new

---

[7] *The Letters of Herman Melville,* ed., Merrell R. Davis and William H. Gilman (New
Haven, Conn., 1960), p. 108.
[8] *Letters,* p. 109.

book mostly done—a romantic, fanciful, & literal & most enjoyable presentment of the whale fishery,—something quite new."[9]

The theory that this narrative was substantially revised is founded in large part on the testimony of these letters. They describe the consistent progress of the narrative. If Duyckinck's observation is correct—and there is no reason to suppose otherwise—then the manuscript could have been ready for publication in late autumn. Its completion a year later suggests the story was extensively revised. Melville's description of the story lends support to this theory, for nowhere is Ahab or Moby Dick mentioned in his letters; rather he describes it in more general terms as a romantic but truthful "whaling voyage."

Evert Duyckinck's unique position as the only person known to have read the early story is significant in that he also reviewed *Moby-Dick* in the *Literary World* (November 22, 1851). In the review he observed, "there are evidently two if not three books in *Moby-Dick* rolled into one."[10] Undoubtedly he recognized the changes Melville had made in the story since he had read it the year before; perhaps it was that which prompted him to divide the novel into books. He had enjoyed the story in manuscript, but he only approved of one of the "books" in the published work: that was Melville's "thoroughly exhaustive account admirably given of the great Sperm Whale . . . [with] its level passages, its humorous touches, its quaint suggestion, its incident usually picturesque and occasionally sublime."[11] Duyckinck's use of words like "humorous," "quaint," and "picturesque" indicates that much of what he had read and enjoyed in the manuscript may have remained in the completed work, for Duyckinck's passage paraphrases Melville's earlier description of the story as a strange sort of tale into which was thrown a little fancy, yet one that also told the truth.

9 *The Melville Log*, p. 385.

10 "Melville's *Moby-Dick; or, The Whale," Literary World*, IX (Nov. 22, 1851), rpt. as "An Intellectual Chowder" in *Moby-Dick: Norton Critical Edition*, ed. Harrison Hayford and Hershel Parker (New York, 1967), p. 613. All quotations from the novel are taken from this edition and cited by page reference in the text.

11 P. 613. Duyckinck objected to the portion of the novel where the crew of the *Pequod* (especially Ahab) act like characters in a German melodrama, and to the poetic conceits, extravagant speculations, and the "piratical running down of creeds and opinions" (p. 615). His objections would seem to include the dramatic and cetological chapters (Duyckinck specifically complains of the "run-a-muck style of Carlyle," an influence in the cetology); he also took offense at "The Ramadan" (17), an early land chapter, for theological reasons.

If the account of the Sperm Whale belongs to the original narrative, then the first whaling story extends far beyond the land chapters (1–22) hitherto identified with the original narrative. Datable evidence supports this possibility, for if Melville wrote his material soon after the events to which he refers (as logic suggests), then two chapters late in the novel are of early origin: "Cistern and Buckets" (78) compares the fall of one of the harpooners inside the head of a sperm whale to the collapse of Table Rock into the Niagara, an event that occurred on June 25, 1850; "Heads or Tails" (90) recounts an anecdote Melville read in the June 29 issue of the *Literary World*.

Also, if there is a chronological correlation between Melville's letters and the composition of the novel, "The Affidavit" (45) was probably written around the time of his letter of June 27 to Bentley, for the chapter is an extension of his phrase, "illustrated by the author's own experience, of two years & more as a harpooneer." In the chapter Ishmael claims authenticity for his story by citing "the author's own experience"—

I have personally known three instances where a whale, after receiving a harpoon, has effected a complete escape; and, after an interval (in one instance of three years), has been again struck by the same hand, and slain; when the two irons, both marked by the same private cypher, have been taken from the body.

. . . .

I say I, myself, have known three instances similar to this; that is in two of them I saw the whales struck; and, upon the second attack, saw the two irons with the respective marks cut in them, afterwards taken from the dead fish. In the three-year instance, it so fell out that I was in the boat both times, first and last, and the last time distinctly recognized a peculiar sort of huge mole under the whale's eye, which I had observed there three years previously. I say three years, but I am pretty sure it was more than that. Here are three instances, then, which I personally know the truth of. (pp. 175–176)[12]

[12] At most Melville may have had some experience as a harpooner on the *Charles and Henry*, a voyage of less than six months. Rather than personal experience in the early narrative, Melville seems to have relied on other whaling books: the account of the "three-year instance," for example, was taken from Rev. Henry Cheever's *The Whale and His Captors* (New York, 1850). Other sources that he used in his chapters of whaling adventure were Fredrick Debell Bennett's *A Whaling Voyage Round the World* (London, 1840); Fredrick Allyn Olmstead's *Incidents of a Whaling Voyage* (New York, 1841); and J. Ross Browne's *Etchings of a Whaling Cruise* (New York, 1846).

"The Affidavit," with its recitation of legendary whales and their feats, fulfills Melville's promise that the story will be based on "certain wild legends in the Southern Sperm Whale Fisheries."

It seems evident that the early narrative underwent some revision after August; otherwise the duration of time Melville worked on a "mostly done" story cannot be logically explained. Also Melville's and Duyckinck's descriptions of this story fail to match the published novel; they suggest the original was a more fanciful (but truthful), less dramatically conceived account of a whaling voyage. Whether chapters like "The Affidavit" (45), "Cistern and Buckets" (78), and "Heads or Tails" (90) are from the original narrative is not absolutely determinable. It is probably true that Melville composed chapters soon after the incidents to which he alludes, and that there was often a temporal connection between what he was writing in the novel and what he was writing to friends, but neither assumption is incontrovertible. However, the consistency with which such references describe and identify the composition of large sequential sections of the novel is convincing. At this point they only suggest that material written in the first stage may occur in *Moby-Dick* as late as chapter 90.

III

The compositional activity of the autumn and early winter had its antecedents in the spring. On May 1 when Melville estimated he was half-way through, he wrote to Dana stating that he was glad the latter's suggestion for the book coincided with his own idea. Dana may have urged him to "give the truth of the thing." Regardless, Melville had already begun gathering his factual sources. On April 29 he withdrew from the New York Society Library two volumes by William Scoresby, *Arctic Regions* and *History and Description of the Northern Sperm Whale Fishery*. Later in the month he asked Putnam's to send to England for Thomas Beale's authoritative work *The Natural History of the Sperm Whale*. Melville's intention in acquiring these sources was to add factual material about whales and whaling to the narrative to give it copiousness and authenticity.[13] Apparently he waited until his copy

---

[13] Howard, *Melville*, p. 162. In previous novels Melville had added factual material to his manuscript in the later stages of writing. For discussion of Melville's compositional habits

of Beale arrived before working on the cetology (informational chapters about whales, in particular the sperm whale).[14]

Melville received Beale's *Natural History* on July 10. However, the ensuing weeks were ones in which he had little time for writing. On July 15 he left New York City for the Berkshires, where he embarked immediately with his cousin on an agricultural tour of the county, returning on the evening of July 20. In the days following Melville read Hawthorne's *Mosses from an Old Manse* and visited the Shaker community in nearby Hancock, where he purchased *A Summary View of the Millenial Church*. On July 24 he returned to New York City and invited several friends to the Berkshires. He then packed up his own family and traveled back to the family home in Pittsfield to make preparations. On August 2 the guests arrived, among them Evert Duyckinck, who read the manuscript. What he read contained little or nothing from Beale's *Natural History,* for Melville had not had time to read and incorporate it into the story. It was probably in this sense that Duyckinck referred to the narrative as "mostly done."

In early August Melville wrote of the impact Hawthorne, and Shakespeare before him, had made on his imagination in his famous review "Hawthorne and His Mosses" (published in the *Literary World,* August 17 and 24, 1850). It is doubtful, however, that Melville found much time in the succeeding weeks for sustained writing. His energies were spent in other activities: "In September he bought a farm near Pittsfield, and returned to New York City only long enough to get his family moved. It was late fall before he was working regularly on the book that had seemed half finished at the first of May and 'mostly done' in August. Even then he worked under bad conditions."[15]

see the appropriate sections in Leon Howard's *Herman Melville;* Howard's "Historical Note" in Melville's *Typee* (Evanston, Ill., 1968); Harrison Hayford, "Introduction" to *Omoo* (New York, 1969); Merrell R. Davis, *Melville's "Mardi": A Chartless Voyage* (New Haven, Conn., 1952); William Gilman, *Melville's Early Life and "Redburn"* (New York, 1951); Hershel Parker, "Historical Note" in Melville's *Redburn,* ed. Harrison Hayford, Hershel Parker, and G. Thomas Tanselle (Evanston, 1969); and Watson G. Branch, "The Genesis, Composition, and Structure of *The Confidence-Man," Nineteenth-Century Fiction,* XXVII (March, 1973) 424–448.

[14] A majority of the cetological chapters are drawn from Beale. Since Melville often added factual material to his narrative in the later stages of composition, it is likely that most of the cetology was added afer he received Beale's *Natural History*.

[15] Harrison Hayford and Hershel Parker, "The Text: History, Variants, and Emendations," *Moby-Dick: Norton Critical Edition,* p. 471.

From early September until the middle of October he was busy
fixing up the house he had purchased. On October 6 he wrote to
Duyckinck describing his continuing labors on the place. He returned to his story in mid-October and by December he was writing
easily and rapidly. On December 13 he again wrote to Duyckinck
requesting "fifty fast writing youths with an easy style & not averse
to polishing their labors . . . . I wish you would [send them],
because since I have been here, I have planned about that number of
future works & cant [sic] find enough time to think about them
separately."[16]

It is generally assumed that Melville began to revise his narrative soon after writing his review of Hawthorne's *Mosses*. Certainly
Hawthorne—and to a greater degree Shakespeare—had a profound
influence on *Moby-Dick,* but evidence suggests it was probably not
until the next year. This does not mean Ahab or the white whale
was absent from the early story. The gam with the *Jereboam* (71)
was presumably written in the months after Melville's visit to Hancock, for he refers to the mad prophet Gabriel as "nurtured among
the crazy society of Niskayuna Shakers" (p. 266), information
about Shaker history he gleaned (and misspelled) from *A Summary
View.* The gam would have been written for the early novel, indi-
cating that Ahab, whose death Gabriel prophesies, was definitely in
the story. (Gabriel's insistence on Ahab's death by the whale's
tail, and his prediction of "fevers, yellow and bilious," and "the
plague" [p. 267] for the ship suggests that the plot of the early
story, particularly the conclusion, was changed considerably in later
months.)

In the period between August and December of 1850, Melville
appears to have been writing cetological material for the story, proceeding with his plan of late spring. This is in part confirmed by
the fact that of the twenty cetological chapters in *Moby-Dick,* nine
borrow from Beale;[17] and three of the Beale chapters refer to events
occurring between August and the end of the year—a strong indication that Melville was working on his cetology at that time.

The most accurately dated chapter is "The Fountain" (85), in

---

[16] *Letters,* p. 117.
[17] The following are the cetological chapters, with B included parenthetically for those
influenced by Beale: 32(B), 55(B), 56(B), 57, 65, 68, 74(B), 75, 76(B), 77, 79, 80, 85(B),
86(B), 88, 92(B), 102(B), 103(B), 104(B), and 105.

which Melville writes, "thousands of hunters should have been close by the fountain of the whale, watching those sprinklings and spoutings—that all this should be, and yet, that down to this blessed minute (fifteen and a quarter minutes past one o'clock P.M. of this sixteenth day of December, A.D. 1850),[18] it should still remain a problem . . ." (p. 310). The ease with which Melville composed the cetological chapters may be reflected in his request three days earlier for fifty fast writing youths to take down his ideas.

The other datable chapters refer to events earlier in the fall. In "Ambergris" (92) the smell rising from the hold of a Greenland whaler is compared to the stench "arising from excavating an old city graveyard, for the foundation of a Lying-In Hospital" (p. 343). The reference is to the excavation of the old cemetery in Pittsfield to make room for the new hospital which was dedicated on September 9. The chapter would have been written after Melville's return to Pittsfield. "A Bower in the Arsacides" (102) was composed after Melville's house guests had left. It describes the skeleton of a whale as "a wonderful sight. The wood was green as mosses of the Icy Glen . . ." (p. 374). Melville and his friends visited the Ice Glen near Stockbridge on August 5.

A final piece of evidence supports the theory that Melville spent this period writing the cetology. On December 30 Melville's father-in-law had charged to his membership at the Boston Anthenaeum a copy of William Scoresby's *Arctic Regions*. More than a month earlier Melville had sent his wife and son to Boston to visit her parents; now at Christmas he had joined them, still working with his cetological sources.[19]

IV

For Melville the final stage of composition was something of an emotional roller-coaster ride. By the early months of 1851 his good humor has passed: he resents intrusions upon his time and becomes irritable with Duyckinck. He then turns to Hawthorne to share his thoughts with his famous neighbor. His letters begin to reverberate with a fresh vigor and renewed energy. The voice and the attitude they reflect are Ahab's, the statements are very much

---

[18] In the American edition the date is 1851, probably a printer's error (p. 483).
[19] *The Melville Log*, p. 402.

those of Shakespeare and Carlyle. Melville's mounting excitement continues throughout the spring and summer months, tempered only by his critical reflection that what he had produced was a "final hash."[20] Both his excitement and harsh judgment were probably prompted by his introduction of dissimilar material into the narrative: the effort exhilarated him, but his statement that his endeavor was a "hash" indicates how poorly, in Melville's opinion, the disparate parts had blended.

The change in Melville's mood is first evident in a letter dated February 12, 1851, in which he refuses Duyckinck's request for a daguerreotype and a contribution to *Holden's Dollar Magazine*: "I am not in the humor to write the kind of thing you need . . . . You must be content to believe that I have reasons, or else I would not refuse so small a thing."[21] Melville goes on to reveal that he has been visiting Hawthorne and reading *Twice-Told Tales*.

February may have been Melville's month of decision. Late in the month or soon thereafter he asked his father-in-law to acquire a copy of Owen Chase's *Narrative* for him. In 1841 Melville had read Chase's account of the sinking of the *Essex* by a sperm whale, and although he mentions the tragedy in "The Affidavit" (45), he apparently did not have Chase's book before him at the time of writing, for quotations from it are footnoted to the history of the *Essex*, evidence of a later interpolation. Melville's request would seem to indicate that Chase's story now had a new importance— perhaps he had been considering a new ending to his narrative, one in which a ship is attacked and sunk by a whale (the *Essex* was stoved and sank within ten minutes). That Melville's original conclusion was revised is suggested by the numerous events that are foreshadowed in the early chapters but never fulfilled.[22] One statement anticipates what may have happened to the crew in the original story (the italicized words were deleted from the English edition): "An Anacharsis Clootz deputation from all the isles of

---

[20] *Letters*, p. 128.

[21] *Letters*, p. 120.

[22] The early chapters look forward to landing on "barbarous coasts" (p. 116), but the *Pequod* does not touch land; they also prepare for an atmosphere of brutality that does not develop in the story—Ishmael, for example, remarks when kicked by Peleg, "That was my first kick" (p. 95), but he is not kicked again. In the original narrative Queequeg may have died in a separate incident, for early in the story Ishmael comments, "From that hour I clove to Queequeg like a barnacle; yea, till poor Queequeg took his last long dive" (p. 61).

the sea, and all the ends of the earth, accompanying old Ahab in the *Pequod* to lay the world's grievances before the bar from which not very many of them ever came back. Black little Pip—he never did—oh, no! *he went before.* Poor Alabama boy!" (p. 108).[23] Inasmuch as Pip does not precede the others in death and only Ishmael returns from the voyage (in contrast to "not very many"), it appears that the original conclusion was altered so that the crew would perish together in a final catastrophic event. A further clue to possible alterations in the story may be found in *The New England Primer,* which Melville acquired on March 6; beside the letter "W" he read, "Whales in the sea/God's voice obey."[24]

Melville's correspondence after receipt of the *Narrative* echoes the intensely dramatic and defiant rhetoric of Ahab. His letter of April 16 praises Hawthorne, but is more descriptive of Ahab:

We think that into no recorded mind has the intense feeling of the visible truth ever entered more deeply than into this man's. By visible truth, we mean the apprehension of the absolute condition of present things as they strike the eye of the man who fears them not, though they do their worst to him,—the man who, like Russia or the British Empire, declares himself a sovereign nature (in himself) amid the powers of heaven, hell, or earth. He may perish; but so long as he exists he insists upon treating with all Powers upon an equal basis.

. . . .

There is the grand truth about Nathaniel Hawthorne. He says NO! in thunder; but the Devil himself cannot make him say *yes.* For all men who say *yes,* lie; and all men who say *no,*—why, they are in the happy condition of judicious, unincumbered travellers in Europe; they cross the frontier into Eternity with nothing but a carpet-bag,—that is to say, the Ego.[25]

The letter paraphrases Ahab's highly dramatic speech in "The Candles" (119), where he asserts his individuality in the face of the fiery Father: "In the midst of the personified impersonal, a personality stands here. Though but a point at best; whencesoe'er I came; wheresoe'er I go; yet while I earthly live, the queenly personality lives in me . . ." (p. 417).

[23] The American reading is recorded in "Substantive Variants Between *Moby-Dick* and *The Whale,*" *Moby-Dick: Norton Critical Edition,* p. 479.

[24] *The Melville Log,* p. 407.

[25] *Letters,* pp. 124–125.

In his next letter, of June 1, Melville returns to an Ahabian topic
—truth: "But Truth is the silliest thing under the sun. Try to get a
living by the Truth—and go to the soup societies. Heavens! Let
any clergyman try to preach the Truth from its very stronghold,
the pulpit, and they would ride him out of his church on his own
pulpit bannister."[26] Melville may have been thinking of "The Sermon" (9) and Father Mapple's message. Later he echoes another
passage from the novel as he writes, "I read Solomon more and
more, and every time see deeper and deeper and unspeakable meanings in him. . . . It seems to me now that Solomon was the truest
man who ever spoke, and yet that he a little *managed* the truth
with a view to popular conservatism . . . ." Ishmael repeats similar
words in defense of Ahab's sorrow in "The Try Works" (96): "The
truest of all men was the Man of Sorrows, and the truest of all
books is Solomon's, and Ecclesiastes is the fine hammered steel of
woe" (p. 355). The letter concludes with Melville's talking of going
to New York City to "work and slave on my 'Whale' while it is
driving through the press."[27] The book is now recognizable as
Moby-Dick: it rocks with Ahab's speech and focuses upon a particular whale.

On June 29 when the book is half-way through the press, Melville tells Hawthorne that he is patching the book together, presumably joining the original and revised portions and inserting
last-minute chapters into the manuscript: "Since you have been here,
I have been building some shanties of houses (connected with the
old one) and likewise some shanties of chapters and essays."[28] He
then discloses the book's secret motto which underscores the philosophic change he made in the early narrative (a change that is
mirrored in his letters). The words are from Ahab's speech in the
dramatic baptismal scene in "The Forge" (113): "This is the book's
motto (the secret one)—Ego non baptiso Te in nomine—but make
out the rest yourself."

The final period of composition seems to have focused on Ahab
as a tragic hero rather than simply the captain of an ill-fated vessel.
In Melville's letters Ahab's language, attitudes, and dark metaphysical questioning are echoed throughout. The increased excitement

---

[26] *Letters,* p. 127.
[27] *Letters,* p. 128.
[28] *Letters,* p. 132.

and the flow of ideas in the letters indicate that for Melville these were months of great creativity. The notion inherent in "Hawthorne and His Mosses," of a character, who, like Shakespeare's dark heroes, would examine what we feel to be so terribly true—this idea seems to have waited until early 1851 to find expression in Melville's dramatic presentation of Ahab. It is this Shakespearean Ahab who enlivens the novel with his "quick probings at the axis of reality,"[29] and his tearing "off the mask" and speaking "the sane madness of vital truth."[30] Melville's excitement can be explained only as the sympathetic involvement of the artist in his character's emotionally consuming quest for metaphysical truth.

V

Moby-Dick is the result of a planned composition extending through the first two stages of writing: progress on the original narrative was steady until August and then the cetology was added to it. The final stage of writing involved the revision and some eleventh-hour patchwork in joining the two narratives. The parts Melville composed during these periods can be identified (the initial chapters have been generally accepted as part of the first story) by following Melville's methodology and tracing datable sources. For example, the cetological chapters were added to the early narrative; therefore, they should lead us back to the remains of the first whaling voyage. The later revision of the book was strongly influenced by Shakespeare; therefore, the echoes and obvious borrowings from the tragedies should allow us to identify the revised portions of the novel.

Cetological chapters may be classified as "fast" or "loose" depending on how well they are attached to the narrative. Those that are "loose" are unattached to their immediate narrative surroundings; in this sense they are movable chapters which Melville could have placed anywhere in the manuscript. Because of their insularity they are of no help in locating the early narrative.[31] On the other

---

[29] "Hawthorne and His Mosses," *Literary World* (August 17 and 24, 1850), rpt. in *Moby-Dick: Norton Critical Edition*, p. 541.

[30] P. 542.

[31] The "loose" chapters were frequently written in self-contained units, a series of chapters concerned with one topic. There are a total of twelve "loose" chapters in the book: 32, 55, 56, 57, 79, 80, 85, 86, 102, 103, 104, and 105.

hand, the "fast" chapters have an expository relationship to the chapters around them. They are attached to the narrative in the manner anticipated in reviewing the book's composition. It is these "fast" chapters listed below that should lead us to the original story:

65. "The Whale as a Dish"
68. "The Blanket"
74. "The Sperm Whale's Head"
75. "The Right Whale's Head"
76. "The Battering Ram"
77. "The Great Heidelberg Tun"
88. "Schools and Schoolmasters"
92. "Ambergris"

The first of these chapters, "The Whale as a Dish" (65), is appended to a chapter sequence that begins with "The Line" (60). It supplies information for "Stubb Kills a Whale" (61), which, in turn, produces the whale steak for Stubb's supper, eaten in chapter 64, and discussed in "The Whale as a Dish." In effect, then, the chapters from 60 through 92 (which is "Ambergris," the last of the "fast" chapters), form a narrative frame in which the remnant of the original story is located. This is supported by the fact that this frame also contains all the dated chapters (listed below) from the first two stages of composition, with the exception of the "loose" and movable cetological chapter, "A Bower in the Arsacides" (102):

71. "The Pequod Meets the Jereboam": August 1850
78. "Cistern and Buckets": June 1850
85. "The Fountain": December 1850
90. "Heads or Tails": June 1850
92. "Ambergris": August 1850

If the early narrative is enclosed within these chapters, then such fanciful and often humorous accounts of whaling adventure like "Stubb Kills a Whale" (61), "The Shark Massacre" (66), "The Pequod Meets the Virgin" (81), "The Grand Armada" (87), and "The Pequod Meets the Rose Bud" (91) were probably part of the original story. These chapters tell of the adventure of whaling in a manner that conforms to the descriptions of the first whaling narrative.

The final stage of composition is the easiest to trace. The importance of Hawthorne and Shakespeare in the revision of *Moby-Dick* needs no comment. It is Shakespeare, however, that is most evident in Melville's reshaping of Ahab: alternately Ahab plays the roles of Lear, Hamlet, Macbeth, Richard III, King Henry, and Timon; he appears in dramatically conceived scenes; his language, its rhythms and allusions underscore the pervasive influence of Shakespeare. This influence has been thoroughly documented by Raymond Long in "The Hidden Sun: A Study of the Influence of Shakespeare on the Creative Imagination of Herman Melville."[32] A tabulation of Long's findings plus the incidence of dramatic elements in the novel (dramatic sub-titles, stage directions, and soliloquies) show that the Shakespearean influence occurs with much greater frequency in certain sections of the books.

Chapters	Total references	Avg. reference per chapter
1–22	6	.27
23–59	72	1.91
60–92	10	.33
93–"Epilogue"	102	2.32

Those sections in *Moby-Dick* that have been associated with the original narrative—1–22 and 60–92—evince only minimal Shakespearean influence. The influence occurs in chapters 23–59 and 93–"Epilogue," but even within these chapters certain ones demonstrate considerably stronger influence. This is evident when they are examined separately.

Chapters	Total references	Avg. reference per chapter
23–59 { 26–34	24	2.67
36–42	35	5.00
93–"Epilogue" { 94 & 99	9	4.50
106–"Epilogue"	93	3.00

[32] Dissertation, U.C.L.A., 1965. Long divides the influence into two types: first, superficial allusions, references either to Shakespeare himself or to his creations (plays and characters), and also quotations and implied quotations; second, deeper influences, which consist of characters of a recognizably Shakespearean type, speeches, scenes, events from the plays, and also Shakespearean devices such as speech patterns and images. Long has noted each occurrence in the novel.

From this tabulation it appears that the revision concentrated on several groups of chapters. Those that introduce the cast of characters (26–34) were apparently revised, although the revision appears to have been superficial; it is more pervasive in the chapters beginning with Ahab at the quarter-deck (36–42). A consistent influence is again discernible in the concluding section (106–"Epilogue").

It is not surprising that Ahab is prominent in these chapters. He is introduced briefly in the initial segment (26–34); he is more dramatically evident in the next group of chapters (36–42); and in the concluding events he is before the reader constantly until he darts his final harpoon into the unconquerable whale (106–"Epilogue").

VI

This study has attempted to describe the composition of *Moby-Dick*. External evidence has been considered, dates have been ascribed to various textual references, and, as a result, stages of composition have been determined and material in the novel assigned to the various stages of writing. Much of the composition still remains a mystery. Nevertheless, certain conclusions—and a few conjectures—can be made about the writing of the book:

1. Melville wrote *Moby-Dick* in three stages. In February, 1850, he began a whaling story, which he worked on steadily until August. In the months following he wrote much of the cetology. In the final phase, begun early in 1851, he revised the narrative and later interpolated material into it. Each period produced the following identifiable chapters:

> *stage one:* chapters 1–22.
> *stages one and two:* chapters 60–92, and probably the "loose" cetological chapters.
> *stage three:* chapters 26–34, 36–42, and 106–"Epilogue."

2. The cetology was written for the original narrative and added to it in late autumn and early winter of 1850.[33]

---

[33] Stewart states in "The Two *Moby-Dicks*" that the revision probably took place in the following order: first Melville conceived of a whale sinking a ship, as in the case of the *Essex;* then he made it a particular whale with a particular name and color; and, after changing the plot, "the author felt the necessity of establishing in the reader's mind such facts as that a whale could be white, could bear a name, and could sink a ship. Hence sprang the cetology" (p. 446). Stewart has the progression of events backwards: the cetology

3. Melville may have revised the first story in two stages. The earliest revision probably involved chapters 26–34; they seem to have been revised before the present ending was added to the book, else Pip's early death would not be foreshadowed in chapter 27. Later, perhaps in the spring of 1851, Melville may have decided to rewrite the original conclusion.

4. The revised conclusion is first evident in "The Castaway" (93). Pip's rescue from a watery grave in this chapter prompts Ishmael to remark that the episode anticipates his own abandonment, thus foreshadowing his solitary state in "Epilogue." But Pip's rescue may also offer a clue as to how Melville revised the original. In the early narrative Pip was to have preceded the others in death; perhaps he was drowned in the first version of "The Castaway" and was resurrected in the revision so that he might play the fool to Ahab's Lear. In a similar manner Melville probably used other scenes from the early novel, transforming them to meet the demands of the plot.

The case of Queequeg illustrates what may have happened to incidents Melville revised. Like Pip's, Queequeg's death is prophesied in an early chapter (13), where Ishmael states that his friend is to take a "last long dive." His death may have occurred as a result of his descent into the ship's hold to search for an oil leak; he does become gravely ill and asks that a coffin be made for him. But in the reshaping of the plot the various deaths are held for the conclusion; thus Queequeg recovers and Melville uses his coffin to save his narrator.

5. In joining the two narratives, Melville used large sections from each, salvaging much from the original. He alternated sections from the two narratives in structuring the novel, beginning with the original land chapters (1–22), and then proceeding to the revised chapters that introduce Ahab, the crew, and their quest (26–42); he then returned to the original story, preserving certain adventure chapters and the cetological chapters that he had attached to the

was written, then the plot was changed, and later, after April 1, when Melville received Chase's *Narrative,* the cetological chapter "The Battering Ram" (76), which does what Stewart suggests of the cetology as a whole (that is, prove that a whale "could sink a ship"), was interpolated into the manuscript. Melville had Chase's *Narrative* before him when writing the chapter, for he borrows verbatim Chase's phrase "paved with horses' hoofs" (Henry F. Pommer, "Herman Melville and the Wake of the *Essex,*" *American Literature,* XX, November, 1948, 295).

early narrative (60–92); he concluded with the revised ending (106– "Epilogue"). Melville stitched these sections together with a pot-pourri of chapters of both early and late composition, including many of the "loose" cetological chapters.

VII

Melville's retrospective view of the composition is recorded in his letter of June 1, 1851, to Hawthorne. In the past sixteen months he had patched two narratives together and in the process had transformed a diverting story into an American classic. Melville's appraisal of his effort is ironic, but also prophetic, for he realized that his *Whale* was the result of antithetical forces that he could no longer resolve—the need to secure an audience for his writing, coupled with an intense compulsion to tell the truth. The artistic paradox finally resulted in his long silence. For Melville his greatest effort was a failure:

My dear Sir, a presentiment is on me,—I shall at last be worn out and perish, like an old nutmeg-grater, grated to pieces by the constant attrition of the wood, that is, the nutmeg. What I feel most moved to write, that is banned,—it will not pay. Yet, altogether, write the other way I cannot. So the product is a final hash, and all my books are botches.[34]

[34] *Letters*, p. 128.

Form as Vision in Herman Melville's *Clarel*
Bryan C. Short

I N HIS FOREWORD to Vincent Kenny's book on *Clarel,* Gay Wilson
Allen recommends three "routes" for approaching the poem. The
first relates *Clarel* to Melville's "spiritual quest for the meaning of
existence." The second reaches *Clarel* by way of Melville's actual trip
to Palestine. The third explores Melville's anticipation of the pessimism so important to later thought.[1] Efforts by such recent critics as
Kenny and William H. Shurr, not to mention all whose contributions Kenny summarizes in his fourth chapter, have moved us far
enough along these routes that another can be glimpsed.[2] *Clarel*
demands a reading in the light of relationships between Melville's
poetic technique and modifications which the practice of verse
wrought in his view of literature. A reverence for organic unity
pervaded Romantic poetics in America;[3] Melville's changing interpretation of this doctrine determines the adapting of versification to
narrative purpose which gives *Clarel* its unique shape. Such a study
promises a better understanding of how Melville's later verse grew
out of the impatient questing of the novels, an explanation of his
curious abandonment of tetrameter in the *Clarel* epilogue, and a
more flattering image of his state of mind than has been current.
The protean nature of Melville's poetry suggests that the promise
of artistic rather than philosophical accomplishment motivated the
varied forms of his mature works. Although his themes reflect the
depression which adorns his family correspondence, his incessant
technical experiments bespeak an undying vitality. Our view of
Melville should include the literary interests, both practical and theoretical, which kept him active at his desk in spite of obscurity, money
problems, family tragedy, poor health, and civil service. *Clarel,* with

---

[1] *Herman Melville's Clarel: A Spiritual Autobiography* (Hamden, 1973), pp. x–xi.

[2] William H. Shurr, *The Mystery of Iniquity* (Lexington, Ky., 1972).

[3] See R. H. Fogle, "Organic Form in American Criticism, 1840–1870," in *The Development of American Literary Criticism,* ed. Floyd Stovall (Chapel Hill, N.C., 1955), pp.
75–111.

its profound dedication to organic poetics, reveals these springs and motives as well as any other work in the cannon.

Battle-Pieces lays the groundwork for organic form in *Clarel* by achieving a well-tested strategy for facing the terrors of experience, a style which both suits and embodies that strategy, and a new confidence, noted by critics, *vis à vis* the spiritual quest whose enticements survived the foundering of Melville's fiction.[4] Without this foundation, *Clarel* is unthinkable, for *Clarel* presents a world as blasted and a plot as depressing as any met previously in Melville's works. A study of organicism in the epic begins with *Battle-Pieces*, upon whose successes rests Melville's decision, in the teeth of his woes, to grapple with old and crushing obsessions in the medium of eighteen thousand tetrameter lines.

The main strategy carried from *Battle-Pieces* into *Clarel* is the abrogation of "deep diving" after "chronometrical" truths in favor of a disciplined objectivity. Melville signals this strategy in a prefatory note:

The aspects which the strife as a memory assumes are as manifold as are the moods of involuntary meditation. . . . Yielding instinctively, one after another, to feelings not inspired from any one source exclusively, and unmindful, without purposing to be, of consistency, I seem, in most of these verses, to have but placed a harp in a window, and noted the contrasted airs which wayward winds have played upon the strings.[5]

Poetry responds to the winds of war without forcing an artificial consistency on them. *Battle-Pieces* wagers that clearly "noted" historical movements may reveal the meaning of existence more effectively than the single-minded vision of a Taji, and that a valuable organic bond can unite fact and verse. This is not to say that Melville eschews fictionalization but that fictionalization plays a more limited and descriptive role than in his novels.

Objectivity suits Melville's main *persona,* an aging observer remote from the action. However, during the course of *Battle-Pieces,* Melville discovers important correspondences between poetic and battlefield deeds; the Civil War gives birth to modern man, brave, self-

[4] Laurence Barrett, "The Differences in Melville's Poetry," *PMLA,* LXX (Sept., 1955), 622. Edwin Fussell, *Frontier* (Princeton, N.J., 1965), p. 378.

[5] Howard P. Vincent, *Collected Poems of Herman Melville* (Chicago, 1947), p. 446. This edition is used for references to *Battle-Pieces,* hereafter cited by page number.

controlled, and fatalistic, and Melville adopts this new hero as a model for his own literary goals. Courageous warriors display the same discipline as the poet, and both stand in the mainstream of history. Praising the pilot of a suicide-launch, Melville writes:

> In Cushing's eager deed was shown
> A spirit which brave poets own—
> That scorn of life which earns life's crown.
> ("At the Cannon's Mouth," p. 83)

Poetry can strive for an organic encompassing of heroic action because it embodies a parallel heroism.

However brave, neither poet nor soldier, art nor experience, can claim knowledge beyond death; in this objective limitation all share equally. The living must be satisfied with mere hints at the meaning of existence without hoping that some heroic act or literary "deep dive" will yield more:

> Obscure as the wood, the entangled rhyme
>   But hints at the maze of war—
> Vivid glimpses or livid through peopled gloom,
>   And fires which creep and char—
> A riddle of death, of which the slain
>   Sole solvers are.
> ("The Armies of the Wilderness," p. 69)

The equality of art and action only partly explains Melville's confidence in an objective, unified poetry. Art goes a step further by so revealing the human heart that it anticipates experience. In " 'The Coming Storm' " Melville takes the example of Shakespeare:

> No utter surprises can come to him
>   Who reaches Shakespeare's core;
> That which we seek and shun is there—
>   Man's final lore. (p. 94)

The truths of the heart cannot transcend mortality, but, as illuminated by art, they predict whatever shocks may come—a function which in *Clarel* takes the place of attempts to penetrate the pasteboard mask of reality. If one picks a great experience—the Civil War, a pilgrimage to the Holy Land—a poetry which reflects its varied aspects organically and without preconception can capture whatever lessons the experience teaches. Imposing transcendental hopes on the experience will only destroy both its heroic discipline and its validity.

In seeking to respond objectively to the winds of history, Melville evolves a style in line with Emerson's organicist dictum that "it is not metres but a metre-making argument which makes a poem."[6] He describes the style in "A Utilitarian View of the Monitor's Fight":

> Plain be the phrase, yet apt the verse,
>   More ponderous than nimble;
> For since grimed War here laid aside
> His painted pomp, 'twould ill befit
>   Overmuch to ply
>   The rhyme's barbaric cymbal. (p. 39)

The plain, apt verse of *Battle-Pieces* matures in "Lee in the Capitol," the penultimate poem in the volume, into the full-blown *Clarel* form; loose iambic tetrameter, a prominent line throughout the collection, falls into unequal verse paragraphs; flexible rhyme patterns intrude on the predominant couplets. The poem presents a dramatic yet essentially verbal scene much like those of *Clarel* and reflects a similar relationship between narrator and character. "Lee in the Capitol" presents the final hero of *Battle-Pieces* abandoning his avowed silence to speak before a hostile public. Both the circumstances of Lee's act and the repetition of his views in a prose supplement suggest Melville's identification with him. Hero and poet come together to climax the hope for both art and experience, a hope which rests on the bravery, aptness, and objectivity of Lee's words, compellingly turned into verse. Out of the narrowed horizons and clouded dreams of war comes a vision of honest courage and unified art. Lee's act, like Melville's bow to history, reveals an ability to anticipate if not transcend experience, for his plea catches "the light in the future's skies" (p. 152). Discipline and self-control sustain most of the *Clarel* pilgrims. The belief that a verse like that of "Lee in the Capitol" can contain metaphysical anxieties within an objective framework and thereby anticipate their ravages is the heaviest weapon carried by Melville from *Battle-Pieces* into the epic. Melville's willingness to fictionalize Lee's speech demonstrates his willingness to sum up the

---

[6] "The Poet," in *Essays, First and Second Series* (Cambridge, Mass., 1929), part II, 9. The idea is discussed by Edwin Fussell, "The Meter-Making Argument," in *Aspects of American Poetry*, ed. Richard M. Ludwig (Columbus, Ohio, 1962), pp. 3–31.

lesson of the war as he sees it; the abandonment of preconceived transcendental goals does not stop art from reaching conclusions. *Clarel* begins on the hope that new, if circumscribed, insights into the "meaning of existence" are possible.

In line with principles of organic unity, Melville's substitution of disciplined objectivity for deep diving dramatically modifies the "diagram" of his characteristic quest.[7] In *Clarel,* the search leads away from rather than toward the symbol which promises resolution. Whereas Taji incessantly follows Yillah, Clarel's pilgrimage leads him from Ruth. This change in direction, to some a structural disharmony, reflects Melville's wish to distinguish spiritual knowledge from emotional satisfaction and to keep the transcendent questing of his earlier works from dominating experience.[8] The lesson of Civil War fatalism permits Melville to build into *Clarel* his misgivings about the nobility of both pilgrims and pilgrimage; vivid adventure gives way to desultory wandering and endless talk; systems of belief no longer command attention on the basis of logical force. Robert Penn Warren comments that "Melville is trying to show ideals not as abstractions but as a function of the life process."[9] This impulse, both objective and organic, leads Melville to conclude that grand ideas have little positive impact on human happiness; they do Clarel no more good than they do the wounded veterans of the war.

Just as the search for knowledge in *Clarel* separates from the promise of satisfaction, the views of the characters have little to do with their importance. The sociability of Derwent, whose meliorism subjects him to derision, keeps him at the center of the group. Vine says so little that his influence on Clarel partakes of the irrational. Rolfe's heartiness outweighs his contradictions. Walter Bezanson concludes that Clarel "goes increasingly from asking whose beliefs are right to asking who is the right kind of man."[10] A concomitant question which Melville asks is not what truth is deepest but what kind of art is both unified and honest, a question which finally undercuts all abstractions. Melville's objectivity challenges even Lee's resigned wisdom. Removed from the realm of historical greatness, experience

[7] John Seelye, *Melville: The Ironic Diagram* (Evanston, Ill., 1970), discusses Melville's characteristic pattern.

[8] R. H. Fogle, "Melville's *Clarel:* Doubt and Belief," *Tulane Studies in English,* X (1960), 103.

[9] "Melville's Poems," *Southern Review,* n.s. III (Autumn, 1967), 831.

[10] *Clarel* (New York, 1960), p. lxix.

offers less comfort than blind faith; the wise soldiers of *Battle-Pieces* condense into Ungar, whose heroism is irrelevant to his needs. Versification follows suit by seeking effects of plainness and tension rather than ease or dramatic brilliance. The tetrameters borrowed from "Lee in the Capitol" come to embody, and finally to symbolize, the hard realities of a wasted world.

Clarel is not, however, without a hint of redemption, but redemption, operating within the sphere of satisfaction rather than knowledge, finally contradicts both the experience of its characters and the outcome of its plot, creating a disintegration which threatens to ruin the organic unity at the heart of the work. Redemption comes second hand in Melville's curiously buoyant epilogue. It is here that Melville redefines organic form in order to escape the objective decorum of his narrative. Like the palinode of a Medieval allegory or the epilogue of an Elizabethan play, the *Clarel* epilogue removes Melville's conclusion from the context of the tale. Clarel is left alone shouldering a greater burden than ever; none of his friends can comfort him; but Melville blithely tells us that things are not so bad. In reevaluating the search for truth, Melville denies the final value of brave and disciplined objectivity, the archetypal virtues of *Battle-Pieces;* art, in the epilogue, is left alone to find its own satisfactions. Melville salvages the principle of organic unity by shifting to a new and fitting form. He abandons the tetrameters which have stood for "apt" art since their emergence and takes on a pentameter line. Once *Clarel* has conveyed its charge of depressing truth it flees into emotional and stylistic exuberance. If, as the epilogue says, "death but routs life into victory,"[11] hard facts seem to rout an art of truth into an art of pleasure in which style answers organically not to experience but to the immediate delights of literature. The *Clarel* epilogue trades tension, plainness, discipline, and objective seriousness for wit, exaggeration, delicate stylistic artifice, and casual sophistication.

In the *Clarel* epilogue, Melville moves away from the typically Romantic organicism of Emerson's "metre-making argument" to a perspective in which poetry, by creating its own decorum, becomes an argument-making meter equally unified but liberated from objectivity. How this happens, and what it implies for Melville's poetics,

---

[11] *Clarel*, p. 523. Subsequent references to this edition will be cited in the text by page number.

reflect in the ways by which Melville prepares for the epilogue. Given Melville's doubts, it is hardly surprising objectivity and organic unity result in the bleak finale of *Clarel,* but the ability of art to anticipate this bleakness enables Melville to detach and distance his poetic voice from experience and finally to elevate it, like "the spirit about the dust" (p. 522) over the predetermined ruins surrounding it. Melville knows what is coming and has time to prepare an escape. The heroism of poetry, discovered in *Battle-Pieces,* has given the created world, the world of literature, an immediacy and a power previously reserved for bold adventure and half-glimpsed spiritual forces; when the potential emotional attractiveness of art rather than either mysterious meanings or observed facts determines the style and form of a work, that work can achieve an expressiveness and beauty denied to an art of objective observation. It is in the context of Melville's shift in focus from truth to beauty that the symbolic value of his versification comes into focus.

In *Moby-Dick,* Ishmael's consciousness is a territory in which opposing views conflict; in *Clarel,* verse itself plays a similar role. Poetry transforms Melville's narrative voice from that of a first-person participant or an objective observer into a less well-defined authorial presence. The constraints of meter, rhyme, and third-person detachment make it difficult for the narrator to submerge himself in the events of *Clarel* as Ishmael does when the *Pequod* sets sail; his voice, identified with versification, is less malleable. How Melville defines this voice and makes it embody the conflict between experience and freedom, truth and beauty, is best illuminated by Northrop Frye's apt description of musical rhythm in English epic verse:

When we find sharp barking accents, crabbed and obscure language, mouthfuls of consonants, and long lumbering polysyllables, we are probably dealing with *melos,* or poetry which shows an analogy to music, if not an actual influence from it.

The musical diction . . . is congenial to a gnarled intellectualism of the so-called "metaphysical" type. It is irregular in metre (because of the syncopation against stress), leans heavily on enjambement, and employs a long cumulative rhythm sweeping the lines up into larger rhythmical units such as the paragraph.[12]

Combined with his assertion that English epic verse naturally tends

[12] *Anatomy of Criticism* (Princeton, N.J., 1957), pp. 256–257.

to a four-beat line, Frye's description suits *Clarel* in all but one respect; the longer line of the English epic tradition—from alliterative
to blank verse—permits four accentual stresses to appear in a line less
frequently than every other syllable, thus providing a hedge against
strict metrics. A pentameter line, for example, can easily show four
major accents, without either contradicting or abandoning its meters,
simply by deemphasizing one metrical stress. If the octosyllabic line
of *Clarel* is to escape from tetrameters into accentual rhythm, it must
resort to extra syllables, feminine endings, violent substitutions, and
continual enjambement. Although these occur with frequency, they
lack the sustained force necessary to efface the movement of Melville's tetrameters, whose effect of disciplined plainness gave few
problems in the shorter compass of "Lee in the Capitol." Consequently, the rudiments of accentual rhythm, *melos,* continually struggle against metrics, producing a tension which Melville finds valuable enough to his theme to reinforce through rhyme and indentation.

Melville generally indents or breaks a line whenever his focus shifts
from one character to another or to the narrator, and whenever the
narrative changes mode (conversation, song, thought, commentary,
description). However, indentation also varies the texture of the
verse, occurring more frequently in passages of agitation such as that
in which Clarel learns of Ruth's death (pp. 512–513). Indentation
speeds the flow of verse by introducing new rhyme sounds and patterns. Melville lends stability to calmer passages by utilizing couplets
and quatrains, as in "Clarel and Ruth"; elsewhere, as in "Celio,"
rhymes change and rhyme patterns mutate so rapidly as to prevent
the easy division of the poem into units smaller than the paragraph.
Taken together, indentations, breaks, rapid rhyme mutations, and
metrical irregularities call attention to the jagged and cumulative
effects defined by Frye, and the absence of these devices returns the
poem to the unchallenged metrics of "Lee in the Capitol." Regular
metrics predominate in many places expressing hope for consolation
within the world of objective experience; accentual freedom struggles
more violently against meter where the discipline of established doctrines threatens to collapse. When the climax of the tale brings utter
despair, Melville escapes to a pentameter in which ease and rhythmic
freedom prevail, thus tolling the death of his organic combination
of objectivity with stylistic plainness and metrical tension. Melville

makes sure that collapses in established order result from events within the sphere of human anticipation, and thus that they pinpoint the poverty of vision which now goes hand-in-hand with both heroic discipline and the commitment of poetry to an organic "noting" of factual trends.

The promise of escape which Melville consummates in the epilogue informs the lyrics of *Clarel*. Although sometimes frivolous, as a group they celebrate freedom from discipline, beauty, and related values which receive little reinforcement from the pilgrims—hedonism as opposed to self-denial, satisfaction as opposed to knowledge, faith as opposed to reason, feeling as opposed to thought. Twenty-two of them, nearly half, are sung by four characters—Glaucon, the Cypriote, the Lesbian, and the Lyonese—who question the asceticism of the pilgrimage; thirteen express a more comforting faith than that of Clarel. The lyrics also give certain characters the opportunity to speak more personally than they can elsewhere. Vine's depth receives a major witness in his two songs; Ungar reveals his hidden wishes in verse. From the beginning, the lyrics undercut the constraint which weighs upon the pilgrimage; they presage Melville's leap into the epilogue by exemplifying the qualities which make art satisfying even in the face of blankness and by employing poetic forms less restrained than that of the narrative.

The first lyric peeps out at Clarel from under the peeling whitewash of his hotel room in Jerusalem. In the only sustained pentameters outside the epilogue, it tells of an answer to doubt found by an earlier tenant who sees the decayed remains of the Biblical world as symbols of a personal, emotional faith:

> So much the more in pathos I adore
> The low lamps flickering in Syria's Tomb. (p. 131)

The lyric embodies the ability to make subjective feelings and alluring symbols into the bases for a satisfying faith—an ability which Clarel lacks. Melville's sophisticated use of alliteration in such lines as "Triumph and taunt that shame the winning side," and "My unweaned thoughts in steadfast trade-wind stream" produces an accentual rhythm which does not jar against metrics. Shortly thereafter, Clarel's actual pilgrimage begins and the message of satisfaction and the pleasing style of the lyric are forgotten.

The start of the journey introduces Glaucon, Melville's first hedo-

nist, who abandons the group after singing four lyrics warning
against the deliberate rejection of beauty for a life of trial. Glaucon's
final song suggests that the psychological effect of a blasted landscape
is dangerous for those who traverse it:

> Tarry never there
> Where the air
> Lends a lone Hadean spell—
> Where the ruin and the wreck
> Vine and ivy never deck
> And wizard wan and sibyl dwell:
> There, oh, beware! (p. 185)

However, the pilgrims continue in their belief that the search for
knowledge supercedes all sensations, a view which prevails until the
final section of the poem.

Following Glaucon's departure, a Dominican friar sings a song of
praise for the Church which is mocked by Margoth in an important
negative example of the lyric promise:

> Patcher of the rotten cloth,
> Pickler of the wing o' the moth,
> Toaster of bread stale in date,
> Tinker of the rusty plate,
> Botcher of a crumbling tomb,
> Pounder with the holy hammer,
> Gaffer-gammer, gaffer-gammer-
> Rome! (p. 230)

Margoth criticizes the Church in a poem whose metrical pounding
and short, parallel, end-stopped phrases produce a mechanical effect
more rigid than any other in the volume. The oppressive meter of
Margoth's poem relates to its meaning in three ways; it symbolizes
his view of church activities, it exemplifies his own rigidly dogmatic
beliefs, and it embodies the danger that repeated formal patterns can
degenerate into empty, deadening convention. Melville satirizes both
the Church and Margoth for the programmed nature of their responses to life, and his metrics demonstrate the need for freedom in
art, personal attitude, and doctrine. For all his scientific sanctimony,
Margoth is as unsatisfied as the others; his trochaic tetrameter merely
offers an exaggerated mirror image of the iambic tetrameter of the
narrative. Margoth's song makes it clear that an organic fitting of

form to theme cannot alone produce a verse of comforting emotional power.

The Dead Sea cantos of *Clarel* contain important lyrics by Nehemiah (p. 241), and Mortmain (pp. 250–251), both of which reaffirm the significance of a faith like that in the first lyric. Mortmain laments the death of the now "unadored" Southern Cross as a Christian symbol, and Nehemiah's psalm paraphrase finds comfort in a candle shining in the "valley of shade." Both seek a religion supported by simple affective symbols comparable to the "low lamps flickering in Syria's Tomb" rather than intellectual abstractions—a religion of satisfactions rather than truths. Mortmain's song conveys an impression of the attractiveness of the dead symbol:

> How far removed, thou Tree divine,
> Whose tender fruit did reach so low—
> Love apples of New-Paradise!
> About the wide Australian sea. (pp. 250–251)

Ultimately, Nehemiah's narrow fundamentalism and Mortmain's bitterness prevent them from accepting the emotional and imaginative freedom which is Melville's key to escape from eternal pilgrimage; neither can create his own symbols of faith; both sing in the iambic tetrameter of the narrative, and both die on the journey. The presence of such delicate yet tragic songs in iambic tetrameter implies that the lyric and narrative sensibilities can merge, that experience can lay the groundwork for freedom if one can achieve the proper combination of sensitivity and aesthetic distance—gifts which begin to replace discipline and objectivity at the center of Melville's art.

"Mar Saba" introduces the Cypriote and the Lesbian, whose songs of love and pleasure contrast with the asceticism of the monastery. Their sensuality awakens Clarel to the attractions of a return to Ruth, thus contributing to the erotic theme discussed by Nina Baym.[13] The Cypriote's first song is particularly symbolic; after two stanzas describing the lasting delights enjoyed by the gods, he finishes with an imperative:

> Ever blandly adore them;
> But spare to implore them:

[13] "The Erotic Motif in Melville's *Clarel*," *Texas Studies in Language and Literature*, XVI (Summer, 1974), 315–328.

They rest, they discharge them from time;
　　　Yet believe, light believe
　　　They would succor, reprieve—
　　　　　　Nay, retrieve—
Might but revelers pause in the prime! (p. 286)

For the Cypriote, earthly and heavenly revelry provoke comparison,
and revelry expresses faith; no gaping dichotomy separates flesh and
spirit, satisfaction and knowledge, beauty and truth. The proper approach to the gods combines adoration, affirmed in the first lyric and
lamented by Mortmain, with respect for the senses. The Cypriote's
anapests and widely varied line lengths again suggest an alternative
to tetrameters. Hearing his song, the central group of pilgrims are
deeply touched.

"Mar Saba" climaxes when Melville brings Vine, Mortmain, and
Rolfe face to face with the famous palm tree of the monastery, while
Clarel looks on. Each of the three undergoes a moment of inspiration, a hint at the unity of dream and experience available to the
liberated mind, and then each reverts to doubt and questioning. In
each, the choice of experience and objective reason over sensuality
and emotion prevents the acceptance of a vision woven out of mo-
mentary ecstasy. In the face of the most eloquent symbol and the
deepest feelings in the poem, they relapse. Mortmain, an Ahab
stripped of his command by Melville's objectivity, dies in anguish.
Moved, Clarel begins to reflect on his love for Ruth; he acknowledges
the importance of erotic symbols to Christianity and the beauty
which they possess, but his belief in his own impurity keeps him
from rejecting a discipline which, unlike the Cypriote, he identifies
with religion. He continues to think of Ruth in abstract terms, as if
she too were an item of knowledge. As the pilgrimage leaves Mar
Saba, the stage is set for Ungar and the Lyonese, who restate the
conflict between order and freedom.

Ungar sings the swansong of Melville's identification with Civil
War heroism. His two fragments, both metrically rigid, express a
philosophy of resignation and a secret hope for revenge (p. 425).
Ungar senses the vanity of his wish and the split between his knowledge of life and his dream of vindication. Rather than finding a way
of uniting himself, he controls his disintegrated personality through
relentless mental discipline. He presides over the now stale pilgrimage which, with the coming of the Lyonese, begins to give way to the

end of Clarel's quest for knowledge and his concomitant acceptance
of satisfaction as a goal.

After arguing with a monk on the importance of sexuality, Clarel
dreams of the choice before him:

> And Clarel dreamed, and seemed to stand
> Betwixt a Shushan and a sand;
> The Lyonese was lord of one,
> The desert did the Tuscan own,
> The pale pure monk. A zephyr fanned;
> It vanished, and he felt the strain
> Of clasping arms which would detain
> His heart from each ascetic range. (pp. 499–500)

Just as a movement from end-stopped to run-on lines gives the passage a sense of emerging freedom, Clarel awakens to feel an "organic change" working within him; the arms of love which draw
him from Mar Saba promise a unity of spirit unknown to him before; he experiences a sudden impatience with his journey. The
Lyonese then sings the folly of a discipline which contradicts nature:

> Rules, who rules?
> Fools the wise, makes wise the fools—
> Every ruling overrules?
> Who the dame that keeps the house,
> Provides the diet, and oh, so quiet,
> Brings all to pass, the slyest mouse?
> Tell, tell it me:
> Signora Nature, who but she! (p. 500)

The four songs of the Lyonese accentuate his freedom from dogma.
They employ such rapidly shifting feet and strong alliteration that
they often attain an accentual rhythm which obliterates metrics,
anticipating Melville's experiments in *John Marr and Other Sailors*:

> Over the river
> In gloaming, ah, still do ye plain?
> Dove—dove in the mangroves,
> How dear is thy pain! (p. 488)

Clarel hears the Lyonese without heeding the elegiac tone central to
his lyrics. Dame nature both brings all to pass and makes all pass
away. The Lyonese, wise compared to the other hedonists, has bought

his freedom by a deliberate distancing of himself from the religion which draws him to the Holy Land. His poems acknowledge and integrate his sense of loss, creating out of pain a promise of consoling beauty. Clarel also ignores the power of time sung by the Cypriote, Ungar, and the Lyonese; he attaches his hopes not to freedom, imagination, beauty, and emotion but to Ruth herself. Fellowship and love may well be experiences in which Melville takes unambiguous pleasure, but his works tell us that only the very lucky gather their fruit; we are unprepared for life unless we prepare for loneliness. When Ruth dies, Clarel, like Mortmain, relapses into anguish.

Melville's final lyric, a dirge on the death of Ruth, firmly establishes the value of an art of expressive beauty; in it, Melville's narrative voice takes its new direction. The dirge sings in tetrameters, hinting that disciplined objectivity can coexist with imaginative freedom for those who are not blind. In order to avoid confusing this possibility with the vain hope that experience will reward the resolute, Melville ends his story on an objective note, leaving Clarel to the fate which has been anticipated.

Melville's dirge places Ruth in a sensually pleasing realm of "honey" and "mosses sweet" where her lover may hope to rejoin her. It creates a mental image of death as gentle and feeling, an imaginative leap which it justifies through literary symbolism rather than experiential data. The final image sums up its main affirmation:

> And if, ere yet the lover's free,
> Some added dusk thy rule decree—
> That shadow only let it be
> Thrown in the moon-glade by the palm. (p. 515)

The palm recalls that of Mar Saba, which cast a shadow over the pilgrims by confronting them with the ephemeral nature of their dreams. And yet, that shadow, the despair of Mortmain, the resignation of Vine and Rolfe, proves the imaginative force of those dreams. The dirge, a sophisticated intrusion of art on ritual, affirms the emotional appropriateness of such dreams even in a context which also proves them insubstantial. Only in the world of personal emotion and aesthetic sensitivity do they persist, yet life inhabits this world as well as the objective realm of physical experience. The dirge shows poetry capable of creating an alluring vision in response to the most pressing tragedy, of establishing an organic symbol of hope comparable to the adored symbols of Christianity. The true artist, lover, or worshipper is he who sustains his faith creatively by keeping the Southern Cross, the low lamps, Ruth, imaginatively alive or by replacing them with equally compelling phenomena.

After the dirge, Melville dissociates his viewpoint from that of his less imaginative protagonist; he describes Clarel's Easter Week activities with reserve and artistic distance in order to fulfill his tale of experience before retreating into the epilogue. However, during the Passion Week canto, Melville imbues Christian ritual with the same imaginative grace and delicate sensuality seen in the lyrics and the dirge:

> With the blest anthem, censers sway,
> Whose opal vapor, spiral borne,
> Blends with the heavens' own azure Morn
> Of Palms; for 'twas Palm Sunday bright,
> Though thereof he, oblivious quite,
> Knew nothing. (p. 517)

Clarel, in his depression, ignores the procession—another of the sources of inspiration which experience offers to those who are sensitive to beauty and uncommitted to doubt. Remaining blind, Clarel vanishes into the "obscurer town" a final victim of Melville's molding of heroism, discipline, and objectivity into an organic art.

The epilogue reaffirms the satisfactions of the *Clarel* lyrics. Not only does Melville abandon his jagged tetrameters for an easier, freer-flowing rhythm, but he displays a wit rare in both *Clarel* and his earlier verse:

> But through such strange illusions have they passed
> Who in life's pilgrimage have baffled striven—
> Even death may prove unreal at the last,
> And stoics be astounded into heaven. (p. 523)

Melville playfully mocks the blinding egoism of the intellect; the urbanity of the verse prevents our reading it as either a true confession of newfound religious faith or as an ironic joke. He offers, above all, an elegant and clever literary antidote to the gloom of the narrative. The determinism of "Darwin's year" can be read into "Luther's day" if one wishes, but for the poet history is the raw material of poetry, which stands on imagination, sensual pleasure, and beauty. Life is a victory if celebrated rather than merely endured. Like Glaucon, Melville abandons the pilgrimage with a warning for those who deem it "life's pilgrimage," the only path to walk.

The *Clarel* epilogue in all its conscious artificiality fits form to theme as carefully as any of Melville's verses. Frequent couplets and quatrains reinforce the witty comparisons which give it an Augustan quality. Images and symbols are tossed off or piled on one another with a breezy casualness which challenges intellectual rigor. Vast generalizations explode into aphorism without warning, and disappear as rapidly, hinting at their own insignificance. The verse coolly recommends to Clarel, wracked by anguish,

> Then keep thy heart, though yet but ill-resigned—
> Clarel, thy heart, the issues there but mind. (p. 523)

Lightness of tone gives the caution a hollow ring which even an image from *The Scarlet Letter* ("like a burning secret which doth go / Even from the bosom that would hoard and keep") cannot counteract. Without the amusing stylistic artifice and exaggeration which frames it, Melville's conclusion would demand a deep evaluation. What the style of the epilogue warns us is that such a conclusion, always objectively problematical, is absurd in an art whose job should be to create attractive, emotionally accessible, organic manifestations of whatever it affirms, and not to give sententious speeches. The lesson of Melville's changing art in *Clarel* is that truth-seeking, whether transcendental or objective, too easily produces a truth which is useless while ignoring opportunity after opportunity for beauty and satisfaction. The *Clarel* epilogue, in its marvelously complex self-consciousness, gives the best proof of Melville's faith in literature and playful delight in creative freedom since the early pages of *Moby-Dick*.

Battle-Pieces and *Clarel* tell the tale of Melville's interest in a serious, disciplined, realistic, and organically unified verse; as such, *Clarel* can be called America's greatest Victorian poem. Melville found in *Battle-Pieces* a new approach to the doubts and ambiguities hovering over his later fiction. As reservations about this approach arose, he built them organically into the structure, the versification, and the lyrics of *Clarel,* evolving an alternative vision at the fringes of his epic. By the end, the alternative—faith in the satisfactions of beauty, imaginative freedom, and art—moves from the fringe to the

center, and the epilogue gives it the last word. Here, Melville prefigures the witty and technically sophisticated verse of his later years.
Clarel proves Melville's tenacity and clear-sightedness in bringing to
completion a staggeringly difficult work, his alertness to sources of
new inspiration, and his willingness to risk stylistic audacity when
his vision warrants.

Moby-Dick: The Transformation of the Faustian Ethos

Gustaaf Van Cromphout

O NE MAJOR DIFFERENCE between *Moby-Dick* and its five predecessors in the Melville canon consists in its being its author's first
exploration of "landlessness." Like *Moby-Dick,* the earlier novels
recount actual or allegorical voyages, three of them even involving,
briefly or incidentally, whaling ships. Like *Moby-Dick* also, those
novels express what Merlin Bowen has rightly called Melville's "principal concern" in all his works, "a concern with the problem of self-
discovery, self-realization." But unlike *Moby-Dick,* those novels also
involve an "otherness" both sufficiently real and sufficiently compre-
hensible to act as a foil in the process of self-definition. Tommo and
Redburn, for instance, learn much about themselves from their con-
frontations with the "other," whether this be the valley of Typee, or
Liverpool, or the complexities of life aboard ship. The same is true,
mutatis mutandis, of the remaining early protagonists. In *Moby-
Dick,* by contrast, this "other" ceases to function as an aid to self-
knowledge because it ceases either to be truly "other" or to be accessible to human understanding, in the former case becoming a mere
reflection of the self and in the latter becoming a world emptied of
meaning and hence emptied of reality. In *Moby-Dick* the voyage is,
literally and metaphorically, one into "landlessness." The formal implication of this "landlessness" have been noted by Edgar A. Dryden: "Unlike its predecessors, *Moby-Dick* is almost completely self-
contained and self-referring. . . . it is always moving away from the
objective or factual world and persistently calling attention to itself
as fiction." Melville's masterpiece brings to full imaginative development a tendency in his thought only implied by such earlier statements as Redburn's "I began to see, that my prospects of seeing the
world as a sailor were, after all, but very doubtful; for sailors only go
round the world, without going *into* it."[1]

[1] Bowen, *The Long Encounter: Self and Experience in the Writings of Herman Melville*
(Chicago, 1963), p. 2; Dryden, *Melville's Thematics of Form* (Baltimore, 1968), p. 83;

The *Pequod*'s voyage into landlessness is Melville's version of the Romantic transformation of the Faustian ethos. When characterizing *Moby-Dick* as Faustian, I am not just referring to Ahab's being "the Faust of the quarter-deck," as Evert Duyckinck put it upon the novel's appearance and as Melville criticism has recognized ever since. Nor am I concerned with *Moby-Dick* as a variation upon the traditional Faust story, complete with a Faust, a devil, a pact, and a damnation, as William W. Betts and Charles Dédéyan have interpreted the book. I consider *Moby-Dick* Faustian in a more pervasive way. Following the lead of such students of our culture as Thomas Mann, Oswald Spengler, and T. K. Seung, I regard "Faustian" as almost synonymous with "Western," in that Faust represents what is most characteristic of the Western psyche: its boundless aspirations, its expansionism, its identification of knowledge with power, its attempt to subdue nature, its yearning for control over its own destiny. Thomas Mann's claim that Faust symbolizes the West's deepest essence receives considerable support from our obsessive concern with the Faust figure through the centuries; and no century was more Faust-conscious than the nineteenth, as a result primarily of Goethe's masterpiece.[2]

In the sense just indicated there is as much Faustianism in an

---

Redburn, The Writings of Herman Melville, ed. Harrison Hayford, Hershel Parker, and G. Thomas Tanselle (Evanston, Ill., and Chicago, 1969), IV, 133.

[2] Duyckinck is quoted in Hershel Parker, ed., *The Recognition of Herman Melville* (Ann Arbor, Mich., 1967), p. 40. Betts, "*Moby Dick:* Melville's *Faust*," *Lock Haven Bulletin,* I (1959), 31–44; Dédéyan, *Le Thème de Faust dans la littérature européenne* (Paris, 1961), IV, pt. 1, 206–224; Mann, *Gesammelte Werke* (Frankfurt am Main, 1960), IX, 599; Spengler, *Der Untergang des Abendlandes,* 2 vols. (Munich, 1922–1923), the most brilliant and elaborate argument for the identification of the Western mind with Faust; Seung, *Cultural Thematics: The Formation of the Faustian Ethos* (New Haven, Conn., 1976). The Western obsession with Faust is amply documented. See, e.g., E. M. Butler, *The Fortunes of Faust* (Cambridge, Eng., 1952); Geneviève Bianquis, *Faust à travers quatre siècles* (Paris, 1935); it took Dédéyan six volumes to chronicle the theme of Faust in Western literature; André Dabezies discovered that he had to take into account hundreds of works in order to produce a reasonably complete survey of *Visages de Faust au XXe siècle* (Paris, 1967). From among the innumerable nineteenth-century reactions to Faust, I select one whose origin (a newspaper article of 1835) shows how widespread even then was the idea of Faust's representativeness; referring to Goethe's conclusion of his masterpiece, the *Zeitung für die elegante Welt* says that "to have abandoned Faust would have meant abandoning the entire modern world, since Faust is all of us" (quoted in Hans Schwerte, *Faust und das Faustische,* Stuttgart, 1962, p. 82; all translations in this essay are mine, unless otherwise indicated). On more exalted levels, Hegel and Schopenhauer, Mme de Staël and Carlyle, Emerson and Margaret Fuller were saying much the same thing. For Melville's familiarity with Goethe's *Faust,* see Henry A. Pochmann, *German Culture in America* (Madison, Wisc., 1961), p. 759, n. 262.

Ishmael or a Bulkington as in Ahab himself. And the *Pequod*—a highly elaborate instrument for subduing nature, as Richard Chase has reminded us—is on a Faustian voyage. Ishmael's experience, as I shall try to show, brings him to an important insight, an insight reflecting Melville's awareness of the profound change then transforming the Faustian ethos. *Moby-Dick,* itself a Faustian venture in its epic ambitiousness, thus represents Melville's endeavor to understand some of the deepest spiritual tendencies shaping Western experience. In fact, Taji's claim in *Mardi,* "This new world here sought . . . is the world of mind," would have made an apt motto for the greatest among Melville's quests on the frontiers of human thought.[3]

There was a time when "limitless space," which Spengler regarded as the "prime symbol" (*Ursymbol*) of the Faustian psyche, made ceaseless striving objectively worthwhile. "The world-embracing metaphysical cupola," as Leo Spitzer put it, gave meaning to man's quest.[4] Such an early manifestation of the Faustian spirit as the Gothic cathedral represented the soul's attempt to escape from the confining heaviness of matter in order to achieve union with a God who was a personal presence rather than an abstraction.[5] Similarly Marlowe's well-known lines about

> Our souls, whose faculties can comprehend
> The wondrous Architecture of the world,
> And measure every wand'ring planet's course

reveal a faith in the objective substantiality of the universe that is in striking contrast with, say, Emerson's "It is the uniform effect of culture on the human mind . . . to lead us to regard nature as a phenomenon, not a substance." A Columbus, a Bacon, a Newton strove to bring within human ken realities that, until their advances in perception, had lain beyond it. And the Enlightenment, having postulated a universally valid and humanly intelligible "order" in nature, then appealed to that "order" to justify its intellectual and artistic endeavors. The Faustian mind aimed at knowledge of and,

[3] Chase, *The American Novel and Its Tradition* (Garden City, N.Y., 1957), p. 101; *Mardi, The Writings of Herman Melville,* ed. Harrison Hayford, Hershel Parker, and G. Thomas Tanselle (Evanston, Ill., and Chicago, 1970), III, 557.

[4] Spengler, I, 229; Spitzer, *Essays in Historical Semantics* (New York, 1968), p. 300, n. 70.

[5] Spengler, I, 264, 512. Cf. D. W. Robertson, Jr., *A Preface to Chaucer* (Princeton, 1962), p. 182: "The God of the Middle Ages . . . may have been ineffable . . . but He was a much more immediate Being than the romantic infinite."

through knowledge, at benefit from or mastery over the forces it perceived. Faustian space symbolized "einen Herrschaftsanspruch der Seele über das Fremde"—the soul's claim to dominance over what is "other."[6]

Occasionally, however, this "other" raised disturbing questions. Pascal's modernity, which consists in what Georg Lukács has called his "phenomenology of despair" rather than in his Jansenist solution, is suggested by statements like "the eternal silence of infinite space frightens me" and "engulfed in the infinite immensity of space, which I do not understand and which knows me not, I am frightened." Space, which Western man had so daringly extended, lost its meaningful content and became the realm of the void. It gradually became, as Alexandre Koyré says, "the infinite, uncreated nothingness, the frame of the absence of all being; consequently also of God's." One Romantic response to this anguish of the void was to turn more emphatically inward. The Faustian quest was interiorized, eventually to culminate in Rilke's claim that the only meaningful space left is the space of the inner world ("Durch alle Wesen reicht der *eine* Raum:/Weltinnenraum . . .").[7]

In *Moby-Dick* Melville confronts this collapse of Faustian space and its consequences. The experience of space, Charles Olson has said, is a central factor in *Moby-Dick,* but "space was the paradise Melville was exile of."[8] At first Ishmael voices the traditional Faustian yearning for "limitless space": "I am tormented with an everlasting itch for things remote."[9] In order to satisfy this yearning, he has repeatedly shipped as a merchant sailor (p. 15). His now opting for a whaling voyage will lead to a very different experience, although his early remarks reveal a duality of purpose consonant with traditional Faustian aspirations: he wants to experience not only the sea, which in the symbolic world of *Moby-Dick* is the mirror of the self,

[6] Christopher Marlowe, *Tamburlaine the Great,* Part I, II, vii, 21–23; Ralph Waldo Emerson, *Nature* (1836; facsimile rpt. San Francisco, 1968), p. 61; Spengler, I, 400.

[7] Lukács, *Die Zerstörung der Vernunft* (Neuwied am Rhein, 1962), p. 103; Blaise Pascal, *Pensées, Oeuvres complètes* (Paris, 1954), pp. 1112–1113; Koyré, *From the Closed World to the Infinite Universe* (Baltimore, 1957), p. 275. On the extension of space see also Marjorie Hope Nicolson, *The Breaking of the Circle* (rev. ed.; New York, 1960). Rainer Maria Rilke, *Sämtliche Werke* (Wiesbaden, 1956), II, 93; see also his seventh *Duineser Elegie:* "Nirgends, Geliebte, wird Welt sein, als innen. . . . immer geringer/schwindet das Außen" (*Sämtliche Werke,* Wiesbaden, 1955, I, 711).

[8] *Call me Ishmael* (New York, 1947), p. 82.

[9] Herman Melville, *Moby-Dick,* ed. Harrison Hayford and Hershel Parker (New York, 1967). p. 16. All page references to *Moby-Dick* are to this edition and will be given in the text.

but also the alien worlds beyond the sea, that is, the truly "other." As he puts it: "I love to sail forbidden seas, and land on barbarous coasts" (p. 16). Somewhat later, replying to Peleg's question why he wants to go whaling, Ishmael reveals the same dual impulse: "Well, sir, I want to see what whaling is. I want to see the world" (p. 69). Perceiving the duality, Peleg brings Ishmael to a sense of its inadequacy:

"Now then, thou not only wantest to go a-whaling, to find out by experience what whaling is, but ye also want to go in order to see the world? Was not that what ye said? I thought so. Well then, just step forward there, and take a peep over the weather bow, and then back to me and tell me what ye see there.". . .

Going forward and glancing over the weather bow, I perceived that the ship swinging to her anchor with the flood-tide, was now obliquely pointing towards the open ocean. The prospect was unlimited, but exceedingly monotonous and forbidding; not the slightest variety that I could see.

"Well, what's the report?" said Peleg when I came back; "what did ye see?"

"Not much," I replied—"nothing but water." (p. 70)

The voyage of the *Pequod* bears out this landlessness, this failure to encounter "otherness":

But how now? in this zoned quest, does Ahab touch no land? does his crew drink air? Surely, he will stop for water. Nay. For a long time, now, the circus-running sun has raced within his fiery ring, and needs no sustenance but what's in himself. So Ahab. Mark this, too, in the whaler. While other hulls are loaded down with alien stuff, to be transferred to foreign wharves; the world-wandering whale-ship carries no cargo but herself and crew, their weapons and their wants. . . . Hence it is, that, while other ships may have gone to China from New York, and back again, touching at a score of ports, the whale-ship, in all that interval, may not have sighted one grain of soil; her crew having seen no man but floating seamen like themselves. So that did you carry them the news that another flood had come; they would only answer—"Well, boys, here's the ark!" (p. 319)

The phrase "no man but floating seamen like themselves" suggests that the gams or near-gams do not modify this "landlessness." The other ships, whalers like the *Pequod,* but mirror back to the *Pequod*'s crew their own hopes, fears, or fates.[10]

[10] For the possible compositional implications of the inconsistency between the book's "landlessness" and Ishmael's earlier stated desire to "land on barbarous coasts" (p. 16), see James Barbour, "The *Town-Ho*'s Story: Melville's Original Whale," *ESQ: A Journal of the*

Bereft of its "otherness," the voyage becomes an experience of the void that leads to a heightened experience of the self. "Boundless solitude," Spengler said, was ultimately "the homeland of the Faustian soul." Ishmael is a cosmic outcast to whom John Seelye rightly attributes the suspicion that nature is but "a hollow sham, hiding absolutely nothing."[11] There is a Pascalian despair in Ishmael's cosmic loneliness, as when he questions "the heartless voids and immensities of the universe," or when he exclaims: "The intense concentration of self in the middle of such a heartless immensity, my God! who can tell it?" (pp. 169, 347).

And yet it is precisely the voyage of the self into this heartless immensity that holds out the promise of one's experiencing "truth." Pip's confrontation with the void has led to the kind of insanity that is "heaven's sense" (p. 347); and Bulkington symbolizes the realization that "in landlessness alone resides the highest truth" (p. 97). But truth has clearly ceased to be an objective structure, identifiable and graspable. Even conventionally honest, upright Starbuck no longer finds its source: "Great God, where art thou?" (p. 422). The abolition of "otherness" had emptied also God and truth of content. The Go dof Faustian man in his Romantic stage is no longer the personal God "climbed after" in the great cathedrals, but instead has become "an impersonal principle, unimaginable, ungraspable . . . an inconceivable abstraction,"[12] much like the "nameless, inscrutable, unearthly thing" (p. 444) that Ahab sometimes holds responsible for his fate. How utterly God has become a *deus absconditus* is suggested by Gordon V. Boudreau in his study of Melville's architectural symbology. When Melville compares the whale to a Gothic cathedral, he commonly omits the "copestone (or its equivalent stone symbol)," which symbolized "Christ as passage-way from earthly city to heavenly city"; and though this "persistent absence of copestone," just because it is so striking, draws the reader's attention to the symbolic significance of the copestone, it is itself, as absence, symbolic of "a

---

American Renaissance, XXI (2nd Quarter, 1975), 111, and "The Composition of *Moby-Dick*," *American Literature*, XLVII (Nov., 1975), 352 and n. 22.

[11] Spengler, I, 241; Seelye, *Melville: The Ironic Diagram* (Evanston, Ill., 1970), p. 64. For a general perspective, see Robert Martin Adams, *Nil: Episodes in the Literary Conquest of Void during the Nineteenth Century* (New York, 1966); pp. 141–148 deal with *Moby-Dick*.

[12] Spengler, I, 512.

God that is always missing."[13] Truth also is nowhere to be found. It has become "shoreless, indefinite as God" (p. 97); it "hath no confines" (p. 144); and it is as inscrutable as the "sphinx" that Ahab questions (p. 264). As Melville already suggested in *Mardi,* truth, like God, has become an unanswerable question. "Tell us what is truth?" asks Mohi; to which the philosopher Babbalanja replies: "The old interrogatory; did they not ask it when the world began? But ask it no more. . . . that question is more final than any answer."[14]

Turning truth into an unanswerable question meant temporalizing and subjectivizing it. If man is, like Bulkington, responsive to the highest imperative of his being, he attempts without cease to formulate the question, whether in thought or in action. And "the presupposition that each man is locked in the prison of his consciousness," which the Romantics, as J. Hillis Miller has noted, shared with many modern thinkers, led them to conceive of truth as a metaphor of self—as a ceaseless attempt "to utter our painful secret," as Emerson put it, in order to achieve self-knowledge. "Truth . . . ," we are told in Goethe and Schiller's *Xenien,* "*My* truth—for I don't know of any other." Georges Poulet is right in stressing that one important aspect of Romanticism was "a taking possession by consciousness of the fundamentally subjective character of the mind." The aesthetic implications of this inward turn of consciousness are obvious. It is not surprising that Hegel, whose *Aesthetik* has been called "the culmination of all romantic theories of art and aesthetics," considered "the true content" of Romantic art to be "absolute inwardness." As suggested above, the real object of the Faustian quest had become the self in all its mysterious complexity. And *Moby-Dick* is emphatically the product of a mind "which has turned away from the chaos and confusion of the world toward a contemplation of its own activity."[15]

13 "Of Pale Ushers and Gothic Piles: Melville's Architectural Symbology," *ESQ: A Journal of the American Renaissance,* XVIII (2nd Quarter, 1972), 76, 79, 78.

14 *Mardi,* p. 284.

15 Miller, *The Disappearance of God* (Cambridge, Mass., 1963), p. 8; *The Complete Works of Ralph Waldo Emerson,* ed. Edward Waldo Emerson (Boston, 1903–1904), III, 5; Johann Wolfgang Goethe, *Gedenkausgabe der Werke, Briefe und Gespräche,* ed. Ernst Beutler (Zurich, 1962), II, 471; Poulet, *The Metamorphoses of the Circle,* trans. Carley Dawson, Elliott Coleman, and the author (Baltimore, 1966), p. 93; Georg Wilhelm Friedrich Hegel, *Vorlesungen über die Aesthetik, Sämtliche Werke,* XIII (Stuttgart, 1964), 122–123; the tribute to Hegel's aesthetic theories is from Paul Frankl, *The Gothic* (Princeton, N.J., 1960), p. 473; Dryden, p. 84.

The *Pequod*'s element, after all, is water—the unlimited watery prospect that Ishmael faces during his first encounter with Peleg, instead of "the world" he expected to see. And as meaningfully as in Baudelaire's "L'Homme et la mer," water is in *Moby-Dick* the mirror of the soul; hence its universal attraction (pp. 12-14). Ahab, who, as a whaler, has preeminently been a man going "*round* the world, without going *into* it," is but universalizing his experience when he attributes the soul-reflecting significance of the sea to the world as a whole. The globe, in his view, "like a magician's glass, to each and every man in turn but mirrors back his own mysterious self" (p. 359). The voyage of the *Pequod* is an endeavor to see more clearly into the mystery of the self, but the endeavor being in vain, the mystery looms for ever unresolved. "The image of the ungraspable phantom of life" (p. 14) fuses with "the overwhelming idea of the great whale," that "grand hooded phantom" (p. 16) whose mystery will for ever encompass our existence (pp. 380, 384-385). Interested as he was in etymology, Melville must have been aware of the historical contiguities in meaning among "idea," "image," and "phantom." Their combined effect is to create an atmosphere of objective unreality in which the thinking "I," standing forth as the only essence, reduces the "other" to merely phenomenal existence.[16]

The confrontation with the whale most clearly reveals the problems facing Faustian man. T. K. Seung has shown that the formative period of Faustian culture (roughly the twelfth to the fourteenth centuries) witnessed a transition from allegorical to literal sensibility and modes of expression, a transition reflecting a shift from a theocentric to an anthropocentric world view. Literalism is a mode of expression revealing man's confidence in the objective validity of his perceptions; it reflects man's assumption that he knows or is able to know that which he perceives. Not surprisingly literalism, as Norman O. Brown has said in reference to its Protestant variety (Luther's *Eindeutigkeit*), did much to foster the modern scientific spirit with its assertion of man's knowledge-based power over nature. This argument can be applied in reverse to the transformation of

---

[16] For a different interpretation, one emphasizing "things rather than ideas," see Robert Zoellner, *The Salt-Sea Mastodon* (Berkeley, 1973; the quotation is from p. 8). Zoellner's argument is best summarized on p. 150: "The true narrative line of *Moby-Dick* is not the pursuit of the White Whale, but rather the transmutation which Ishmael's sensibility undergoes as that pursuit is prosecuted—and the essence of this transmutation is the gradual displacement of the conceptual whale by the perceptual whale."

Faustianism in the Romantic age: if the emergence of the Faustian ethos involved a transition from allegorical to literal sensibility, the Romantic transformation of that ethos may be said to have involved a transition from literal to symbolic sensibility. From the end of the eighteenth century onward the inadequacy of the literalist-scientific view became obvious. "The letter killeth" acquired a new and poignant meaning for Blake or Wordsworth or Keats observing the human spirit atrophied by the scientific mentality. The creative and unifying power of the symbolic imagination appeared to be the road to a new spiritual integrity. From a Faustian point of view, however, symbolism involved limitation. In much the same way that the allegorical sensibility reflected man's ultimate powerlessness in a theocentric universe, symbolism confronted man with a universe that exploded his pretense of knowing and controlling it. In *Die romantische Schule* (1836) Heinrich Heine pointed to the conceptual and formal implications of the shift from a literalist to a symbolist sensibility: "Classical art had to represent only the finite, and its forms could be commensurate with the artist's idea; Romantic art had to represent, or rather to suggest, the infinite and the purely spiritual."[17]

Ishmael approaches the whale on both the literal and symbolic levels. As exemplified by him, the literalist sensibility has clearly lost confidence in its own validity. The cetological chapters are riddled with confessions of inadequate treatment. The collapse of meaningful space, the disappearance of identifiable "otherness" is evidenced by the literalist inability to establish any real links between the "me" and the "not-me," an inability illustrating "how impassable is the gulf between the mind and its object."[18] The mind has no "hold" upon the whale; it cannot force him into any graspable forms. "If the Sperm Whale be physiognomically a Sphinx, to the phrenologist his brain seems that geometrical circle which it is impossible to square" (p. 293). Moreover, "If I know not even the tail of this whale, how understand his head? much more, how comprehend his face, when face he has none?" (p. 318). The whale shows "his great genius" by "his doing nothing particular to prove it" and by "his pyramidical silence" (p. 292). He cannot even be properly *seen:* "there is no earthly way of finding out precisely what the whale

---

[17] Seung, *Cultural Thematics;* Brown, *Love's Body* (New York, 1966), pp. 191–200; Heine, *Sämtliche Werke* (Munich, 1923), V, 351.

[18] Bowen, p. 122.

really looks like" (p. 228). Clearly we have here an instance of that "solipsistic unease" which, as A. D. Nuttall has brilliantly demonstrated, has affected many minds from the eighteenth century onward.[19] Ishmael's whale does "exist," but his insusceptibility to the mind's efforts at analysis and understanding, to the mind's attempts at assimilation, makes his objective existence ultimately irrelevant to the self. All the dissecting and analysis in the cetological chapters merely demonstrate the failure of literalism to bring us any closer to the "truth" about the whale. "Dissect him how I may . . . I but go skin deep; I know him not, and never will" (p. 318).

But if there is "no earthly way" to get to the truth about the whale, there is perhaps a "landless" way, a seaway (pp. 228, 97). The whale as symbol certainly brings us closer to the Faustian quest in its Romantic stage than the whale as objective reality: what is sought after is no longer knowledge of the "other," but knowledge of the self. Furthermore, Moby Dick as symbol transcends the connotations associated with the whale in traditional symbology and has thus lost that protection against merely personal interpretation which a culture confers upon its symbols. Moby Dick, like his element water, has become a portrait of every individual contemplating him: he means what anyone reads into him. Ahab, who, in Charles Olson's words, "had all space concentrated into the form of [the] whale,"[20] has come "to identify with him, not only all his bodily woes, but all his intellectual and spiritual exasperations. The White Whale swam before him as the monomaniac incarnation of all those malicious agencies which some deep men feel eating in them" (p. 160). To Gabriel of the *Jeroboam* the white whale is "the Shaker God incarnated" (p. 267). To Captain Boomer of the *Samuel Enderby* he has become a noli me tangere. Honest, upright Starbuck sees in Moby Dick the indifference and basic innocence of nature. The sailors in general, regarding Moby Dick with superstitious awe, credit him with ubiquity and immortality (p. 158) and with being an instrument of God (p. 208). Ishmael's interpretation in "The Whiteness of the Whale"

---

[19] *A Common Sky: Philosophy and the Literary Imagination* (London, 1974). See also William Ellery Sedgwick, *Herman Melville: The Tragedy of Mind* (New York, 1962), pp. 111–112: ". . . the solipsism of consciousness, a theme which Melville continually broaches in *Moby Dick*"; and Thomas Woodson, "Ahab's Greatness: Prometheus as Narcissus," *ELH: A Journal of English Literary History*, XXXIII (Sept., 1966), 362: "Ahab is haunted by the unknowability of 'things,' and turns desperately to solipsism."

[20] *Call me Ishmael*, p. 12.

is the least definitional of all, and it is for that reason symbolically the truest: more than anyone else Ishmael hints at the insoluble ambiguities, the endless mysteries suggested by the whale, whose color serves to reinforce his role as "phantom" and "idea," since whiteness "in its profoundest idealized significance . . . calls up a peculiar *apparition* to the soul" (p. 166; my italics). The paradox inherent in such a view of reality is well conveyed by a statement of Paul Brodtkorb's: "The emotion that constitutes white makes vibrantly visible as a presence the nothingness with which all existence is secretly sickened."[21]

Having been reduced to a medley of interpretations, the whale can no longer provide a meaning transcending individual perception. Reality has been reduced to the content of one's perceptions, as is demonstrated in "The Doubloon" and as Pip in his divine madness realizes: "I look, you look, he looks; we look, ye look, they look" (p. 362). Herein lies the ultimate loneliness of the Faustian soul and its inability to achieve self-definition. As long as the world was "real," the soul was "possible," Spengler suggests; what gave direction and meaning to the soul was its striving to comprehend reality and in the process to realize its possibilities and thus its idea of its self. But the "other" having been abandoned as unreal, there remained only the self and that hypersubjectivism which Werner Kohlschmidt has called "Fichte's Greek gift [i.e., Trojan horse] to Romanticism" ("das Danaergeschenk Fichtes an die Romantik"). While ostensibly exalting the self, subjectivism undermined it: Romanticism, in Wylie Sypher's words, "created the self and destroyed the self."[22] Without the context of the "other," the self became indefinable; alienation became the crisis of identity. Teufelsdröckh's "unanswerable question: Who am *I*; the thing that can say 'I?'" echoes through the nineteenth century.[23]

Moby-Dick demonstrates that when the "not-me" becomes a mystery inaccessible to the mind and thus, in effect, a void, the "me" becomes a mystery insusceptible to definition. Ahab, who does not

---

[21] *Ishmael's White World: A Phenomenological Reading of* Moby Dick (New Haven, 1965), p. 119.

[22] Spengler, I, 75, 107; Kohlschmidt, *Form und Innerlichkeit* (Bern, 1955), p. 162; Sypher, *Loss of the Self in Modern Literature and Art* (New York, 1962), p. 19.

[23] Thomas Carlyle, *Sartor Resartus* (New York, 1937), p. 53; Ralph Harper, *The Seventh Solitude: Metaphysical Homelessness in Kierkegaard, Dostoevsky, and Nietzsche* (Baltimore, 1965), pp. 11–13.

know whether the whale is "agent" or "principal," inscrutable mask or inscrutable essence (p. 144), has the same questions concerning the whale's counterpart, himself: "Is Ahab, Ahab? Is it I, God, or who, that lifts this arm?" (p. 445). Thomas Woodson's comment is to the point: Ahab "is continually in doubt of his identity. . . . [He] is never sure whether he is everything or nothing. . . . The mystery of things and the mystery of self become the same problem to him."[24] Ahab's plight is prefigured in his fantasy of the artificial man that he wants the blacksmith to forge. He does not want him to have "eyes to see outwards," but instead "a skylight on top of his head to illuminate inwards"; within, however, there is only a void, since the artificial man, though endowed with a "chest modelled after the Thames tunnel," will have "no heart at all" (p. 390).

In reference to the lack of progress into knowledge characterizing his quest, Ahab claims that "we are turned round and round in this world" (p. 445). The loss of "otherness" entails a reduction of the Faustian quest to an endless solipsistic circle from which there is no escape into something even resembling an absolute. Whether or not the circular quest destroys the quester, it never provides him with an answer, as Ishmael recognizes:

Round the world! There is much in that sound to inspire proud feelings; but whereto does all that circumnavigation conduct? Only through numberless perils to the very point whence we started. . . . Were this world an endless plain, and by sailing eastward we could for ever reach new distances, and discover sights more sweet and strange than any Cyclades or Islands of King Solomon, then there were promise in the voyage. But in pursuit of those far mysteries we dream of, or in tormented chase of that demon phantom that, some time or other, swims before all human hearts; while chasing such over this round globe, they either lead us on in barren mazes or midway leave us whelmed. (p. 204)

The anacoluthon in the last sentence but reinforces the message that the quest leads nowhere.

The passage just quoted is not, however, Ishmael's final word on the subject. His emancipation from traditional Faustianism is incomplete so long as he has not transcended what Kierkegaard considered man's self-defeating desire "to lay hold of something so really

[24] "Ahab's Greatness: Prometheus as Narcissus," pp. 363–364.

fixed that it can exclude all dialectics,"[25] so long, that is, as he even desires a "final" answer. As a participant in the action of *Moby-Dick*, Ishmael shares with Ahab, Bulkington, and the others the dilemma inherent in the pursuit of an aim fatally beyond human reach, a dilemma well expressed by Charles Feidelson: "The phantom is ungraspable as long as we stand on the bank; and the ocean is annihilative once we dive into it."[26] But Ishmael dives and is not annihilated. He survives to become the narrator of the action he participated in, and it is as narrator that he best exemplifies the essence of Romantic Faustianism, the recognition that "the goal of the journey of life [is] the experience of the journey itself."[27]

My argument involves a distinction between the "two Ishmaels" in *Moby-Dick*. In Walter E. Bezanson's words, "the first Ishmael is the enfolding sensibility of the novel, the hand that writes the tale, the imagination through which all matters of the book pass. He is the narrator. . . . The second Ishmael is not the narrator, not the informing presence, but is the young man of whom, among others, narrator Ishmael tells us in his story. . . . This is forecastle Ishmael or the younger Ishmael of 'some years ago.' "[28] Narrator Ishmael, moreover, is concerned with both narrative and narration. When focusing on narrative, he tries imaginatively to recapture the moods and hopes and perceptions of forecastle Ishmael and his companions; his narrative deals with the *then*, with an experience already completed. When focusing on narration, Ishmael's concern is with the *now*—with his ongoing endeavor to put into words what happened *then*. The *now*, representing an experience not yet completed, puts its stamp upon the book as emphatically as the *then*: *Moby-Dick* "is always in process and in all but the most literal sense remains unfinished. For the good reader the experience of *Moby-Dick* is a participation in the act of creation."[29] Authorial Ishmael's endeavor to give form and tentative meaning to his journey in the *Pequod* resulted in a book that is as much about the experience of writing a

[25] Søren Kierkegaard, *Concluding Unscientific Postscript*, trans. David F. Swenson and Walter Lowrie (Princeton, N.J., 1941), p. 35, n.

[26] *Symbolism and American Literature* (Chicago, 1953), p. 29.

[27] M. H. Abrams, *Natural Supernaturalism: Tradition and Revolution in Romantic Literature* (New York, 1973), p. 216.

[28] "*Moby-Dick*: Work of Art," in Moby-Dick: *Centennial Essays*, ed. Tyrus Hillway and Luther S. Mansfield (Dallas, 1953), pp. 36–37.

[29] Ibid., p. 56.

book as about the experience recalled in the book. And in a sense, the writing turned out to be as frustrating as the journey: both experiences fail to provide answers to the questions they evoke. The difference consists in Ishmael's responses to these failures; and his responses reveal different Faustian selves.

Forecastle Ishmael regards life as an Ixionic experience, as in the "Round the world!" passage quoted above, or as in this meditation on human destiny from "The Gilder":

There is no steady unretracing progress in this life; we do not advance through fixed gradations, and at the last one pause:—through infancy's unconscious spell, boyhood's thoughtless faith, adolescence' doubt (the common doom), then scepticism, then disbelief, resting at last in manhood's pondering repose of If. But once gone through, we trace the round again; and are infants, boys, and men, and Ifs eternally. (p. 406)

Whether these words be Ishmael's or not,[30] the fact remains that as long as Ishmael is the Ishmael evoked in "Loomings," an Ishmael questing for answers and solutions, he identifies himself with the other seekers and is bound to be as cruelly frustrated as they. Their quest tends to become his quest ("Ahab's quenchless feud seemed mine"—p. 155), and the despair inherent in their quest tends to become his despair, as in "The Lee Shore" (pp. 97-98), because like them he seeks answers, and through them he realizes the fatal impossibility of finding answers. The quest, for Ishmael and his companions alike, is thus reduced to an Ixionic experience in which the Faustian dream of knowledge and mastery has become the nightmare of total contingency. In this sense Carl F. Strauch is right in claiming that "If" is "the most important word in *Moby-Dick*."[31]

In the "Epilogue," however, Ishmael ceases to be "another Ixion" (p. 470). Though his final self-characterization as "orphan" sounds like a conceptual echo of the "Call me Ishmael" of the opening, and though we might thus be tempted to conclude that in his beginning was his end, such a conclusion seems unwarranted in view of the striking tonal difference between the "Epilogue" and the opening. "Orphan" and "Ishmael" both suggest, to be sure, a crisis in self-

---

[30] The Hayford-Parker edition of *Moby-Dick* follows textual tradition in attributing this passage to Ishmael; however, the editors note the possibility of Ahab's being the speaker of the passage (see p. 494).

[31] "Ishmael: Time and Personality in *Moby-Dick*," *Studies in the Novel*, I (Winter, 1969), 471.

definition: metaphorically they both stress the absence of any meaningful relation to the "other" and hence of any real understanding of the self. This point also is made in the "Ifs" passage in "The Gilder": "Our souls are like those orphans whose unwedded mothers die in bearing them: the secret of our paternity lies in their grave, and we must there to learn it" (p. 406). But whereas Ishmaelism or spiritual orphanhood is associated with bitterness and anguish in "Loomings," in the "Epilogue" it is accepted with a casualness that in no way disturbs the preternatural peace pervading the scene. Ishmael, in other words, has ceased tormenting himself about the ever-elusive answers to his questions concerning his place in the scheme of things and hence concerning his identity.[32]

Ishmael's new attitude does not amount, however, to his turning his back upon Faustian striving. The soul's "last limit," we were told in *Mardi,* "is her everlasting beginning."[33] And at the end of his *Pequod* experience Ishmael, a true embodiment of undying Faustianism, faces indeed a new and equally arduous task: "AND I ONLY AM ESCAPED ALONE TO TELL THEE" (p. 470). In his end is his true beginning: as author he embarks on another endless journey, and as author he demonstrates the principal lesson to be learned from his experience with the *Pequod*—that the journey itself is the goal of the journey. When Ishmael is at his most authorial, he sees virtue rather than horror in the absence of finality: "God keep me from ever completing anything" (p. 128), or, in reference to his cetological "books" and "chapters": "I promise nothing complete; because any human thing supposed to be complete, must for that very reason infallibly be faulty" (p. 118). Like Emerson, he regards Cologne Cathedral, not finished until 1880, as an apt symbol of the highest intellectual or artistic achievement: its very incompleteness, its "ever leav[ing] the copestone to posterity," is a measure of its greatness (pp. 127–28). For authorial Ishmael, as for Hölderlin's Hyperion, man's want and incompleteness have become grounds for self-congratulation.[34]

In its demonstration of the failure of traditional Faustianism,

---

[32] Cf. Warwick Wadlington's interesting discussion of the cycle of experience in *Moby-Dick* and its role in generating an ever-contingent identity: *The Confidence Game in American Literature* (Princeton, N.J., 1975), pp. 73–103.

[33] *Mardi,* p. 230.

[34] Emerson, *Complete Works,* XII, 70; Friedrich Hölderlin, *Hyperions Jugend, Sämtliche Werke und Briefe* (Munich, 1970), I, 524: "Das ist die Herrlichkeit des Menschen, daß ihm ewig nichts genügt. In deiner Unmacht tut sie dir sich kund. Denke dieser Herrlichkeit!"

Moby-Dick is a deeply pessimistic book: all the aspirations of the captain and crew (including Ishmael as actor in the drama), whether outer-directed or inner-directed, meet with frustration or disaster. But once "the drama's done" and a "dirge-like main" (p. 470) has mourned the death of an illusion, Ishmael is ready for his exercise in negative capability—the capability, in Keats's words, "of being in uncertainties, Mysteries, doubts, without any irritable reaching after fact & reason." The result is a highly inconclusive book and, through authorial Ishmael's recognition of the value of such inconclusiveness, ultimately a book that transforms man's epistemic limitations into a glorious challenge. Its very inconclusiveness also makes *Moby-Dick* a fit chapter in the totality of Melville's oeuvre, which, as Albert Camus maintained, but consists of "le même livre indéfiniment recommencé."[35] Perhaps Melville was afraid of finality. In an age that predicted the death of art,[36] there was great value indeed in an undying artistic effort, especially since, as Nietzsche was to say, "we have art so that we won't perish of truth," or, in Ishmael's version, "clear Truth is a thing for salamander giants only to encounter" (p. 286).[37]

[35] *The Letters of John Keats*, ed. Hyder Edward Rollins (Cambridge, Mass., 1958), I, 193; Camus, "Melville: Un Créateur de mythes," in Moby-Dick *as Doubloon: Essays and Extracts*, ed. Hershel Parker and Harrison Hayford (New York, 1970), p. 248.

[36] Hegel's *Vorlesungen über die Aesthetik* have often been considered a "funeral oration on art." See, e.g., René Wellek, *A History of Modern Criticism* (New Haven, Conn., 1955), II, 321, 334; Benedetto Croce, *Aesthetic,* trans. Douglas Ainslie (New York, 1968), p. 302; Erich Heller, *The Artist's Journey into the Interior and Other Essays* (New York, 1968), p. 115. Cf. also Macaulay's claim, in his essay on Milton (1825), that "as civilisation advances, poetry almost necessarily declines" (*Critical and Historical Essays*, London, 1961, I, 153). See also the references to the "Extinction of poetry" in Wellek, II, 456.

[37] Friedrich Nietzsche, *Gesammelte Werke* (Munich, 1926), XIX, 229.

Melville's Comic Debate:
Geniality and the Aesthetics of Repose

John Bryant

A<small>FTER</small> *Pierre,* Melville published in rapid succession a portfolio of tales, the serialized novel *Israel Potter,* and a "comedy of thought," *The Confidence-Man.* The feverish pace brought him financial solvency but also a near breakdown, and by 1856 he had abandoned fiction writing altogether. Scholars have held that the bitter and exhausted author lost control of his later narratives and that his once sportive yet genial comic spirit suffered a similar "pattern of decline."[1] Some even argue that Melville's failure was inevitable; he simply lost faith in the power of fiction and language itself to "tell the truth."[2] But recent critics deny that any decline in Melville's narrative skill occurred.[3] The same may be said for his comic sensibility. Rather than deteriorating, Melville's comic spirit was seeking a new voice, one that could subsume a knowing mind within a warm heart and yet remain critically detached from the author's personality or subject matter. In his magazine pieces, Melville experimented meticulously with comic types and narrative

---

[1] Edward H. Rosenberry, *Melville and the Comic Spirit* (Cambridge: Harvard Univ. Press, 1955), p. 7. The belief that Melville's powers declined began with F. O. Matthiessen who considered *Israel Potter* and *The Confidence-Man* to be products of "a miserable compulsion." See *American Renaissance: Art and Expression in the Age of Emerson and Whitman* (1941; rpt. New York: Oxford Univ. Press, 1967), p. 491. The present essay is an expanded version of a paper delivered before the Melville Society, December 1977.

[2] See Edgar Dryden, *Melville's Thematics of Form: The Great Art of Telling the Truth* (Baltimore: Johns Hopkins Univ. Press, 1968) and Nina Baym, "Melville's Quarrel with Fiction," *PMLA,* 94 (1979), 909–21.

[3] William B. Dillingham argues that Melville used irony as an artful means of mediating his "profundity" and the vapidity of his audience's expectations. See *Melville's Short Fiction, 1853–1856* (Athens: Univ. of Georgia Press, 1977), pp. 4 and 370. From a different perspective, Warwick Wadlington argues that Melville invites his readers to engage in a "godly gamesomeness" that exercises the heart rather than obscures truth. See *The Confidence Game in American Literature* (Princeton: Princeton Univ. Press, 1975), pp. 96 and 147.

American Literature, Volume 55, Number 2, May 1983. Copyright © 1983 by Duke University Press.

voice.[4] To be sure, the author severely challenged the utility of Ishmael's jaunty sociability, but ultimately he strengthened his commitment to geniality.

During this experimental phase of his career, Melville's object was to create an effective third-person speaker. A comparison of the endpoints of his experimentation reveals the degree of his success. *Pierre* (1852) is something of a "botch"; *The Confidence-Man* (1857) is masterfully controlled by a distant, self-effacing, third person who is himself a kind of confidence man.[5] The genesis of this comic voice is complex. The confidence man first appears as a character; he is the dialectical counterpart of Melville's familiar "genialist," an American version of what Stuart Tave has called the amiable humorist.[6] Gradually acquiring a psychological depth that enhances his comic potential, the knavish figure unites with the genialist to form the prophetic "genial misanthrope" of Melville's last novel. Along with this synthesis of comic types, Melville also used the confidence man in his experiments with unreliable narration. Moving beyond the limits of the ironic, first-person speakers of his early tales, he gradually introduced into his fiction the "metaphysical scamp" as a detached, third-person voice.

What guided Melville's search for comic detachment was the need to contain himself within, rather than expose himself through, his humor. Far from exhibiting a decline, the magazine pieces testify to a vigorous artistic growth along the positive principles of an "aesthetics of repose." Although he was an artist in transition, Melville was, nevertheless, an artist in control.

I

The genialist is often the butt of Melville's satire or burlesque.[7] But

---

[4] Evidence of the diversity and intensity of Melville's experimentation can be found in the fact that in the Spring of 1855 he composed or saw through publication five pieces, each with a different kind of narrator. In March, April, and May, Melville published the ninth installment of *Israel Potter* (third-person, omniscient narrator), "The Paradise of Bachelors and the Tartarus of Maids" (first-person, unreliable), and "The Bell Tower" (third-person, omniscient), respectively. By April, he had also proofed "Benito Cereno" (third-person, central consciousness), and in July he composed "I and My Chimney" (first-person, reliable).

[5] Dryden, p. 195.

[6] *The Amiable Humorist: A Study in the Comic Theory and Criticism of the Eighteenth and Early Nineteenth Centuries* (Chicago: Univ. of Chicago Press, 1960).

[7] For Elizabeth Foster, *The Confidence-Man* is a "philosophical satire on optimism." See Introd., *The Confidence-Man: His Masquerade*, by Herman Melville (New York: Hendricks

while Melville frequently "lacerates his persistently genial men,"[8] he never rejects geniality. For him, geniality is an unavoidable *instinct* urging man toward an integrative vision of life. Melville could no more reject it than he could his "instinct of the knowledge of demonism."[9] The genial instinct is part of the fabric of humanity. It is that force revealed to Babbalanja on May mornings, or (as Melville puts it in *John Marr*) "that something . . . the flower of life springing from some sense of joy in it. . . ."[10] Without it, Pierre's mind grows "maggotty," and Ahab becomes a "self-consuming misanthrope" (*MD*, XCVI, p. 353). With it, Ishmael can "perceive a horror [yet] . . . be social with it" (*MD*, I, p. 16). But this "sense of joy," or " 'all' feeling" (as Melville characterized it in a letter to Hawthorne) is ephemeral, and an over-indulgent pursuit of it inevitably leads to a shallow hedonism or facile optimism that blinds man to the world's "demonism." Tommo embraces cannibals; Delano dandifies a "monster." Their genial instinct is a sign of grace but also a tragic flaw. It is a "humor" that can preserve or destroy, humanize or delude.[11]

Melville's "persistently genial men" should not be damned. They are complex beings who must balance geniality and their growing recognition of life's darker side: a lawyer is obsessed with his scrivener's dis-ease; a seedsman shivers over the vain mechanisms of human sexuality. Poised on the brink of self-awareness, these admittedly impercipient men are stunned by their new knowledge yet preserved by their genial instinct. If they are to be condemned, it is because they serve only limited rhetorical ends. Only beginning to grasp the demon spirit, they know less than they would like. They lack assurance and control over the tales they attempt to tell. In

---

House, 1952), p. xiv. Similarly, Joseph Flibbert sees the novel as a "burlesque reconstruction of [the age's] philosophy of geniality." See *Melville and the Art of Burlesque* (Amsterdam: Rodopi, 1974), p. 149.

[8] Marjorie Dew, "Black-Hearted Melville: 'Geniality' Reconsidered," in *Artful Thunder: Versions of the Romantic Tradition in American Literature in Honor of Howard P. Vincent*, ed. Robert J. DeMott and Sanford E. Marovitz (Kent: Kent State Univ. Press, 1975), p. 177.

[9] *Moby-Dick*, ed. Harrison Hayford and Hershel Parker (New York: Norton, 1967), XLII, 169. Hereafter cited as *MD*; Roman numerals refer to chapters.

[10] *Collected Poems of Herman Melville*, ed. Howard P. Vincent (Chicago: Hendricks House, 1947), p. 161.

[11] In an examination of Melville's uses of the word "genial," Merton M. Sealts, Jr., concludes that the author remained at best ambivalent toward geniality. See "Melville's Geniality," in *Essays in American and English Literature Presented to Bruce Robert McElderry, Jr.*, ed. Max Schulz (Athens: Univ. of Ohio Press, 1967), pp. 3–26. Dew explicitly contradicts Sealts's interpretation.

creating the "genial misanthrope," Melville was able to surpass these ironic spokesmen and shape characters and voices (such as the speaker in "I and My Chimney" or Charlemont and Goodman in *The Confidence-Man*) who could more readily accommodate awareness and sociability.

Geniality serves an aesthetic as well as a moral function. After *Pierre*, Melville abandoned the Byronic mode of self-exposure that typified much of his earlier works. His later fiction adheres to a more restrained, reposeful conception of art. Melville's chief problem was to compress the chimeras of selfhood within a genial shell, to contain the demonic within the comic, to master the tensions between conflicting instincts. What impressed Melville about the ancient statues he viewed in Rome was their "tranquil, subdued air such as men have when under the influence of no passion."[12] Even Laocoön's anguished face, a "symbol of human misfortune," partakes of this tranquility. For Melville, the ancient sculpture evokes a modern dilemma in its embodiment of "the doubt and dark groping of speculation in that age when the old mythology was passing away and men's minds had not reposed in the new faith."[13] Just as Laocoön's creator buried within reposeful shapes in stone his agony over the "passing away" of one belief, Melville aspired toward a reposeful voice in prose that could articulate his own problem of faith without exposing too sharply his "dark gropings." His goal, too, was restraint: to objectify passions and subdue selfhood within art itself. Hence, one of "the finest . . . statements of truth" for him was Maurice de Guerin's remark that "There is more power and beauty . . . in the well-kept secret of one's self and one's thoughts than in the display of a whole heaven that one may have inside one."[14] Well before Melville underscored this passage in 1869, he had found a model for his principle of concealment in Nathaniel Hawthorne.

"Hawthorne and His Mosses" (1850) is as much an essay on the artful function of geniality as on the recognition of "blackness, ten times black." In praising his friend's covert "snatches" of truth and "quick probings," Melville argues that the "great Art of Telling the Truth" is a process of concealment. But more, its mechanism for

[12] Merton M. Sealts, Jr., *Melville as Lecturer* (Cambridge: Harvard Univ. Press, 1957), p. 150.
[13] Sealts, *Lecturer*, p. 139.
[14] Jay Leyda, *The Melville Log* (New York: Harcourt, 1951), pp. 703–04.

restraint is the heart. Refraining from "all the popularizing noise and show of broad farce, and blood-smeared tragedy," Hawthorne is "content with the still, rich utterances of a great intellect in repose, and which sends few thoughts into circulation, except they be arterialized at his large warm lungs, and expanded in his honest heart."[15] The heart's dual function is to *express* an inner being but also to *humanize* that dark entity and make its expression palatable. Governing the heart, the genial spirit "arterializes" deep thought. It gives human dimension to demonic revelations and repose to the mind.

Like the heart, Hawthorne's "contemplative humor" rises above the hail-fellow's "rollicking rudeness." It is "so high, so deep, and yet so richly relishable. . . . It is the very religion of mirth" (*MM*, p. 403). Hawthorne's "relishable" yet spiritual tone is transformed under Melville's scrutiny into images of suppressed fire and light. The fireplace in "Fire Worship" (quoted at length by Melville) illuminates the link between geniality and art. A metaphor for both the heart and art, it exhibits Laocoön's tense repose. Here, the hearth contains the fire's potential for "mischief" and "mad destruction" within its warm "domestic kindness." Just as Shakespeare has his "flashings-forth," the fire, Hawthorne writes, may "[betray] his wild nature," but its "red tongue" rarely escapes the stony hearth whose warm heart atone[s] for all" (*MM*, p. 404). In its containment of fiery truths, the fireplace resembles Melville's crucible of "Art" in which "unlike things must meet and mate" and where "Humility— yet pride and scorn" are fused within the "mystic heart."[16] Hearth, heart, and art—the three are similar emanations of the same genial spirit.

In fusing the domestic and the sublime, Hawthorne's art achieves the ripeness of "Indian Summer sunlight" that unifies the landscape in "one softness" yet "still reveals the distinctive hue of every towering hill, and each far-winding vale" (*MM*, p. 404). Hawthorne's "mirth" gives an artful presence to the variable topography of the self; and yet it subdues the realities of "hill and vale" beneath "one softness." For Ishmael, nature "paints like the harlot" (*MD*, XLII, p. 170), but for Melville, as artist, the "distinctive hues" of art give

---

[15] *The Portable Melville*, ed. Jay Leyda (New York: Viking, 1952), p. 408. Hereafter cited as *MM*.
[16] Melville, *Poems*, p. 231.

palpable form to otherwise incomprehensible truths. The darkness within us is not total. Indeed, its presence "gives more effect to the ever-moving dawn, that forever advances through it, and circumnavigates [the] world" (*MM*, p. 406). Melville's art, like Hawthorne's, does not deny darkness; it subdues and "forever advances through it." The voice of "a great intellect in repose" is built upon the fusion of mind within "the all-engendering heart" (*MM*, p. 405). It is the expression of dark inner truths which intrude upon but never fully possess the bright world.[17]

Melville's search for a voice that could match Hawthorne's repose reached a plateau with Ishmael's "free and easy sort of genial, desperado philosophy" (*MD,* XLIX, p. 196). Although Ishmael plays many roles, his multiplicity suggests a fruitful pliability of mind that does not detract from his reliability as a narrator.[18] He possesses many "distinctive hues." Moreover, although his ironic humor conveys the despair of his failure to name what he knows is "dreadfully nameless,"[19] Ishmael can contain the emptiness of his white world within the "one softness" of his genial voice. And yet, the very dominance in *Moby-Dick* of this semi-autobiographical character, full of "hypoes" and obsessions, denies Melville the narrative distancing, the critical freedom from personality, that could lead him to authorial "repose." By turning to third-person narrative, he was in effect rejecting the notion of art as a sounding board for personality and adopting an aesthetic based upon an effacement or abnegation of selfhood. Moreover, in doing so, he could promote the growth of a genial voice more securely located within the transcendent "mystic heart."

To a large degree, Melville's decision to write *Pierre* in the third-person stems from his readiness to fulfill the Hawthorne model. But unlike Ishmael who probes and yet is separate from Ahab's mind, the narrator in *Pierre* fails to sustain an even distance from his "infatuate" protagonist. He brands Pierre a "blind fool, and a million times an ass"[20] for his insufferable idealism, an idealism which the proud

---

[17] Melville's most memorable expression of this aesthetic principle is found in his ruminations on "Two Sides to a Tortoise": ". . . keep [the bright side] turned up perpetually if you can . . . and don't deny the black." See *Selected Writings of Herman Melville* (New York: Random House, 1952), p. 56. Hereafter cited as *SW.*

[18] Wadlington, p. 73. See also Dryden, p. 110.

[19] Paul Brodtkorb, Jr., *Ishmael's White World: A Phenomenological Reading of Moby-Dick* (New Haven: Yale Univ. Press, 1965), p. 131.

[20] *Pierre; or the Ambiguities,* ed. Harrison Hayford, *et al.* (Evanston and Chicago: Northwestern Univ. Press and The Newberry Library, 1971), p. 171.

speaker, it seems, has already overcome. The narrator is like an obsessed personality hurling salvoes of indignation at himself through the flimsy guise of a third-person pronoun. As Lawrance Thompson notes, the "furiously derisive bitterness" in *Pierre* undermines the novel's "genial, jovial, comic" effect.[21] Thus, in attempting to create a congenial third-person voice, Melville found himself ironically removed from the sensibility of a "great intellect in repose." He could not duplicate what he had admired in Hawthorne.

To be sure, *The Confidence-Man* is not a novel that reposes in the bosom of either an old or new faith, but its elusive speaker and central character, the cosmopolitan, conform in significant ways to Melville's aesthetic. As Elizabeth Foster concludes, "the finest and quietest irony of the book is a sort of constant whisper . . . in the very manner of the book, which in a style suggesting kindliness and impartial good nature and gentle, sometimes jaunty, ease, leads quietly up to the most bitter conclusions."[22] By engaging readers in a rich experience of doubt, the novel promotes a balanced understanding of doubt: it is as much a suspicion that *belief is possible* as it is that *disbelief is inevitable*. The cause of this reader experience lies in the narrator's abdication of authorial responsibility. By refusing to judge or establish norms, Melville pushes the reader into a quagmire of speculation on motives and meanings. The speaker's coy equivocations only tease us deeper into doubt. And though his "ponderous stuttering" lacks repose,[23] his voice evinces total effacement of the author's personality. Unlike *Pierre*, this novel contains little that is autobiographical. In it, Melville's presence (aside from three intrusive chapters) is thoroughly concealed. If anything, the author's "self and thought" remain, in Guerin's words, a "well-kept secret."

If *The Confidence-Man* lacks the traditional, normative speaker, it also lacks a hero. A tentative "moral center" amidst the knaves and fools on board can be found, however, in Frank Goodman, the cosmopolitan. Prophesying the coming of "the genial misanthrope," Goodman offers a clue to his own identity: ". . . under an affable air, he will hide a misanthropical heart. In short, the genial mis-

[21] Lawrance Thompson, *Melville's Quarrel with God* (Princeton: Princeton Univ. Press, 1952), pp. 247–48.

[22] Foster, p. xciv.

[23] Warner Berthoff, *The Example of Melville* (1962; rpt. New York: Norton, 1972), p. 166.

anthrope will be a new kind of monster . . . [who, unlike Timon] will take steps, fiddle in hand, and set the tickled world a' dancing. In a word, as the progress of Christianization mellows those in manner whom it cannot mend in mind, much the same will it prove with the progress of genialization."[24] In being "genialized," the misanthrope will "take on refinement and softness." The cosmopolitan also possesses "a healthy balance . . . between meekness . . . and misanthropy."[25] In fusing such "unlike things," he spiritualizes pragmatism; he can both recognize man's potential for good yet remain wary of his capacity for evil. Like Machiavelli's Prince, he can dissemble as well as show good faith. And like the novel's narrator, he is a gadfly or "metaphysical scamp" who can cheat cheaters and even "con" others into a leap of faith. Annihilating our readiness to believe, he paradoxically goads us to entertain new beliefs. In words Melville also used to describe Hawthorne, Goodman seems "to dispense a sort of morning through the night" (CM, p. 207). The cosmopolitan's genial misanthropy, therefore, highlights the utility of the genial spirit. Like a great intellect in repose, the genial misanthrope will suppress thought within the heart and put on "softness."

These thumbnail sketches of *Pierre* and *The Confidence-Man* isolate the salient features of Melville's experimentation—the parallel growths of the genial misanthrope as a character and the confidence man as a narrator. In bridging the two works, certain tales and *Israel Potter* display the choices Melville made in molding his fiction to his aesthetic requirements.

II

Although historical antecedents for Melville's confidence games have been traced in the popular culture,[26] the device grows naturally

[24] *The Confidence-Man: His Masquerade,* ed. Hershel Parker (New York, Norton, 1971), p. 154. Hereafter cited as *CM*.
[25] Elizabeth Keyser, " 'Quite an Original': The Cosmopolitan in *The Confidence-Man,"* *Texas Studies in Literature and Language,* 15 (1973), 280.
[26] Richard Chase identifies Melville's confidence man as a variation on the Yankee Peddler; see *Herman Melville: A Critical Study* (New York: Macmillan, 1949). Daniel Hoffman considers the figure to be "an amalgam of America's popular comic figures" in *Form and Fable in American Fiction* (New York: Oxford Univ. Press, 1967), p. 283. For an additional tracing of the confidence man motif see Susan Kuhlman, *Knave, Fool, and*

from his own fictive patterns. Throughout such tales as "Bartleby," "The Paradise of Bachelors and the Tartarus of Maids," and "Jimmy Rose," Melville relates the same conflict between impercipient *genialist* and *isolato*. His confidence game emerges in other tales as a specialized version of this recurring pattern when the *isolato* is recast as a *false genialist* or confidence man. Whereas a Bartleby may bewilder his genial interlocutor, the false genialist schemes and attacks beneath a show of consanguinity. Out of this "comic debate" between integrative (genialist) and subversive (confidence man) sensibilities, the "genial misanthrope" evolves, uniting the identities of both types into a "wary confidence" suited for humane survival. The magazine pieces contain seven confidence men: Oberlus in "The Encantadas"; the lightning-rod man; Israel Potter, Benjamin Franklin, and John Paul Jones in *Israel Potter*; Babo in "Benito Cereno"; and, interestingly enough, the chimney in "I and My Chimney." Each character advances in seriousness and complexity beyond his predecessor.

Melville's confidence games also have a narrative dimension. In everyday experiences a confidence game requires a knave and a fool, but in fiction someone must also relate the particulars to an audience. An author may designate either the confidence man or his unwitting dupe as first-person observer. Neither is particularly reliable since the former is a cheat, and the latter a fool. Through a third-person speaker, the author may attach himself to the central consciousness of either confidence man or fool, and hence be unreliable. Or as an omniscient consciousness, the third person may be thoroughly reliable. Of course, an omniscient speaker may also acquire knavish traits by violating the expectations of a readership that has willingly surrendered its disbelief unto him. In his early tales Melville relies upon the first-person perspective of an intended victim, but in later works he develops the voice of a "tainted" omniscient speaker, one whose very refusal to direct our judgments awakens us to the fragility of confidence.

Throughout the magazine pieces, Melville's confidence games progress through four phases: the experimentation with comic villains in certain early tales; the exploration of the confidence man's

Genius: The Confidence Man as He Appears in 19th Century American Fiction (Chapel Hill: Univ. of North Carolina Press, 1973). For specific references to confidence men in the newspapers of Melville's day see Johannes D. Bergmann "The Original Confidence-Man," *American Quarterly*, 21 (1969), 560–77.

social and psychological potentials in *Israel Potter*; the full articulation of the comic debate in "Benito Cereno"; and the genesis of the genial misanthrope in "I and My Chimney."

After *Pierre*, Melville returned to his familiar first-person mode, but his short narratives were not complete retrievals of his earlier, Ishmaelian voice. The speakers in "Bartleby" and "Cock-A-Doodle-do!" grope for meaning; their growth toward a higher consciousness is questionable. The lawyer's simplistic equation, "Ah, Bartleby! Ah, humanity!" is as meaningless in its generality as the inarticulate crowing of the speaker at the end of "Cock-A-Doodle-do!" Such tales ironically expose the intellectual limitations of geniality. "The Encantadas," however, marks a recovery of the Ishmaelian voice, but as if to compensate for this elevation of the genial spirit, Melville introduces for the first time the genialist's nemesis, the confidence man.

Melville's comic voice interlaces and unifies the wasteland imagery of the "The Encantadas." Both a metaphysician and a gourmand, his speaker expounds and then literally devours his thoughts. The tortoise, for instance, is a highly allusive symbol of Melville's bright and dark philosophy, but in the end it makes for good soup. Such "genialization" hints at a comic union of spirit and flesh that emerges again in the final sketch when the speaker picnics in repose on the graves of castaway sailors. Like a "religion of mirth," Melville's "genial, desperado" tone transcends these doleful sketches and even the penultimate tale of Oberlus, the hermit and confidence man.

A broadly-drawn, incompetent villain, Oberlus connives and lusts but is doomed to failure. The surly misanthrope's first impulse is to seize power by blunderbuss. In need of slaves, he abducts a "righteously suspicious" black sailor. But when the victim's mates retaliate and leave Oberlus in chains, the hermit devises a more genial strategy: he "makes up" to his new victims "like a free-and-easy comrade, invites them to his hut, and with whatever affability his red-haired grimness may assume, entreats them to drink his liquor and be merry" (*SW*, p. 107). The false genialist's dominion grows until, rejected in his suit for an island queen, he seeks revenge by arson and is jailed. His failure stems from his inability to repress his fiery passions, and his incompetence as a villain suggests that, at best, fortune reigns indifferently over good and evil. In rationalizing his antipathy for Oberlus, Melville strives for a more positive conclusion:

"it is religion to detest [the hermit], since it is philanthropy to hate a misanthrope" (*SW*, p. 112). The paradox inherent in this redefinition of love as hating those who hate does not disturb the speaker; it is a witty accommodation of conflicting impulses. The wordplay also indicates the speaker's control. Once again, geniality subsumes malignancy. In its earliest phase, then, the confidence man figure teases the genialist into deeper self-awareness.

"The Lightning-Rod Man" is Melville's first full-length portrait of a confidence man actively pursuing a genial victim. Even though he is more richly satanic than Oberlus, the title character also fails. Basing his rhetoric on fear, he sells his rods during thunderstorms. And deeming isolation from man and nature to be the most effective insulation, he sedulously avoids hearths and tall men because they draw lightning. His misanthropy, however, pales before his victim's braggadocio. Standing by his hearth, the genial speaker takes comfort in the notion that lightning can strike from earth to heaven. The lightning-rod man is a poor rhetorician. He cannot modify his fearful arguments to address his fearless and witty victim. The speaker out-talks the salesman and even carves masks for him, a function that a self-respecting confidence man is obliged to do for himself. The peddler is labeled an undertaker, a god of thunder, Satan crying before God, and a modern-day Tetzel, all before he gets his cloven foot in the door. If this devil seems a shape-shifter, it is the speaker's doing, not his. The genialist's victory, then, is as much rhetorical as theological, and his verbal skills prefigure the controlled confidence of the knave-killer, Frank Goodman.

Melville's earliest confidence men are foiled by their own obsessions and incompetence. Their desperate misanthropy merely "gives more effect" to the genial spirit. But in *Israel Potter* these straw men grow into a figure of threatening psychological verisimilitude. Based upon a "sleazy gray" pamphlet, *The Life and Remarkable Adventures of Israel R. Potter* (1824), the serialized novel also explores new narrative strategies. It is another and more successful experiment in self-effacement. With such ironic, first-person tales as "Bartleby," Melville could project a speaker whose dim awareness is radically distinct from his own consciousness. But the Potter tale goes even farther to surpass the autobiographical mode of earlier works. Avoiding the excesses of *Pierre*, this new attempt at third-person narration effectively balances bitterness and repose. Playing the biographer and historian, Melville records the intimate thoughts of a fellow wanderer and yet remains distant, critical, and dispassionate.

Claiming to have reprinted the original story with only "a change in the grammatical person,"[27] Melville, in fact, refined words, raided history for additional characters, reduced and expanded scenes, and added a veil of allegory. At times indignant, the novel's reliable third-person narrator has nevertheless purged the "bitter derisiveness" that marred *Pierre*. Any bitterness Melville may have had at this time is transformed into a critique of Potter's failure. Of course, muted scorn can be sensed in the novel's facetious dedication and the allegory of the bricks, but these hints never erupt into derision. The novel exhibits the author's growing control. As John Freeman notes, Melville had "resolved . . . to restrict himself to the dry husk of language, putting an external constraint upon his genius."[28]

This tale of an expatriate's vain longings for home is also Melville's most extensive characterization of the confidence man as an embodiment of self and society. Throughout its complex network of diddling, Israel must play all three roles in the confidence game. He is Franklin's slowly comprehending *dupe* but later a *confidence man* himself, and he is an impartial *observer* of Franklin's diddling of Jones and of Jones's own games.

Franklin is Melville's first substantial confidence man. With damning, faint praise, the narrator exposes the common sense diplomat in his "honorable hat" and "worsted hose" (*IP*, p. 48). It is a portrait of subtle deficiencies. Franklin's thoughtladen mind buzzes—like a "hogshead on the wharf" swarming with flies (*IP*, p. 39). He is "the type and genius of his land" but not "a poet" (*IP*, p. 48). He urges men to be trustful, for too much distrust "is the worst consequence of a miserable condition" (*IP*, p. 41). And yet securing trust is his first step in manipulating men. Franklin's geniality is only a pasteboard calling card for seeking entrance into other men's favor and possessions. When Israel attempts to slake his thirst for Otard and a chambermaid, Ben spirits the temptations away—for Israel's sake and

[27] *Israel Potter: His Fifty Years of Exile*, ed. Harrison Hayford, *et al.* (Evanston and Chicago: Northwestern Univ. Press and The Newberry Library, 1982), p. vii. Hereafter cited as *IP*.

[28] Raymond Weaver, Introd., *The Shorter Novels of Herman Melville* (New York: Horace Liveright, 1928), p. xxxv.

Franklin's pleasure. An apprentice in the devious arts, Israel quickly catches on to the false genialist: "Every time he comes in he robs me with an air all the time, too, as if he were making me presents" (*IP*, p. 53). Franklin is "sly, sly, sly" (*IP*, p. 54).

Although Jones's savage heart counters Franklin's Tuscan head, he, too, is a confidence man. Still, he plays Franklin's fool. When Jones demands more ships, the narrator mimicks Franklin's byzantine response. Impressed by empty wit, Jones attempts to display his own verbal skills with an obvious play on the diplomat's name: "Thank you for your frankness . . . ; frank myself, I love to deal with a frank man" (*IP*, p. 58). Franklin manages an incredulous smile. The narrator's refusal to interpret the smile and what it signals to Israel prefigures the wordy manipulation of later works.

Although a victim in the parlor, Jones is a victor at sea. Franklin depends upon the "mild superiority of successful strategy" (*IP*, p. 52) to manipulate, but Jones, a "gentleman-wolf," plays a different game. He survives through relentless bravado in a world "subject to organic disorder" (*IP*, p. 114). Unlike Franklin, he is "a bit of the poet," and yet his passions, like his tattoos, are "elaborate, labyrinthine, cabalistic" (*IP*, p. 62). A deadly practitioner of the confidential arts, he slides into enemy ports to plunder by night as though insinuating himself "into human harbors or hearts" (*IP*, p. 99). His "hoodwinking" battle tactics genially conceal powder and shot: ". . . . The two ships glided on freely, side by side; in that mild air exchanging their deadly broadsides, like two friendly horsemen walking their steeds along a plain, chatting as they go" (*IP*, p. 113). "Intrepid, unprincipled, reckless, predatory," Jones, like America, is "civilized in externals but a savage at heart" (*IP*, p. 120).

As confidence men, Franklin and Jones are all-too successful; they characterize the glory of America's shallow pragmatism and predatory power. Israel's schemes also succeed but afford him little more than subsistence and anonymity. For him, the confidence game erodes identity. Israel is shrewd enough to know that it is better "to plough, than be ploughed" (*IP*, p. 12), and his native optimism brightens his frequent seclusions in dark jails and hideaways. But not all Yankees are winners, and the flaxen-haired Israel quickly learns that no amount of scheming can insure success in a world governed by chance. Escaping the British in "ditcher's rags," Israel artfully eludes his pursuers but is nevertheless arrested, not as an American but as a deserter from the British army. The enemy's misperception ironically conceals Israel's true identity but still lands him in jail. This comic lesson in the futility of disguise foreshadows Israel's grandest larceny on board an enemy ship. But here, Israel's confidence game makes him a "nobody."

Left dangling in the rigging of a British man-of-war, Israel must manipulate his foe to his favor. A stranger in alien waters, he claims to be a member of the British crew and "a poor persecuted fellow" whom no one is "willing to remember" (*IP*, p. 138). Israel glad-hands his incredulous "mates" urging them to be sociable. Grudgingly, they accept the disguised Yankee but pass him unwanted from foretop to hold, where he persists in his lie. Despite his "general sociability" (*IP*, p. 141), the once boastful American becomes a friendless Wandering Jew with "no end in the world" and "no final destination" (*IP*, p. 140). Israel's false geniality secures him a safe but sullen anonymity. His complaint, "Who ain't a nobody," echoes Ishmael's "Who ain't a Slave," but it lacks the jocularity, even the capitalization. Israel is a lower-case nonentity whose necessary self-annihilation is a game he must play merely to survive. He has taken to heart Franklin's assurance that God will help him if he helps himself, but in the end he is a victim of his own "helping," the butt of a cruel joke, the punchline of which is that chance outstrips human will. Israel's conclusion is that man "succeeds better in life's tragedy than comedy" (*IP*, p. 160).

Israel's tragedy lies not so much in his loss of identity as in his necessary misuse of the genial spirit. He must deceive to exist; hence, he is fated to fall from grace. In "Benito Cereno" Melville explores the implications of this fall more carefully when he brings Delano, Cereno, and Babo together to debate the uses of geniality. Ultimately, the debate between acceptance and resignation remains precariously unresolved. The tale also marks another development in Melville's narrative technique. Whereas the author of *Israel Potter* disguises himself as a biographer; in "Benito Cereno" he fashions a voice so seemingly non-commital that it becomes unreliable. The central consciousness narrator exhibits no bitterness toward Delano's naïveté or Cereno's despair, no repulsion over Babo's treachery. He is reposefully detached from his material.

This tale of Amasa Delano's inadvertent discovery of a slave revolt on board a Spanish vessel centers upon the complex confidence game that the slave leader has designed to cover-up his rebellion. Forcing his captive captain to resume his former role, Babo plays the Cheerful Negro; Cereno, the indifferent master. Delano, the intended victim of this masquerade, is the tale's central consciousness. As one of the densest lambs in Melville's flock of impercipient genialists, he is ill-prepared to penetrate Babo's pretense. Like the lawyer in "Bartleby," he is a man of "assumptions": his "household boat" is the touchstone for "a thousand trustful associations" (*SW*, p. 297); all black men are, to him, willing servants. Amidst the thinly-veiled tensions, Delano benignly transforms a nursing slave (planted to evoke a "sunny" and "quite sociable" sight for the American) into the epitome of "naked nature, . . . pure tenderness and love" (*SW*, p. 292). Delano takes to "negroes" as "other men to Newfoundland dogs" (*SW*, p. 307). For him, the black man is the spirit of geniality. But Delano's benevolent racism is dangerously flawed; it denies the black man his humanity and therefore ignores his capacity to lie and kill.

In a confidence game, the dupe frequently asks to be duped. He perceives the knave to be an ally, discloses his innermost desires, and in effect suggests to the knave the rhetorical strategies by which he can be undone. Convinced of the black man's innate "good humor," Delano attempts "to tickle the negro" with his jokes. Playing the servile Newfoundland dog, Babo tailors his game to Delano's genial "assumptions" and obliges him with ingratiating smiles. Although Babo eventually fails, his rhetoric (which must be judged by its thorough use of the available means of persuasion) dupes Delano so completely that the American cannot distinguish black from white. A mulatto's "display of elegance," for instance, proves to Delano that, despite popular beliefs ascribing treachery to mixed breeds, such men are *not* masked "devils" (*SW*, p. 313). The irony, however, is that Delano does not know that black and white blood has already been *mixed* (and will again be mixed) not in the heart but on the battle deck. Delano's convictions are so strong that he even forces a genial construction upon Babo's climactic attempt to murder Cereno, an action the slave performs (Delano believes) "as if with desperate fidelity to befriend his master to the last" (*SW*, p. 326).

Early on, Delano sights a medallion depicting "a dark satyr in a mask, holding his foot on the prostrate neck of a writhing figure, likewise masked" (*SW*, p. 259). The emblem prefigures the story's *dénouement* when Delano, "his right foot [upon] . . . the prostrate negro," detains the "snakishly writhing" Babo (*SW*, p. 327). Like a *tableau vivant*, the scene freezes for a moment a dramatic rendering of the comic debate between the genial and the demonic. Delano is the satyr-like genialist; Babo, the snakish confidence man. Both wear genial masks: Delano's faithfully projects his sunny disposition; Babo's promotes trust only to conceal savagery. The unresolved tension between the two continues after Babo's demise as Delano attempts at the end to reinvigorate Cereno's dying confidence.

For the Spaniard, Babo's piked head is a "hive of subtlety "(*SW*, p. 353), a haunting symbol of the peril, if not impossibility, of human confidence.[29] Forced to play comrade to the murderer of his best friend Aranda, Cereno has lost all taste for congeniality. He is a tormented monk whose quarters, like his very being, blend the auras of a "cluttered hall of some eccentric bachelor-squire" and a torture chamber (*SW*, p. 305). "Again and again," Cereno repeats "how hard it had been to enact the part forced on [him]" (*SW*, p. 350). But enact he did, and so well that Delano believed Cereno, not Babo, to be the "monster." Just as Potter plays a "nobody" and thus becomes one, Cereno's monstrous performance unleashes in him a fearful recognition of human duplicity not unlike Babo's. The Spanish *isolato* chooses to die rather than assimilate this darker side. Delano, however, reaffirms his genial spirit and in the tale's final dialogue argues that his instinctive trust preserved him "when acuteness might have cost [him his] life" (*SW*, p. 351). Delano urges Cereno to forget: ". . . the past is passed; why moralize upon it?" Bright sun, blue seas and sky—they can forget. But, Cereno responds, that is "because they have no memory, . . . because they are not human" (*SW*, p. 351–2). Memory—as both the immediate recollection of Babo's treachery and as the primal violence that Babo represents—is an unrestrainable human function. But equally instinctive is Delano's impulse to "turn over new leaves," to reset his genial mask. The debate ends in a draw: memory destroys; geniality preserves. Neither can be denied.

[29] To some extent, Babo combines features from Franklin who also possesses a "hive of a head" (*IP*, p. 59) and Jones whose friendliness conceals a savage heart.

The tale's problematic narrative structure contributes to the carefully poised irresolution of this conflict between genial and misanthropic instincts. Students of the tale are familiar with its shifting voices. When Babo attempts to kill Cereno, Melville suddenly abandons his third-person, central consciousness perspective for a narratorless deposition relating the details of the bloody revolt prior to and after Delano's arrival. The tale concludes with the voice of an omniscient speaker who records the final dialogue. Melville's earlier critics considered the deposition to be an unfortunate bit of padding, but the shifting narrative serves more precise rhetorical ends. Each new voice marks a subtle effacement of an authorial presence. Locked into Delano's central consciousness, the opening speaker provides no explanation of events beyond one or two coy hints that something is wrong. On the whole, he transmits uncritically Delano's flawed perceptions. In the deposition and final dialogue, Melville abandons authorial guidance altogether. "Facts" and speeches are left to speak for themselves. As with *The Confidence-Man*, the reader's perspicacity is at issue. But the gradual elimination of voice also serves a dramatic and philosophical end. If Delano is to be taken seriously, his seemingly superficial affirmation must appear as formidable an alternative as Cereno's resignation. As we shall see, Melville's shifts in voice are, in fact, a ploy to strengthen the American's rhetorical credibility in the final debate with Cereno.

The abandonment of the central consciousness narrative occurs precisely at the moment when the battle between Babo's rebels and Delano's men takes center stage. Details of this unseemly violence are recorded in the legalistic jargon of the deposition. We, therefore, do not read Delano's immediate ruminations on the savagery that unfolds before him nor on his own stupidity for not uncovering Babo's treachery earlier. We do not experience the American's "shock of recognition." Instead, we see through secondary sources his "noble" attempts to contain the ensuing bloodbath. The deposition, then, functions somewhat like the messenger in classical tragedy who reports what is too graphic to be staged. Of course, in fiction the reader is automatically spared the immediacy of staged violence through whatever dampening devices the author wishes to impose. But if Melville had maintained his central consciousness perspective, no amount of dampening could have mitigated the brief but intense moment of disillusionment that the American genialist must endure. Could the reader, after observing at first hand Delano's thoughts of battle and possible self-recriminations, readily accept as valid his final "sunny" speech without branding him impossibly insensitive? To make his audience more receptive to Delano's optimism, Melville willfully removes us from Delano's consciousness to conceal his anguish in the heat of action and lend credence to his advocacy of the genial spirit.

The carefully contrived abandonment of central consciousness narration is only one of Melville's manipulative strategies. Like a confidence man, the narrator is also intent upon testing and teasing his reader. He faithfully reports all that Delano sees and thinks, but he consistently refrains from judging those perceptions and thoughts. He seems to know the truth about Babo but is not telling. At the outset, he challenges "wise" readers to determine if Delano's geniality signifies "*more* than ordinary quickness and accuracy of intellectual perception" (*SW*, p. 256; my italics). But at tale's end, we realize that Delano's instinct, although a saving grace, signifies *less*. The narrator has led us astray. Moreover, Melville's narrator seems bent on legitimizing Delano's errors. Because the speaker rarely signals his shifts from Delano's thoughts to his own, the reader can easily lose track of whether the narrator speaks for Delano or himself. At times, the speaker adopts the American's consciousness so thoroughly that he lends authority to the captain's false assumptions. Thus, when the narrator proclaims the black man's propensity for geniality as firmly as Delano (*SW*, p. 292), he draws the reader more readily into Delano's dangerous frame of mind. If Melville's strategy succeeeds, our discovery of Babo's scheme will be as shocking as the naïve American's. The speaker dupes the reader, then, just as Babo dupes Delano.

In "Benito Cereno," the reader's game is to grow beyond the confines of Delano's mentality. But the odds are against us, for the narrator plays fast and loose to trap us in Delano's faulty assumptions. To a large degree, this at times unreliable speaker is an early version of the confidence man narrator in Melville's last novel.

III

In referring to the Civil War's only positive effect upon the American character, Henry James remarked that ". . . the good American

. . . will be a more critical person than his more complacent and confident grandfather." But though "he has eaten of the tree of knowledge," he will not become a "cynic" or "skeptic" but rather an "observer."[30] Even before the Civil War, Melville had also sensed the need for one who could assimilate both prelapsarian complacency and the modern dogma of doubt, keeping uppermost (as Cereno fails to do and Delano overdoes) the preserving warmth of the heart. For Melville, the "genial misanthrope" was such a character.

No tale comes closer to realizing this new comic type than "I and My Chimney." As a "gray headed old smoker" whose "warm heart" and "gentle heat" conceal "secret recesses" best left untouched, the chimney accommodates both complacency and doubt. It is the speaker's alter ego and endures with him the onslaught of old age, impotence, and domesticity. After the speaker unwisely digs for hidden meanings at the chimney's "druidical" foundations, he abjures further self-exposures, fearing that they will lead to "infinite sad mischief" (*SW*, p. 406); he prefers the hearth upstairs where genial flames beckon him to "philosophize" safely on human nature. This is Hawthorne's chimney in "Fire Worship," for it keeps control of the fiery "red tongue" of self awareness. Like "old Montaigne, and old cheese, and old wine" (*SW*, p. 386), the old chimney is an image of ripeness and repose.

But the chimney is a trickster, too. Its placement at the center of the house creates a "labyrinthine . . . abode" with a maze of passageways and doors that forces inhabitants "to be forever going somewhere, and getting nowhere" (*SW*, p. 389). When one of the daughter's suitors, an affected youth, leaves with a protracted flurry of pretentious adieus, he steps out of what he thinks is the front door and into a pantry. Afterwards the boy drops his airs and becomes "more candid" (*SW*, p. 390). The chimney has, in a way, duped the lad into being more congenial. Like Frank Goodman, this prototypical genial misanthrope is both confidence man and genialist; it suppresses dark impulses beneath a philanthropic aspect in order to promote among others a new sense of geniality. As a projection of the speaker's own stable sensibility, the chimney survives external and internal assaults; and like the warm-hearted edifice, the speaker attains the voice of an "intellect in repose."

<hr/>

[30] Henry James, "Hawthorne," in *The Shock of Recognition,* ed. Edmund Wilson (New York: Farrar, Straus, 1955), pp. 536–37.

"I and My Chimney" is the final phase of Melville's experimentation with the literary confidence game. Although the tale reverts to the genial and reliable first-person voice of "The Encantadas," it resolves the stalemated debate in "Benito Cereno." By recording the genesis of the genial misanthrope, the tale allows for the assimilation of Delano's blue sky optimism with Babo's secret savagery and Cereno's fated awareness. To be sure, the genially misanthropic speaker of "I and My Chimney" is not the gadfly that Goodman plays in Melville's last novel. Nor, for that matter, is the somewhat unreliable narrator of "Benito Cereno" the same voice as *The Confidence-Man*'s thoroughly unreliable speaker. Rather, the two tales are experiments in character and voice, stepping stones *en route* to *The Confidence-Man*.

Behind Melville's experiments are the dynamic principles of restraint and fusion which make up the aesthetics of repose. On the one hand, the author sought a detached voice that could conceal rather than expose the "secret recesses" of the self. From *Pierre* to *Israel Potter* to "Benito Cereno," his third-person speakers become increasingly non-committal and indeed unreliable. If, however, they seem to lack the full repose that characterizes reliable narrative, they nevertheless represent decisive steps toward a sense of repose in their self-restraint and detachment. Moreover, Melville wanted an "original" hero for his age, a character capable of surviving with heart and mind not only intact but harmoniously united. The confidence man figure grows to fit this need, first as a comic villain, then as a more substantial nemesis for the naïve genialist, and finally as the catalyst for the genial misanthrope. The twin developments of voice and character in the magazine pieces suggest that the concept of geniality plays a profound role in Melville's aesthetics and that the author, far from having lost his creative power, was actively engaged in the direction of his work. He was an artist at the helm.

Index

This index is centered on Herman Melville. The titles of his writings appear as main entries, and an unqualified entry such as "appearance *vs.* reality" refers directly to the content of those writings. The names of fictional characters (e.g., Captain Vere) are listed as commonly referred to by critics and are not inverted for alphabetical ordering.

Notes on Contributors

James Barbour (1933–). University of New Mexico, 1969–. Edited *Romanticism* (1986); *Essays on Puritans and Puritanism* (1986).

John Bryant (1949–). Pennsylvania State University, Shenango Valley Campus, 1980–1986; Hofstra University, 1986–. *Melville Dissertations 1924–1980: An Annotated Bibliography* (1983); *A Companion to Melville Studies* (1986).

John G. Cawelti (1929–). University of Chicago, 1957–1980; University of Kentucky, 1980–. *Apostles of the Self-Made Man* (1965); *The Six-Gun Mystique* (1970); *A Focus on Bonnie and Clyde* (1973); *Adventure, Mystery, and Romance: Formula Stories in Art and Popular Culture* (1976); *The Spy Story* (1987).

Hubert H. Hoeltje (1898–1969). State University of Iowa, 1928–1947; University of Oregon, 1947–1961; Union College (Kentucky), 1961–1968. *Sheltering Tree: A Story of the Friendship of Ralph Waldo Emerson and Amos Bronson Alcott* (1943); *Inward Sky: The Mind and Heart of Nathaniel Hawthorne* (1962).

R. W. B. Lewis (1917–). Bennington College, 1948–1950; Smith College 1951–1952; Newark College, Rutgers University, 1954–1959; Yale University, 1959–. *The American Adam: Innocence, Tragedy, and Tradition in the Nineteenth Century* (1955); *The Picaresque Saint: Representative Figures in Contemporary Fiction* (1959); *Trials of the Word: Essays in American Literature and the Humanistic Tradition* (1965); *The Poetry of Hart Crane* (1967); *Edith Wharton: A Biography* (1975).

Sidney P. Moss (1917–). Murray State University, 1954–1964; Southern Illinois University, Carbondale, 1965–1987. *Poe's Literary Battles: The Critic in the Context of His Literary Milieu* (1963); *Poe's Major Crisis: His Libel Suit and New York's Literary World* (1970); *Charles Dickens' Quarrel with America* (1984).

John W. Nichol (1921–). Denison University, 1953–1966; University of Hawaii, Manoa, 1976–1978; University of Southern California, 1966–86.

Sherman Paul (1920–). Harvard University, 1950–1952; University of Illinois, 1952–1974 (M. F. Carpenter Professor, 1967–1974); University of Iowa, Carver Distinguished Professor of English, 1974–. *Emerson's Angle of Vision: Man and Nature in American Experience* (1952); *The Shores of America: Thoreau's Inward Exploration* (1958); *Louis Sullivan: An Architect in American Thought* (1962); *Edmund Wilson, A Study of Literary Vocation in Our Time* (1965); *Randolph Bourne* (1966); *The Music of Survival: A Biography of a Poem by William Carlos Williams* (1968); *Hart's Bridge* (1972); *Repossessing and Renewing: Essays in the Green American Tradition* (1976);

Olson's Push: Origin, Black Mountain, and Recent American Poetry (1978); *The Lost America of Love: Rereading Robert Creeley, Edward Dorn, and Robert Duncan* (1981); *The Onward Way* (1984); *In Search of the Primitive: Rereading David Antin, Jerome Rothenberg, and Gary Snyder* (1986).

O. W. Riegel (1902–). Dartmouth College, 1927–1929; Washington and Lee University, 1930–1973. *Mobilizing for Chaos: The Story of the New Propaganda* (1934); *Crown of Glory: The Life of James J. Strang, Moses of the Mormons* (1935).

Beryl Rowland (1918–). University of Toronto, 1962–1963; York University, 1963–1987; University of Victoria, 1987–. *Blind Beasts: Chaucer's Animal World* (1971); *Animals with Human Faces: A Guide to Animal Symbolism* (1973); *Birds with Human Souls* (1978); *Medieval Woman's Guide to Health* (1981). Edited *Companion to Chaucer Studies* (1968, 1979); *Essays in Chaucerian Irony* (1985).

James Schroeter (1927–1985). Temple University, 1961–1962; Illinois Institute of Technology, 1962–1974; University of Lausanne, 1974–1985. Edited *Willa Cather and Her Critics* (1967).

Merton M. Sealts (1915–). Wellesley College, 1946–1948; Lawrence University, 1948–1965; University of Wisconsin, 1965–1982 (Henry A. Pochmann Professor of English, 1975–1982). *Melville as Lecturer* (1957); *Melville's Reading* (1966); *The Early Lives of Melville: Nineteenth-Century Biographical Sketches and Their Authors* (1974); *Pursuing Melville, 1940–1980* (1982). Edited by *Billy Budd, Sailor* (1962); *Emerson's "Nature": Origin, Growth, Meaning* (1969).

Bryan S. Short (1942–). Northern Arizona University, 1967–.

Eleanor E. Simpson (19 –).

Judith Slater (1938–). Canisius College, 1970–1975; Clinical psychologist, 1980–.

Christopher W. Sten (1944–). George Washington University, 1970–.

Gustaaf Van Cromphout (1938–). State University of Ghent, 1966–1968; Northern Illinois University, 1968–.

Charles N. Watson, Jr. (1939–). Washington State University, 1968–1975; Syracuse University, 1975–. *The Novels of Jack London: A Reappraisal* (1983).

R. E. Watters (1912–1980). University of Washington, 1941–1944; Indiana University, 1944–1946; University of British Columbia, 1946–1961; Royal Military College of Canada, 1961–1976. Edited *A Check List of Canadian Literature and Background Materials* (1959; 1972); *Canadian Anthology* (1966, 1974); *The Sam Slick Anthology* (1969).

Library of Congress Cataloging-in-Publication Data
On Melville / edited by Louis J. Budd and Edwin H. Cady.
    p.   cm.—(The Best from American literature)
  Includes index.
  1. Melville, Herman, 1819–1891—Criticism and interpretation.
I. Budd, Louis J. II. Cady, Edwin Harrison. III. Series.
PS2387.05   1988   813'.3—dc 19   88–18897
ISBN 0–8223–0867–3